Applause for *C*

Excerpts from G

"The author's passion for music is awe-inspiring."

"A gripping book of an enigmatic journey which intrigues the reader from the start."

"A heart-full story . . . a true and deep search."

"An intimate, heartwarming true story of one woman's journey to find "the one.""

"Using her love of music, Linda glides us up and down the scale from one adventure to the next. Like any favorite song, it's over way too soon, but the joyous feeling remains long after."

"A story with a never-ending sense of *joie de vivre*."

"A treat to be taken along on her courageous journey."

"A memoir that read like an adventurous romance novel!"

"Her surprising spiritual connection with Mother Mary on her journey is beyond breathtaking. A psychic, music, travel, food, Mary, love . . . what more could you want from a memoir?"

"A page-turner . . . the suspense kept me at the edge of my seat the whole way through."

"Descriptions of foreign cities and people peppered with exotic language and traditions make this a book in which every reader can find a treasure."

"There are so many wonderful things about this book. The rich descriptions of vibrant cities and their major attractions, the history of past politics of place, the cultural clashes in both language and practice: all compelling and noteworthy."

"If you love music, literature, the search for ancestral roots, and the ever-changing quest for love eternal, this book is for you."

"Enjoy the bumpy, enticing ride to a rich and lasting love, a love well-earned in its telling."

Odyssey
of *Love*

LINDA JÄMSÉN

Odyssey
of *Love*

Cover Design by Michelle Fairbanks

Interior Formatting by Melissa Williams Design

Paperback ISBN 978-1-948604-99-4
eBook ISBN 978-1-948604-26-0

Library of Congress Control Number: 2021902510

Published by Tulipan Press

TULIPAN
——press——

To Otto,
for waiting

My entire life has been nothing but an odyssey of love . . .
I was fitted only for loving . . .

Franz Liszt

Night at the Opera House

As the concertmaster warmed up the strings onstage, the overhead lights in the distance dimmed to tiny flecks, like stardust in the Judea Desert. Bass singers discreetly loosened their bow ties while altos fidgeted with beaded earrings from Tel Aviv markets. I plucked a page from the Rossini score and fanned myself, hoping not to tip over in three-inch heels onto the trumpet section—a minor concern compared to our overriding fear: a suicide bomber lurking in the Opera House.

I gazed out over the audience and prayed for another appreciative crowd. Ours was the only foreign chorus brave enough to travel to Israel at a time of increasing turmoil. So far, we'd been warmly welcomed on the three-week tour. Festival organizers had reassured us of less violence at Christmastime, but it was difficult to ignore all the heavily armed soldiers patrolling the streets and metal detectors looming at every tourist site that December in 2002.

In anticipation of Maestro José Serebrier's entrance, the stage fell silent and turned momentarily pitch-black, plunging my thoughts into even darker terrain. I reached back into the soprano section for Zsuzsa's hand. "You don't hear any loud ticking sounds, do you?" I whispered to my friend.

"Only your heartbeat," she said. "Breathe deeply and relax, Linduska. Think of Mary."

Yes, Mother Mary. She'll protect us. Earlier that day, Zsuzsa and I had lit candles at the Church of the Holy Sepulchre in Jerusalem and asked for Mary's protection. Recalling the serenity of that moment, my pulse simmered down. After all, a group of eighty Hungarians singing another *Stabat Mater* was a most unlikely terrorist target. Well, eighty Hungarians, one Brit, and this American. I slinked closer to the tenors and pulled a few strands of chestnut hair across my forehead.

Finally, Maestro Serebrier entered onstage with the soloists to rousing rounds of applause. With a flourish of his frizzy reddish mane, the Uruguayan conductor raised a baton-less arm toward the skies and summoned the cellos, which crept in with a sigh. Their ascending *arpeggios* were topped off by the twinkling of flutes, followed by strident *staccatos* from the string basses, foreshadowing the pain of Christ's mother standing at the foot of the Cross. The conductor made a cradling movement with his arms; the opening wailed like a desperate lullaby.

As the male vocals joined in, I cleared my throat and internally searched for the right starting note—was it G or B-flat? It was too late to check the score without rustling the pages and creating a commotion. I opened my trembling mouth and let out an amorphous sound that magically blended with the angelic ones. As the top of my head started tingling, I closed my eyes and imagined floating up with the music toward the heavens.

Over two years ago, I had stood onstage under very different circumstances, cloaked in familiar academic surroundings amid family and friends. Never had I imagined singing at an opera house so far from home. Then again, much of what Angelica had predicted, like this musical immersion, had already come true.

I thought back to how my Odyssey began . . .

Part One

The Seven-Year Glitch

*Life is either a daring adventure
or nothing at all.*

Helen Keller

Angelica

Unlike other homes on the gentrified Cambridgeport street, the faded triple-decker with peeling gray shingles needed a sprinkling of fairy dust. Scraggly, overgrown weeds poked out through patches of cracked dirt in the front yard; a hornet's nest lodged snugly inside a broken cellar window. I glanced around for a pointy black hat but spotted only the telltale broomstick parked against the sunken porch. *Why had I let my best friend Jenni talk me into seeing a psychic?*

Climbing the sagging wooden steps, I remembered my mother's story of how she had turned to the supernatural as a young woman, also after a failed romance. A fortune-teller had predicted she would soon meet a new man with the initial "J" and marry him six months later. Right on schedule, Mom met and then married Joseph, my father. If their long, happy union was a testimony to the power of the tea leaves, maybe there was hope for me, too. *I'm only following a family tradition, right?*

As I fumbled for the buzzer marked "Angelica," the

front door creaked open, and a petite figure floated out to greet me.

"My, my, you must be Linda," she said in a singsong voice.

I tried to respond but could only stare, entranced by her otherworldly appearance. Tinsel-like threads wove through Angelica's golden tresses, which spiraled Rapunzel-like down a high-collared, ruffled ivory shirt. Her diaphanous skin and delicate features reminded me of a Pre-Raphaelite model. A timeless aura hovered over her, making it difficult to determine exactly how old Angelica might be.

With a graceful hand she directed me inside, the hem of her pink organdy skirt sweeping up cat hairs in the hallway. I was tempted to feign a migraine and flee, but the oasis of her opal blue eyes steadied my nerves. "Isn't this heat stifling?" she said. I forced a smile.

A battalion of rusty metal fans welcomed us into the living room, where I braced myself for an onslaught of tarot cards and UFO replicas. Instead, her home reminded me more of The Cloisters than Coney Island. A marble statue of Mother Mary, adorned with necklaces of dried red rose petals, gazed up from an Early American style end table. Ancient-looking paintings of Saints Sebastian and Peter hung from paint-chipped walls next to crucifixes and framed variations of the Lord's Prayer.

Angelica motioned me toward a cavernous wooden chair and glided over to the purple velvet one opposite. She requested I refrain from crossing my legs and arms, and then asked, "Are you willing to hear all the news I pick up on, even if it's negative?"

"Yes." Ever since the big blowup with my longtime boyfriend, Hank, one month earlier, I had already hit rock bottom. I sat up straight and discreetly aired out the clingy top beneath my navy jacket.

Angelica began by inviting my "Higher Guides" to

envelop us in a "golden circle of healing light and protection." As soon as she closed her eyes, I made the sign of the cross, lest any wayward spirits slipped in through the screen windows. After a long silence, she described a church ceremony and "an older man with a cane." *Is that Dad?* I wondered. *Maybe I am getting married after all!* "You're wearing a flowing burgundy dress," Angelica continued. *Burgundy?* She squinted her eyes. "It appears you're a bridesmaid. Do you know anyone who is getting married?"

"The bride could be Wendy," I said, not wanting to divulge too much. Jenni might have told Angelica about my sister's upcoming nuptials, but I doubted my best friend would have sabotaged the session she'd taken such trouble to organize as my birthday present.

"A wedding, how lovely," she said before shutting her eyes. Moments later, she continued, "I see you used to live on the West Coast. California, right?" I nodded. *Well, anyone could have googled my former address.* My body language eased up as I realized that this psychic—or "visionary," as she preferred to be called—was more Glinda of Oz than the Wicked Witch of the West. Perhaps she could wave her magic wand and change Hank's aversion to marriage and children.

While Angelica concentrated intently, a furry white cat that answered to Luna sprang to her lap, seeking attention. I thought of my calico, Squeak, bouncing between the banished Hank in the living room of our Somerville apartment and the bedroom, where I'd staked my claim. Seeing my eyes moisten, Angelica leaned forward and uttered her first prediction: "Soon you'll be living in Eastern Europe."

"What?" I gasped. "Why would I be *there*?" Not an unreasonable question, given the vast amounts of time and money I'd invested the last four years as a student in the Graduate Management Program at Harvard-Radcliffe. One

LINDA JÄMSÉN

month earlier, on my forty-first birthday, I'd delivered—
and sung—the student commencement address.

Angelica dropped her dreamy eyelids again. "You're
not a tourist, that's for sure. It seems you're doing meaningful work and getting paid for it." She poured herself a
glass of water and offered me one. "Have you been thinking of moving overseas, Linda?"

Lady, your sixth sense needs some fine-tuning. I
explained that my professional focus was on taking my
fundraising career to the next level, hopefully as vice president of a large nonprofit organization. For over three
years, I'd been toiling away as director of development at
The Guidance Center in Cambridge and was overdue for a
promotion.

"I understand, but *is* this something you've considered?"

Sure, I'd fantasized about exploring family roots in
Poland and Russia and seeing the landscapes that had
inspired my musical idols, Chopin and Liszt. But anything
more than a two-week trip to Europe seemed overindulgent
to this workingwoman.

Upon hearing these sentiments, Angelica tugged on her
delicate pearl necklace and asked my Higher Guides for
more details. Moments later, she revealed: "You are going
to be teaching abroad."

"You must mean music," I chimed in. It had been my
major in college and was the only subject I felt qualified
enough to teach.

"No, no, it's not music I'm picking up on." Her long
fingernails wove through Luna's fur; the cat's purrs filled the
silence. "You're standing in front of a classroom, writing
on a chalkboard. It sounds like you're teaching English to
a group of foreigners." She turned toward me. "Have you
ever considered teaching English as a Second Language—
you know, ESL?"

Teaching any subject didn't fit my romantic bill of living abroad. Instead, I imagined sauntering through museums lined with Van Gogh landscapes, swooning to Puccini arias at the opera, writing in well-worn journals while sipping Earl Grey at elegant Jugendstil cafés, and being swept away into a heated love affair with a dashing cellist, complete with Franz Liszt-like features: dark, penetrating eyes, chiseled cheekbones, and a smoldering sexuality. I reached for a nearby envelope and fanned my flushed cheeks.

"I'm sorry, Linda, if this isn't what you want to hear, but the message is coming across loud and clear." She tossed aside a few shimmery strands of hair and gazed into my wary eyes. "Aside from your job, what's keeping you from exploring this possibility?"

Although I didn't want to provide too many clues, Angelica was so off base that I needed to enlighten her as to why, in my seven years with Hank, I'd not once considered leaving him and heading abroad. "You see, my boyfriend and I . . ." My voice started to crack; Angelica nodded gently for me to continue. "I really love him and was hoping we would settle down and start a family."

Angelica refreshed our drinks. "But he has other ideas."

I nodded. "Hank is happy with the ways things are and wants them to stay that way. I'm torn because ours is the best partnership I have ever had." I mentioned the worst: my stormy four-year marriage that had ended years earlier. "Now that I'm over forty," I said, gazing at the statue of Mary, "I think a lot about having a baby. But Hank isn't interested, and time is running out." Angelica handed me a box of Kleenex; I exhaled into a tissue. "I don't know how I could have misread his motives. I was so certain he was going to propose on my birthday, especially after last year's dress rehearsal."

Hank is building a rock sculpture on the beach, and by instinct, I rush over and remove the uppermost stone.

Perched atop a handful of sand is the delicate emerald Victorian ring I'd admired months earlier at an antique store.

"Happy fortieth!" he says, beaming.

"You remembered!" I clutch my chest and wait for him to drop down on bended knee. Gazing into Hank's glowing eyes, I hastily slip the band onto my wedding finger. My heart palpitates in sync with the pounding surf.

Hank tilts his head in bewilderment and reaches for my left hand. I close my eyes and wait. He pulls at the ring, slowly inching it off my finger. "What's he doing?" I wonder. After a final tug, he removes it and guides it over to my right hand.

"This is where it belongs," is his only explanation.

"Oh, dear." Angelica's fair forehead creased into a web of concern.

"It might seem odd to expect that Hank would give me an engagement ring a year later, but weeks before my birthday, he'd been acting secretive, leading me to believe a proposal was in the works." I told Angelica about the "creative projects" that had kept Hank up until the wee hours of the morning, his hushed phone calls with "tele-marketers." "How was I supposed to know he was organizing a surprise party for my birthday-graduation instead of phoning my parents for their blessing?" I twirled my hair up into a loose bun.

"Let's see what this is about." Angelica leaned back into her cushy chair. "Now it's clear. Your relationship with Hank isn't working because he's not your soul mate."

I grasped the armrest and fought the knee-jerk reaction to defend Hank, but even I was running out of excuses. "Until recently, I thought Hank *was* my destiny."

Angelica flashed a sympathetic smile. "What we want for ourselves and what's part of the Universal Plan aren't always one and the same." I furrowed my dark eyebrows.

"Hank is holding you back and already slowing down his pace." *True.* Hank often complained that his managerial job at the bookstore was zapping his energy. "You, on the other hand, are getting ready to leap forward." Her words roused the nagging inner voice that occasionally surfaced about the eleven-year age difference, especially when Hank was mistaken for Al Pacino, whose fans asked to meet me, his "daughter." I bristled at the memory.

"Regardless of what you think," the clairvoyant continued, "you *are* going to teach English overseas and pursue music again." She fell back into a trance. "I see you in ornate concert halls surrounded by clarinets and strings." *Strings! That must be my dashing Liszt look-alike!*

I glanced over at the clock; my boss at the family service agency was expecting me in one hour for a board meeting, which meant fifteen minutes remained to wrap up this psychic session. "Well, even if I were interested in this pipe dream, how could I afford it? An English teacher can't command much of a salary, especially in Eastern Europe."

"Money won't be a problem," she said. "On the contrary, a nice lump sum is coming your way."

Ah, the windfall. That's what had plunged my relationship with Hank into turmoil. I thought back to the night of my birthday-graduation, when my parents had given Hank and me a generous check toward a down payment on our first home. When he and I were alone later that night, he nixed those plans at once, stunned as to why my folks would assume he was ready to invest in property with me. I was still smarting from his refusal to at least consider what seemed the next logical step in our relationship.

"Linda?" Angelica cleared her throat a few times, giving me a moment to collect my thoughts. "What I'm getting at is that your true love isn't here in the U.S."

"He's not?" I glanced around the room. "Then, where is he?"

"I'm not being shown a location, but it's definitely the other side of the pond."

"You mean Walden?"

Angelica smiled. "No, your future spouse is waiting for you in Europe."

I jolted. "Can you at least tell me what he looks like?"

She squinted her eyes again. "I see a tall man with glasses." *That narrows the field down to a few million.* His image was "fuzzy," which meant he wasn't coming into my life for a while. Or perhaps my "Higher Guides" didn't want me to know more details. *Exactly who are these Guides? Maybe they have me mixed up with her next appointment.*

Angelica also claimed that this Odyssey would reignite my passion for music and lead me to discover ancestral roots. "I'm picking up on a Russian connection," she said, her eyes panning the collection of leather-bound Bibles on the shelves. "Are you Orthodox?"

"No, but my Russian grandmother was." I remembered the one time my paternal grandmother, Nana, had taken me to a service at St. Nicholas Cathedral in New York City. At age ten, it was all so mysterious—the solemn expressions of the priests, a strange language, the sweet aroma of honey wax candles mingling with musky incense that made me cough.

"I feel your grandmother's presence strongly around you," Angelica continued. "She loves you and will lead you to the right place."

"Would that be Russia?" I asked, my interest piqued. Although Nana had died years earlier, I most identified with her side of the family because of our similar physical features—dark green eyes, olive complexion, high cheekbones—although at five feet, six inches, I was a good head taller than she had been.

"Not necessarily. But I believe a Russian icon will lead you to your future husband."

Highly doubtful, as I hadn't seen a Russian icon up close since that outing to the cathedral thirty years earlier. I leaned forward and dug my nyloned feet into the braided rug. "Listen, if I'm going to leave everything behind and chase umlauts and accents across the sea, I need more to go on than 'Russian icon' and 'tall man with glasses.'"

"I understand, Linda, but can't you see that a whole magnificent world awaits if you have the courage to embrace it?"

"The magnificent world of what, ESL teaching?" Luna leapt down from her mistress's lap and shot me a sideways glance. *Maybe she was a language instructor in a previous life.*

"That's only one way of getting to the finish line— marrying your intended." She waved an arm toward the willow tree outside the window. "You could go overseas on vacation and see what happens, but that's not what your Higher Guides are telling me. You'll be there much longer."

After our meeting, I thanked Angelica, and then sulked my way back to work. She hadn't offered any affirmation about Hank, nor did her predictions seem to make sense. While it was exhilarating to think the future held so much possibility, I had only traveled abroad three times in four decades and never solo. *Why would I ditch my career, shelve my hard-earned diploma, and leave family and friends to embark on this so-called Odyssey?* I needed to meet Jenni ASAP. She'd help me sort through this hocus-pocus.

Hearing a faint cry down the street, I turned around to find Angelica waving me back from her porch. As I approached, she offered some final advice: "Bring plenty of journals and a camera, as you'll want to record every-thing. Have fun!" She spun around, scooped up Luna, and vanished inside.

Settle *Down*, Not Settle *For*

Jenni was already waiting inside our favorite Harvard Square eatery when I arrived in a huff the following afternoon. From outside, I watched as she pulled a compact mirror from her tote bag and touched up her thin lips with her trademark peach gloss. Her usually fine golden wisps of hair looked plumped up, most likely from the relentless New England humidity.

"Thanks for rushing from work to meet me," I said, entering Mr. Bartley's Burger Cottage and disappearing into my best friend's comforting arms. "Sorry, but I couldn't let this wait until tomorrow."

"Hey, anything that saves me from facing another Lean Cuisine," Jenni said, lifting her roomy caftan and squeezing into a plastic chair at one of the long picnic-style tables. "John thinks I'm out doing an assessment," she said about my former boss at Elder Services.

"Well, this is an assessment of sorts." Jenni still worked at the agency where we had met and shared an office five years earlier. Despite the fifteen years between us, we'd become fast friends, bonding over our New York backgrounds and High Tea habits. Her long career as director of the ombudsman program made her a natural magnet for those seeking advice on all matters, personal and professional. I figured that our intimate chats had saved me a small fortune in self-help books and psychotherapy fees.

Jenni nodded toward the waitress heading in our direction and handed me a laminated menu. "Let's order first. Then I want the full psychic scoop."

"Can I interest you in the 'John Kerry Lite' burger, today's special," the waitress asked, "or are you loyal to other politicians?" I breezed through the long list of personalized patties and picked the "plump, liberal Ted Kennedy." Jenni chose the "Hillary," which promised to "feed a village." We both ordered fresh-squeezed lime rickeys, the specialty of the house.

As soon as our orders were scribbled down, Jenni pounced. "Now tell me everything Angelica said. I've been dying to know about your future with Hank."

"Apparently, we have none. Angelica had lots to say— most of it *way* off the mark."

"Really? That wasn't my experience with her." Jenni reminded me that the seer had correctly predicted her second marriage and the birth of her son Joel.

"I'm glad she clicked with you. But if what she said is true, Hank and I are history."

Jenni sipped politely on her straw. "After the events of the last couple of months, I can't say I'm surprised."

I felt the waterworks cranking up and pulled a wad of napkins from the dispenser. "Angelica said that Hank isn't my soul mate. How can that be after all this time?"

"After all this time, *exactly,*" she said. "You've come up against another commitment snag, Linda, like when you lost your lease four years ago, and Hank wouldn't budge from his place to move in with you."

"That was because his home was rent-controlled and close to his workplace."

"Yes, but you cried for weeks!"

"Jenni, we both know it doesn't take much to make me cry." I dabbed my eyes. "To his credit, Hank *did* wind up moving in."

"True—but it took a year."

"Isn't it better to work with what I've got rather than ditch Hank and find someone who may have the same issues, or worse? At least he's not a cheater, beater, or alcoholic."

"We're all familiar with Hank's fine qualities, Linda. The question is: are you willing to hang in there for the long haul?" She poked at the ice cubes in her plastic cup. "If Hank can't commit after seven years, ten or fifteen might not be enough either."

"But I'm forty-one now, Jenni, and the idea of starting over at this age—"

"Excuse me, my dear," she said, clearing her throat. "You're forty-one. *Only* forty-one! I'd give anything to turn back the clock."

"But I've been out of the singles scene for ages," I reminded her. "Plus, no one meets in real life anymore, only online." I thought of my vivacious college friend, Eve, who was active on Match.com, often lining up breakfast and dinner dates with different men on the same day. Several female colleagues had found mates through paid dating services. In contrast, I'd always met my partners in person, usually through mutual friends or by chance. As a serial monogamist, I'd gone from one long-term relationship to another with little experience in the dating scene.

Fortunately, our Democratic foodstuffs arrived before I gave one more thought to cyberdating. I smothered Ted with ketchup, Jenni pulled the extra cheese from Hillary, and we enjoyed our Bill-sized bites.

"Forget about Hank for a moment," Jenni said. "What else did Angelica predict?"

"That I'll be quitting my job and moving overseas, where my intended is—the 'tall man with glasses.'" It seemed crazy to go to such lengths to meet my true love; then again, putting enough geographical distance between Hank and me would make it difficult to run back to him if I felt myself caving out of loneliness. *Maybe Angelica is on to something . . .*

"Have you told your parents any of this yet?"

"No, I'm dreading it. They were so excited to help us buy our first home."

"Don't worry about them," Jenni said. "They want you to be happy. They'll get over it." She patted my hand. "If you do leave Hank, you may be lonely at first, but trust me, settling for second-best is far worse than being alone. You need to settle *down*, not settle *for*."

I repeated Jenni's words several times. "Thank you, my dear. You've just coined my new mantra."

As we finished our meals, she filled me in on the office gossip and flagged over our waitress, who removed our spotless plates. After ordering "the usual"—two teas and pumpkin pies—Jenni shifted the conversation back to the paranormal. "Angelica's prediction of your moving to Europe sounds so exotic. You often mention traveling but are always thwarted by Hank's resistance to flying."

I envisioned the collage of postcards from wayfaring friends pinned to my office bulletin board at work. When boredom set in, I imagined coasting down Amsterdam's tulip-lined canals, sniffing saffron at Istanbul's Grand Bazaar, and dipping into the pristine waters of Santorini. Until now, I'd stifled any pangs of wanderlust by focusing on my career and studies but had the nagging feeling I was missing out. I had once been more open to possibility, so ripe for adventure. *Is that part of me disappearing? Has she disappeared already?*

"Did Angelica say how you're going to pay for all this?" Jenni asked, pulling me away from these haunting thoughts.

"This one's a stretch. She envisioned me as an ESL teacher."

"Get out!" Jenni smacked the table with her palm. "Well, your father will be thrilled."

"But after the salary I'm making now, how could I manage on much less, especially with all the travel she mentioned?"

Jenni dunked her teabag repeatedly into the mug, as was her habit when on the verge of a brainstorm. "I've got it!" she said moments later. "Ask your parents to redirect the money they gave you. Instead of using it for a down payment on a home, ask them to fund your Odyssey." I reminded Jenni that my folks were generous, but only in helping with the essentials, such as tax payments or utility bills. Plus, there were always strings attached. "Well, in that case, tell them that teaching is something you're curious about and this is the perfect opportunity to find out if you're suited for the profession."

"You seriously think they'd fall for that?"

"Your father was a professor, wasn't he? And he's encouraged you now and then to consider a teaching career, hasn't he?"

True. But Dad's espousals on the alluring benefits of teaching paled in comparison to the thrill I got raising big bucks for causes close to my heart. I also knew that my parents' strong Protestant work ethic precluded them from encouraging the Odyssey Angelica had in mind.

"Aside from your parents being a bit on the quirky side, I can't imagine they'd be upset you asked," Jenni insisted.

"And remember, you're a fundraiser. It's high time to raise some moolah for yourself!"

A small brass ensemble parading down Massachusetts Avenue interrupted our conversation. "That reminds me," I told my friend, "Angelica also said I would reconnect with music." With regret, I remembered the broken promises to revisit my piano repertoire from college. Over the years, other priorities had left little time to pursue this hobby. *Hobby.* Was my former passion now denigrated to hobby status, like bowling or doll collecting? Music had always provided an outlet for expressing the most intimate longings of my heart, like a sacred prayer.

"Well, I, for one, will never forget your performance of Beethoven's *Pathetique* Sonata at the French Library's AIDS fundraiser last year," I heard my friend say.

"That makes one of us."

As Jenni settled the tab, I stared with envy at the musicians and considered her suggestion. Perhaps it was time to test the fundraising waters with a visit to my folks in Amherst. I hadn't seen them since the surprise party, and a visit was way overdue. But first, it was time to pay my respects to a trusted, yet neglected friend.

Ave Maria

Despite the long hiatus, my fingers traveled agilely up and down the Kawai keyboard, reuniting with eighty-eight forgotten friends that had been gathering dust in the living room. As Schumann arpeggios leapt from my long-ago memory bank, I reveled in the smooth sensation of ivory and ebony against my fingertips. The pedals creaked slightly, my feet shifting back and forth between them. But I barely noticed. I was playing again!

The Romantic compositions stirred up memories of how music had sustained me through decades of heartbreaks and losses. Playing Chopin's *Andante Spianato* always soothed my spirits after a failed romance. When Nana and other loved ones left this world, I listened nonstop to the *Transcendental Etudes* by Liszt.

Music had also played a pivotal role in my last two relationships, sounding the death knell of one and announcing the overture of another. Toward the end of my turbulent marriage, I had been practicing a Chopin Nocturne when my soon-to-be ex-husband suddenly appeared on the piano stool and patted my hand. "Give poor Frédéric a rest," he begged, a drained expression on his face.

Hank, on the other hand, had embraced my musical abilities from the start. The first night we met, we'd talked reverently about our respective passions. When he said he'd give anything to hear me play, I was smitten. A week later, I lured him to my apartment with the promise of a hearty steak and serenade. Fortunately, the melodic Mendelssohn had trumped my culinary skills.

How different our conversations were seven years later, mostly heated arguments over making our partnership a permanent one. I resented the way Hank made me feel like a freak for wanting to get married and explore the idea of motherhood and longed to be with someone who shared the same personal goals. Hank's knee-jerk rejection of my parents' gift was the final unresolvable impasse; our love song would have no more encores. Jenni was right. It was time to settle *down*, not settle *for*.

Tears welled up, spilling over onto the ivories. I attached all my anxieties and fears to the music notes; the felt hammers hit the steel strings and vibrated through the soundboard, releasing them into the air. Light as wind, the music propelled my hands up and down the peaks and valleys of the keyboard. As my fingertips tingled in remembrance, I wondered how and why I had put my creative spirit on hold for so long, allowing it to shrivel. *Not anymore!* I had to recapture this part of myself, even if it involved extreme measures, such as moving to Europe and embarking on the Odyssey Angelica had foreseen. *If only Mom and Dad will agree and offer their support . . .*

As the last ethereal notes of a Liszt Consolation reverberated up my spine, I bowed my head into the music stand and with outstretched arms, hugged my piano.

∞

After what seemed like hours, I heard Hank's work boots thudding across the front porch of our apartment. Wanting the musical reverie to linger and not be broken by the unresolved tensions between us, I scooped up our cat, Squeak, and glided into the bedroom, latching the door behind us. After sinking beneath the cotton quilt, I listened to the familiar sounds of Hank washing up in the bathroom and laying out his work clothes for the next day before finally settling into the futon, where he'd been sleeping since the party. *How I miss our closeness!* Usually on Friday nights we mapped out our weekends. I hugged Squeak close to silence my sobs and hoped her warmth would radiate into the tightness of my chest. Finally, when all was still in the living room, my calico and I drifted off to sleep.

A few hours later, Squeak jumped from the bed to the top of the armoire, scattering a handful of earrings and coins onto the floor and rousing me from my snug state. Although the alarm clock showed that it was just after three, the room was already awash in light. I rolled over onto my back, sat up against the pillow, and squinted toward the lamps. They were off.

I blinked multiple times, and after my eyes adjusted to the brightness, I saw a golden orb shimmering at the foot of my bed. A distinct female figure appeared to float within. She wore a long white dress with a sash, which gathered flowing fabric at the empire waist. A light blue robe was draped around her shoulders and across to outstretched hands gracefully hanging open at her sides. The luminous veil covering her head made it impossible to distinguish her facial features. Slowly, a whirl of recognition came over me, and a light chill swept up my spine to the crown of my tingling head. *Mary! She looks like Mother Mary!*

My conscious mind told me I should be afraid. Uncle Stan had seen his two deceased siblings the day before he passed away. I'd had some prophetic dreams over the years but had never experienced a vision like this. *Oh, God, have I conjured her up? Is this the end?*

I ducked under the bedsheets and tightly shut my eyes, but the light penetrated through my eyelids. When I slowly peered out, Mary was still glowing away. I wanted to ask her why she was here, but my lips seemed stuck together. I could only stare, transfixed, at the vision. Despite my confusion, a deep serenity infused my whole being. Although Mary spoke no words, her presence reassured me: "Don't worry. Everything will be okay." For some reason, I believed her. Feeling much lighter, I slipped back into deep, blissful slumbers.

∞

The next morning, I tried to fathom why Mary would visit *me*, someone who had slighted and doubted her. *It must be all those Catholic masses I've been attending with Hank.* For years, I had accompanied him to St. Paul's Church in Harvard Square, mostly because I loved listening to the Boys' Choir there. However, much of the liturgy I found far-fetched, and my musings about the Virgin Mary often led to heated discussions afterward.

"Why is it so difficult for you to wrap your head around the Nativity story?" Hank would ask over brunch. "If God's God, He can do whatever He pleases, can't He?" I'd never had a good rebuttal. After all, the God I was familiar with *could* make miracles happen.

When I was seven years old, my family moved to a new neighborhood on Long Island, where I was having difficulty making new friends. When winter came, but invitations to birthday parties did not, I marched outside onto our snow-covered front yard and into the welcoming arms of an enormous evergreen. Falling to my knees, I clasped my hands the way Mom showed me as she tucked me in every night, and prayed for God to send me a friend. I had no doubt that He would. God had not only answered that prayer but countless others. Despite my faith, I still struggled with much of what I read in the Bible—on the rare occasion I opened it—and these talks with Hank only generated more questions than answers.

It was tempting to tell him about seeing Mary, but we were breaking up. Jenni was a non-believer, as were many of my other friends. Mom was a staunch Lutheran, who uttered Mary's name once a year, during Advent when arranging the Holy Family crèche figurines atop the piano. Dad was more interested in meditation and astral projecting to the moons of Jupiter than in tagging along with Mom to church.

Despite my Sunday outings with Hank, I didn't have a personal connection to any of the local priests. There was no one I could share this vision of Mother Mary with. *No one.* But perhaps that wasn't important. Mary hadn't given me a message for the Pope or requested a chapel be built in her honor, as she had with Bernadette of Lourdes. No, this vision was a blessing meant to comfort and encourage me at a time of deep distress and uncertain beginnings.

For what might have been many hours, I sat on the edge of the bed, basking in the lingering radiance of my supernatural encounter with Mary. Yes, perhaps it was best to keep this a secret until I found a kindred spirit with whom to share it. *Please, Mother Mary, let that be the "tall man with glasses" on our wedding night.*

Fantasie-Impromptu

On Saturday morning, I waited for the front door to slam shut before crawling out of bed. Once Hank was safely out of earshot, I wrote him a brief note saying I would be spending the night at my parent's house in Amherst and asked him to reserve the next evening for an important discussion. Still aglow from Mary's visit, I finally had the courage to end our doomed union and approach my parents, per Jenni's suggestion, about redirecting their gift.

During the two-hour drive to Western Massachusetts, I practiced my pitch: "Mom, you've been encouraging me to travel more and re-engage with music. Maybe now's the time?" And, "Dad, you'll be delighted to know I want to try teaching for a while." But my voice kept faltering; I was much more adept when fundraising for the homeless, people living with AIDS, and disabled seniors. Not even a glimpse of the Berkshire Mountains through the lush foliage along the Turnpike could keep my hands from rattling the steering wheel.

My parents had left New York ten years earlier, lured by Amherst's bucolic beauty and prestigious colleges.

Shortly after connecting with other lapsed Manhattanites, they founded the Expat New Yorker's Club, where Mom serenaded members with songs by George Gershwin and Cole Porter while Dad led a sing-along. Soon they stopped reminiscing about the Big Apple and talked only about the "Happy Valley," the insider's name for the lush, leftist area. Every time I visited Amherst, I felt a bit blissed-out, too.

I exited north of Springfield and followed Route 9 to their adopted village, where the stately Lord Jeffrey Inn, with its white gabled façade and black shutters, dominated the Town Common full of Victorian-style university build-ings, cozy cafes, and boutique shops. I turned my Geo Prizm onto Main Street for a quick glimpse of the Homestead, birthplace of Emily Dickinson. The nineteenth-century poetess had lived most of her adulthood cloistered inside the family's brick house, now a museum, venturing outside only to tend to her beloved garden. I often stopped there to reflect or simply marvel at the robins weaving through the majestic maples and the daffodils "untying their yellow bonnets." But today there was no time to dally.

After driving a few minutes through the leafy outskirts of town, I turned into my parents' driveway and was greeted by an unfamiliar white Cadillac, their old Ford Taurus nowhere in sight. I walked up the cherry tree-lined path of the sprawling ranch-style home to the unmistakable beat of "A Night in Tunisia" blaring through the windows. *Great! Dad's home.*

Loud whistling emanated from his office; I tiptoed inside. From behind the leather recliner, I watched Dad's head of still-thick dark brown hair sway side to side in time with the imaginary jazz band he was conducting. Since retiring and recovering from hip replacement surgery, my father spent most of his time listening to his cherished jazz albums, often improvising solos along with those of his idols, many of whom he'd seen at the Apollo Theater as a youngster growing up in the Bronx. I wanted to announce my arrival but knew better than to disturb his Bebop session with Dizzy Gillespie, and went in search of Mom.

As I approached the kitchen, I heard her on the telephone. Seeing me, she abruptly hung up. "Oh, Linda! Wendy and I were just talking about you." *No doubt about that.* If my sister was to be believed, Mom had been burning up the phone and computer wires, chomping at the bit for Hank's reaction to their gift. I had confided in Wendy but made her promise that I would be the one to break the news to our parents.

I handed my mother the bouquet of magenta carnations I'd hastily purchased at a gas station along the Pike. She plucked one and placed it behind her wavy, shoulder-length auburn hair. "How do I look, dear?" she said, sashaying into the living room and glimpsing her reflection in the antique mirror above the fireplace.

"Like you're going to the prom." She pecked my cheek. Now in her mid-sixties, Mom still radiated youth and vitality. Her vivacious nature meshed well with Dad's more laid-back, introverted style. "Where's Hank?" Her cornflower blue eyes darted over to the driveway.

"I came by myself. Thought I might spend the night."

"What a rare treat. We have you alone!" She rushed to Dad's office and banged on the door. "Joe, your firstborn's here for a visit!" When the musical melee continued, she banged harder. "Come on out, Joe. That night in Tunisia is long over!"

After Dizzy tooted his last note, Dad shuffled into the hallway, a tad disoriented, and pulled me in for a hug with his wooden cane. My parents had already eaten lunch, but Mom served me leftover tofu spaghetti. As I sprinkled parmesan onto my meal, Dad sank slowly into his seat and motioned toward the driveway. "Well, Linda, what do you think of White Beauty?"

"You mean that..." I bit my tongue to keep from saying pimpmobile, "...Caddy out front?" Dad nodded. "You win her in a raffle or something?"

"Goodness, no," Mom said, joining us at the table. "Your father likes all the electronic gizmos on the driver's side. Plus, it was time for another car."

"That's not the real reason for the upgrade," Dad said. "Tell her, Gloria."

Mom beamed at Dad, and in a voice brimming with anticipation, she said, "Well, now that Wendy's getting married, and soon *you*, Linda, we want to escort our girls to church in style on their wedding days."

I reached for a napkin to stifle my giggles. "You *must* be joking."

"It's not a laughing matter, but an economical one," Dad said. "We'll save by not having to hire limousines." His logic didn't make any sense, unless he was counting on the quickest of nuptials before the Cadillac started to depreciate.

"Imagine!" was all I could muster. I twirled some pasta around my fork, and from the corner of my eye, I saw my parents exchange inquisitive glances.

Dad shifted in his seat. "So, why's a busy gal like you visiting your old folks on a beautiful day like today?"

"Obviously, Linda has an important announcement to make," Mom said. She tilted her head toward me. "Don't you, dear?"

I pushed a piece of garlic bread into my mouth and tried to recapture snippets of my pitch. While I planned to tell my parents about Angelica's predictions, I wasn't sure how to broach the subject. "Yes, I have something important to share, but it's not what you and I were expecting." I explained how Hank was uncomfortable accepting money from them, as he had never done so from his own parents, and steered away from the commitment issue. Mom, who had gotten up to toss me a salad, dropped the utensils, along with her jaw. Dad, who'd recently quit smoking, began puffing on his tobacco-less pipe. "It's not as if he doesn't appreciate your thoughtfulness," I continued, "only that it feels like he's getting a handout."

"This is most unfortunate," Dad said. "Your mother and I were hoping that our gift would put your financial future—and relationship—on more secure footing."

"I appreciate that, Dad." *Okay, Linda, take a deep breath. This is your cue to start fundraising.* As my mouth opened, Mom broke in.

"Where does this leave you then, dear?" She looked at me with lines of concern etched on her otherwise smooth face.

Avoiding her gaze, I got up to heat the teakettle. "In Eastern Europe, perhaps?"

"Hank's finally getting on a trans-Atlantic flight?" Dad asked in an incredulous tone.

"No." I filled the pink Spode Tower teapot with loose Darjeeling leaves.

"Then what's this all about?" Mom said.

I poured the hot beverage into a porcelain cup and stared through the light golden waters at the bottom, where succulent tea leaves swirled around, as if dancing in an autumnal wind. Then I remembered why I had agreed to see Angelica in the first place. "Mom. Dad." I nodded at each of my parents. "I took a page from your love history and went to see a psychic."

"You don't say!" Mom struck the tabletop with her reading glasses. "Someone like Lady Olga?"

"Sort of." Mom reminisced about having found Dad, the mystery man with the initial "J," in the tea leaves; he expressed relief that his name hadn't been George or Al. Then I shared Angelica's prophecy—from the music and travel-filled Odyssey to the "tall man with glasses."

Dad arched his eyebrows at Mom. "Maybe you should think about it, Linda, and give it a go. Especially the teaching part." *Good call, Jenni.*

"Actually, I've been mulling over the possibilities, but there are some issues."

"Like Hank." Mom studied my face for a reaction. "Do you plan on inviting him to Europe?" That idea had never crossed my mind, as my change and travel-averse partner would never consider uprooting and moving to another country, when he rarely left the county.

"No, that wouldn't work. I'm ending our relationship tomorrow."

"I see." Dad jotted down a note in shorthand, his secret way of communicating with Mom, and slipped it to her. She read it with interest and nodded.

"Well, dear," she said, "what's keeping you from realizing this dream? If I were you, I'd get out there and kick up your heels! You've been so serious these last few years with that stressful job of yours and mounds of college homework on the weekends. Maybe you need to step away from it all and get a fresh perspective."

"Precisely," Dad added.

I reached into my bag and placed their birthday check on the table. "Now that Hank and I won't be buying property together, I'm returning this." I patted their gift, as if saying goodbye to a very dear friend. "Thanks so much for your generosity. Maybe one day . . ."

Dad reached over to retrieve the check and tucked it into his shirt pocket. "If Hank is no longer a consideration in terms of going abroad, then what is, dear?"

"*Gelt,*" I blurted out. "I can't afford it without dipping into my retirement."

"Have you thought of borrowing the money?" he said.

"A loan?" *Maybe I don't need a gift!* "Yes, a loan would make this Odyssey doable."

Dad slowly lifted himself to his feet, requesting to speak with Mom in private. She gave me an encouraging pat on the shoulder and followed him out of the kitchen. After cleaning up, I fought the temptation to eavesdrop by curling up inside the hammock next to Mom's garden of holly-hocks and tiger lilies. With envy, I watched the bluebirds splashing around the birdbath without a care in the world. Every few minutes, I checked my watch. *What's taking so long?* After thirty minutes dragged by, I closed my eyes and tapped into the sweet serenity of Mother Mary's nocturnal visit. "Yes, everything will be all right," I whispered to myself, dozing off.

Suddenly, a loud, sustained chord jolted me; I sat up and tried not to tip over. A graceful fluttering of notes followed, sounding as if my virtuosic mother was playing a Chopin masterpiece. *Why is she practicing now, with such an important talk looming?* I swung out of the hammock and rushed inside the screened-in porch to the living room, where Dad motioned for me to join him on the sofa.

Mesmerized by the music, I gazed at the photo above the Yamaha of Mom as a fourteen-year-old in an elegant yellow gown, curtseying to a smitten audience after her performance of *Malagueña* at Little Carnegie Hall. At age twenty, she had given up a promising career as a concert pianist to get married and start a family. During my childhood, she had given music lessons and wowed her students and our Long Island neighbors with moving renditions of the Romantic repertoire. I especially loved the third *Liebestraum* by Liszt and would dance around the living room in a sparkly pink tutu, swooning to the harp-like melodies and imagining I was the Sugar Plum Fairy from *The Nutcracker.*

When I was seven years old, Mom had put me on her lap and shown me how to find middle C on the piano. Soon I was learning "Do Re Mi" and making my way through the John Thompson beginner course books. After years of studying with her, she and Dad granted me my wish to major in music at Bard College. At my senior recital, I performed many demanding pieces, but a career as a concert pianist had never appealed to me—not that I remotely had the chops. Instead, I wanted to see the world, fall in love, and help people, not be tied down to the stage.

"What about a *Fantasie-Impromptu,* Linda?" Mom said, her fingers gliding nimbly up and down several octaves on the keyboard.

"It is an amazing piece but way out of my artistic league."

She grinned and returned her eyes to the frayed music score. "No, not this one," she said, craning her head toward me, "but a *Fantasie-Impromptu* for *you.*"

I cocked an eye at Dad, who was all smiles. "Perhaps Poland is a good place to begin your Odyssey?"

Stunned, I joined Mom on the piano bench. "Does this mean what I think?" She raised a finger to her mouth and launched into Liszt's *Liebestraum.* I clutched my chest and sighed.

"Or perhaps Hungary?" Dad continued, referring to that composer's homeland. "Maybe a 'Love Dream' is more appropriate."

As Mom moved her feet between the pedals, I held on to the edge of the upright, my heart pulsating in sync with the *fortissimo* octaves reverberating in the strings. After the Liszt faded to a prayer, I shouted, "Bravo!" and rejoined Dad on the couch. He unfolded a piece of notebook paper.

"Your mother and I have gone over the figures, Linda, and it seems that a loan isn't feasible."

I tried to still my jittery knees. "Oh, that's okay, Dad. I understand."

"No, that's not what your father means," Mom interjected.

Dad fumbled for a small envelope on the coffee table

and placed it on the pillow next to me. "There's to be no loan because we're giving back half of our original gift," he said. "And what's more, if all goes well next year, you'll get the rest, too."

Wow! I tore open the envelope and waved around the check like the latest Publishers Clearinghouse Sweepstakes winner.

"Of course, there will be some conditions," Dad said. *Pluck! I knew there would be strings attached.* "First of all, your mother and I expect you to work while you're abroad."

"Of course. That's a major part of this whole experience."

"Your father's tickled that you want to teach for a time," Mom said with a wink. "Perhaps pursuing this in the land of your ancestral roots and musical idols is a good place to begin."

I stared at the black and white wall photo of Nana and her Polish-Lithuanian husband, Vincent, on their wedding day and imagined the fears and challenges they had experienced as young immigrants seeking a new life in America. If they'd managed under the most adverse circumstances, surely I could seek work in their homelands under more pleasurable ones.

As my parents and I discussed the logistics of ESL teaching, it became clear that I would need to get certified because I had no classroom experience. Their gift would pay for the mandatory teacher training course and supplement the modest teacher's salary I could expect, as well as allow me to travel around Europe during school holidays. Dad figured that with their help, I could afford to stay overseas for two academic years.

"That sounds like a deadline," I said.

He wiped the lenses of his wire-rimmed glasses. "I

wouldn't put it that way. Your mother and I expect you'll be wrapping up your Odyssey by then anyway."

I thought of the "tall man with glasses" and hoped that two years was enough time to meet him. In light of Mom and Dad's generosity, the timeline sounded reasonable enough. "I accept," I told them. "With much gratitude."

An hour later, I joined my parents in the luxurious splendor of White Beauty as we cruised through sprawling tobacco farms and down winding country roads on our way to the local Whole Foods. The soft breeze seeping in through the window made ribbons of my hair and caressed my sunburnt face. As Dad fidgeted with the control panel and Mom thumped out Dvorak on the dashboard, I hoped that someday we'd be putting White Beauty to the use they intended. But for now, I reveled in the company of my dear parents, whom I'd soon be leaving to pursue my own *Fantasie-Impromptu.*

Part Two

Hungarian Rhapsody

If adventures will not befall a young lady in her own village, she must seek them abroad.

Jane Austen

Madame Butterfly

Six months later, as my Malév Airlines flight descended into Budapest's Ferihegy Airport, I gazed down at the panoramic view from my window seat. The impressive Gothic-Revival Parliament Building with its recognizable deep burgundy dome sprawled out along the eastern banks of the Danube, which divided the city in two. Several bridges connected hilly, residential Buda with the flat, more commercial Pest. Even from this height, I could see the august splendor of Budapest: the dense gilding and passionate colors of the Renaissance blending with exotic Moorish domes and fairy-tale turrets. I wondered on which side of this "Paris of the East" my apartment was situated, and if it had a river view.

After touchdown, I collected my luggage and searched for the downtown shuttle service. Vali, a secretary at International House, where I had enrolled in a three-month ESL teacher training course, had suggested the minibus ride to District XIII and agreed to meet me there at ten o'clock. I reserved a spot on the next run and stepped outside into the balmy February morning, relieved to have escaped yet another New England Nor'easter.

As the minibus tore through the suburbs, I turned over stray cushions and suitcases, desperately seeking a seat belt to prevent me from flying through the windshield—a likely scenario, given the driver's tendency to accelerate while passing trucks across double lines. I yanked the nearest belt and forced it repeatedly into the buckle, without success. Several passengers groaned until a wizened elderly man leaned over and tapped me on the shoulder. "*Nem működik,*" he said in a raspy voice.

"Excuse me?"

"*Nem működik,*" he repeated, shaking his head. I knew from my basic knowledge of Hungarian that "*nem*" meant "no." Before I could respond, he quickly slipped into passable English: "It no work." I clung to the door handle.

As we hurtled through the city, billboards promoting swanky sports cars and mobile phone services bombarded my jet-lagged brain. Lingerie ads featuring voluptuous models in plunging necklines and string bikinis also zipped by, confirming Budapest's growing reputation as a top European destination for bachelor parties. Perhaps I'd picked the wrong country in which to begin my search for a life partner. Only an hour after touchdown and already my Odyssey looked more like a Bodyssey.

Thankfully, the gentle ripples of the not-so-blue Danube soon waltzed into view, and we zoomed over the Freedom Bridge, leaving the upscale Gellért Hotel on the Buda side in our wake. Approaching Pest, I glimpsed the gray-green dome of St. Stephen's Basilica majestically dominating a skyline of Baroque cathedral towers and government buildings. The roof of the Nagycsarnok marketplace sparkled with green and yellow porcelain Zsolnay tiles; inside, tourists and locals plowed through ten thousand square meters of paprika, goose liver pâté, embroidered tablecloths, and other Hungarian specialties. When I spotted other Art Nouveau architectural marvels, I almost burst with excitement. Budapest was more fantastic up close than in my guidebook photos.

The driver dropped off all the other passengers at various stops before heading north on Váci Street into the industrial suburbs. I glanced at the address Vali had given me, tapped on his window, and pushed the piece of paper against it, raising my right hand in a "Where the hell are we going?" gesture. He mumbled and shook his middle finger in a forward direction.

As Communist-style blockhouses and IT companies popped up along the asphalt, I shuddered to think of the late-night commute from the school, located far away on the Buda side. My fears were confirmed when we stopped in front of my new home: a gray-blue four-story building with steel window bars protruding from its façade. The narrow street could barely contain the pile of Trabants and Škodas parked with half their wheels on the sidewalk. Down the lane, a once-elegant building with a statue-encircled fountain was spray-painted with profanities, both in English (shit) and its Hungarian equivalent (*szar*).

I exited the minibus, exhausted from the flight and deflated by the lackluster surroundings. Moments later, a woman with a short brown bob wearing ultra-tight black jeans rushed over. It was Vali, who introduced herself and kissed me once on each cheek. Stunned, I pecked at the air, not quite sure of the correct response. She reached for one of my suitcases and explained that the landlady, Mrs. Lehel, was en route for the "inspection," although it wasn't clear whom or what she'd be inspecting.

Entering the lobby, Vali turned left across the chipped tiled floor and opened the door to my rental, which was secured with a metal grating. The three-hundred-square-foot digs included a large, albeit sparsely furnished living room with a small wooden table and outdated television. An enormous animal skin covered the wall above the sofa. Fake electric candles dangled from the light fixture above. The bedroom, with a single bed and dresser, was the size of my former pantry in Somerville.

The tiny bathroom was equipped with a tub but had no freestanding showerhead or curtain. Patches of tape struggled to hold up the cracked tiles. Vali told me I was lucky to have a washing machine, as most other student flats lacked this "*luxus.*" When I inquired about the clothes dryer, she flashed a curious look and handed me a stack of loofah-like towels.

While I was examining the same kind of pull-chain toilet that Nana used to have in her Bronx tenement, Mrs. Lehel shuffled through the doorway. Somberly adorned in black, from open-toed shoes to her draped head, my new landlady motioned for us to join her in the living room. She spoke no English but let her eyes do the talking as they moved from my unkempt braid to the red silk Chinese shirt billowing over my black wool pants. As she grunted some barely audible mouthfuls in my direction, I smiled politely but was already conspiring to skedaddle to more livable quarters. Next week I'd ask Vali about other living options, but I didn't want her first impression of me to be that of a spoiled American.

After ten minutes, Vali excused herself and told me we'd meet on Monday at International House. "If you need anything before then, buzz your neighbor across the hall. She speaks English." She kissed me again on each cheek and exited the building with Mrs. Lehel. "*Szia!*" they shouted, which sounded like its English counterpart, "See ya!"

I locked up and dove straight into what looked like a bed but was a hard-cushioned sofa. Hugging the coffee table-sized pillow and snuggling up with a thick acrylic blanket, I marveled at how everything—from the minibus driver's blatant disregard for highway safety and Vali's kissing ritual, to curtainless showers and exfoliating towels—was much different from what I'd been used to in the States. Of course, learning to adjust to this new culture could be a positive experience, once I got over the initial shocks and discomforts. At that moment, however, only one thought mattered: making up for a lost night of sleep.

∞

Six hours later, I woke up disoriented and headed to the kitchen area for a tea fix. Despite multiple attempts, the gas burner wouldn't ignite. *Shit! Nem működik!* Recalling Vali's advice, I tiptoed across the dimly lit hallway and knocked on the door of my neighbor, Vencel Heléna, remembering that Hungarians gave their family names before their birth ones. As Heléna opened the peephole, her eyes darted from my roomy Cape Cod sweatshirt to faded blue jeans.

"Ah, it's you, the *American*," she said, smiling broadly. She unlatched the door and motioned me inside, kissing me as Vali had. The cramped vestibule was bulging with winter coats, plastic shopping bags, and homespun handicrafts. "Vali told me you coming. I am happy to meet you."

"Likewise," I said, extending a hand. "I'm Linda."

She asked me to exchange my brand-new Nikes for the blue flip-flops sitting outside the closet. Not quite understanding the logic, I obeyed and followed her into the living room.

Heléna, who looked about my age, had short, layered copper-colored hair offset by soft, peachy skin and delicate freckles that danced about deep-set hazel eyes. Her thinly plucked eyebrows arched over a Romanesque nose perched regally above rose-stained lips. A low-cut pink pullover revealed ample, slightly saggy breasts. The tight matching skirt hung over an absent bum in the latest low-rider fashion, showing off slender, toned calves. Despite these provocative stylings, the overall effect was one of grace and sensuality.

"I arrived earlier today and my stove *nem működik*," I told her, sitting down on the sofa and feeling a bit frumpy in my sweatshirt. "Can you help me light it?"

"No problem, my dear." She patted my shoulder. "I show a little later, but first we enjoy some Tokaji." She explained that the world-famous Hungarian beverage was revered as the "Wine of Kings, King of Wines," and then selected two crystal flutes from the wall unit.

"Please don't go to so much trouble," I said, desperate for a caffeine jolt.

"Not at all." She uncorked the gold-labeled bottle. "I'm celebrating today." I was curious as to the source of her excitement but didn't want to pry. "Cheers!" she said, clinking my glass and knocking her head back. "Vali tells me you study become English teacher."

"That's the plan, although I've never done this type of work before." I told her that after getting certified, I hoped to teach ESL in Poland or Russia.

"Maybe you teach me. I always look for ways improving my English knowledge."

"Perhaps," I replied, on heightened alert that the bubbly was more than an icebreaker. "Where have you studied English?"

"At International House—IH—same place where you go." Heléna told me that she had first started learning English after her divorce five years earlier by participating in the school's "guinea pig" sessions. These classes were taught by aspiring ESL instructors who tested their lesson plans on willing students not put off by their teachers' lack of certification. The trade-off in this "experiment" was that these evening sessions were more affordable than IH's daytime ones.

Between dainty sips, she asked if I had a family and handed me a photo of her fifteen-year-old son, Róbert. She had married his father after getting pregnant in her mid-twenties. "Róbert's English much better than mine," Heléna said with pride.

"Such a good-looking boy," I remarked. "Just like his mother." She flashed an appreciative smile, reminding me of a celebrity, although I couldn't pinpoint whom.

"You have boyfriend?" she asked, her voice rising above the battering of soccer balls in the parking lot outside.

"Not anymore." I swooshed the remaining bubbles around my glass and gave Heléna a quick overview of my relationship with Hank and our split six months earlier. With some anguish, I thought back to the final, tearful breakup scene and how he had made no last-ditch effort to keep me in his life. After learning I was strongly considering moving overseas, he had simply said, "I can't possibly go with you." To his credit, he had released me to follow my heart and dreams, and never would have made false promises to entice me to stay. Although I knew it was in my best interests to leave Hank, it still hurt deeply that after my seven years of steadfast devotion, he could not envision us as a married couple. Luckily, I'd had my Odyssey to look forward to, as well as the love and support of my parents and friends. Time had also helped heal the lingering wounds.

"Since leaving Hank, I've been waiting for an opening in IH's teacher training program," I told Heléna. "Budapest was my first choice because I'm a huge Liszt fan." *And I'm hoping to meet a Liszt look-alike.*

Heléna smiled and put down her glass. She pointed her nail-polished pinkies symmetrically at me. "How old you are?"

"Forty-one."

45

"You kidding!" she said. "Can't be! You still looks young and pretty for age."

"Thank you." *I think.* "And you?"

"About same," she said with a mischievous smile. "You find Magyar man. Magyar man logical solution to your problem."

"Magyar?"

"Another word for Hungarian."

As we had only just met, I didn't feel comfortable telling Heléna about the "tall man with glasses." Maybe I would confide in her another time, but for now, I fudged. "I'm not in any rush at the moment. I need a little time to adjust . . ."

"But sex best cure for lonely feeling," she insisted. "Magyar man helps."

I quickly diverted the subject to Heléna's love life, a colorful mélange of Hungarians and foreigners she had attracted at various city museums and spas. As she named "Alastair," "Jack," and "Juan," her arms flailing in animated recall, I understood why many men would find her alluring. *And which celebrity does she remind me of?*

Heléna confided that she was dating István, a married man ten years her junior, whom she had met months earlier at a travel and hospitality conference. His way of courting her had been to complain about his sexless marriage and lethargic wife, who doted more on their two tots than her horny husband. When he'd handed Heléna his business card before dashing home to his family in his sporty BMW, she hadn't been surprised.

"At first, our relationship start in daytime," she said. "István visit me here in flat when Róbert at school." My eyes panned around the matchbox-sized love nest, trying to imagine the possibilities for such intimacy. "Now we grow closer, and he wants me weekends, too. So, you see why I celebrating!" Heléna poured herself another glass of Tokaji; I covered mine.

"What's so special about today?" I asked, blotting a few stray champagne drops from the coffee table with my sweatshirt.

"István's wife away in countryside, so he free. We can make love whole night to his house." *If only Heléna were as familiar with prepositions as she is with propositions.*

"That's wonderful," I lied, not sure how to respond to this tale of infidelity.

"And imagine—no cooking, cleaning, or ironing!"

"What exactly do you mean? He doesn't expect you to do his housework while you're over there, does he?"

"No, no, no!" Heléna waved my suggestion away with her hands. "I'm not wife. But Hungarian man *expects* when married or has life partner." No wonder István's wife wasn't easily aroused, when she had so many other responsibilities, child-rearing included; I shared these observations with Heléna. "Such is life," was her final word on the subject.

As the wall clock neared five-thirty, I stood up to leave, allowing Heléna ample time to primp for her dream date.

"We meet István's house at seven. Can you imagine? I never been there before." She guided me to the kitchen nook. "But first I go hair appointment." I couldn't imagine anyone improving on her hairstyle. *Geez, Magyar men sure are picky.*

After reminding Heléna of my stove problem, she demonstrated the correct ignition technique and showed me how to operate the washing machine. Every inch of her bathroom was filled with Avon products and smelled like roses. She promised to help me put together a grocery list in Hungarian and suggested I drop by at eleven the next morning, after her return from István's.

"*Köszönöm,*" I thanked her, slipping back into my sneakers. "And don't forget to behave." I wagged a finger, knowing full well she wouldn't heed my advice.

With a wiggle in her booty and a flirty wink, she wished me "*Jó éjszakát*" and kissed me good night. High on Tokaji and our newfound friendship, I floated back to my flat.

∞

"Meryl Streep!" I blurted out the next morning, my blurry eyes straining to find the travel alarm. My neighbor was a double for the famous film star, circa *Silkwood*. I rushed to the refrigerator, devoured what was left of my airplane sandwich, and watched the minute hands go by in anticipation of my neighbor's return. At eleven, I crept across the hallway.

Heléna slowly opened the door, rubbing bloodshot eyes. "Oh, it's you," she slurred.

"Is this a bad time? I can come back."

"No, it's okay." She yawned and headed for the kitchen area, her patchwork robe swaying by her silver anklet. "You like coffee?" she said. "I know I need."

"*Nem, köszi.* I'm a tea drinker." I hovered as she made a beeline for the java machine. "When I was here yesterday, you reminded me of a movie star, but I was so jet-lagged I couldn't think—"

"The Meryl, of course." She added a pinch of paprika into a cup of strongly brewed coffee. "Only Meryl without talent."

"How did you guess?"

Heléna dismissed the idea with a flip of her hand. "I hear all the time." She quickly changed the subject to her exploits the night before, including István's five-room sprawl in the Buda Hills, the featured waterbed, and details as to why he was "great in the sack."

"I'm not surprised your date went so well," I told her. "You looked hot last night."

"Thanks, I know," she said with confidence, not conceit.

As she leaned over to pour me a glass of water, I noted that her hairstyle looked much the same as it had the day before, other than it having been tousled from her roll in the reef. I needed to have my chestnut locks touched up and asked Heléna to recommend a hairdresser.

"My dear, I didn't have *this* hair done," she said, touching her head, and then pointing her index finger downward. "I had crotch wax job."

I nearly gagged on the water. "You paid someone—a stranger—to do that?" I knew there were such places in the States but had never set foot in one.

"Kati's not stranger anymore. Plus, I like her design."

"What design?" I asked, assuming she was talking about the salon's interior.

"I had *pillangó* this time."

"What's *pillangó*?" I imagined some tortuous hair removal technique.

"Sorry, but I don't know English word. Am checking." She pulled a Hungarian-English dictionary from the wall unit and quickly thumbed through the "P" section.

"Ah, *butterfly*." I craned my neck to see the word. "But I don't understand."

"My dear, Kati made butterfly design down there using wax and shave combo." I flinched, but Heléna defended her primping session. "It don't hurt so much. It's art." She returned the book and joined me on the sofa. "You really need try. Hungarian man *expects*."

I shook my head. "You mean, Magyar men expect their women to stay fit, cook meals, clean and scrub, work full-time, raise children, and help with the bills?" Heléna nodded; I expelled a sympathetic sigh. "What's in it for them?"

"Ahh." She slinked back into a pillow, most likely reminiscing scenes from her sexcapade the night before. "Hungarian men best lovers in the world." A factoid apparently glossed over by my Frommer's travel guidebook. "Even the Marilyn say her best lover was Hungarian."

"And if that was good enough for Miss Monroe, it's good enough for us?"

"Linda, you genius." She slurped down the remaining coffee.

I was about to remind Heléna of my shopping list when a loud noise startled us. She wiped her hands and peered through the blinds. "That be my ex-husband bringing Róbert home," she said. Understanding this was my cue to leave, I put my sneakers back on and headed toward the door. Heléna promised to take me food shopping later in the week.

Back at my place, I tossed and turned in bed for hours, wondering how I could handle this racy society. Finally, a familiar Puccini aria wove through my weary mind, and with a grin, I flitted off to dreamland and rested up for my long-anticipated first day of teacher training classes at International House.

Gabi

I arrived early for the five o'clock class, allowing time to report to Vali and walk around IH's premises, situated one block from a busy tram stop on Margit Street at the foot of the Buda Hills. Surrounded by small shops and a handful of bars and cafés, the school occupied a spacious three-story building on leafy Bimbó Street; I hoped the name wasn't an omen.

Despite the cool late-winter weather, female students pranced around the courtyard in low-cut pants and plunging V-neck sweaters, exposing svelte stomachs and narrow hips. Their attentive male counterparts were more reasonably dressed. I wondered why they were outside braving the elements instead of nestled inside the lobby's elegantly sculpted archways, when a haze of smoke arose from the patio tables. I'd read that Magyars smoked more than most Europeans; the overflowing ashtrays offered proof.

Vali's colleague informed me that she'd left for the day and handed me a registration form and a large packet of documents. He pointed toward the stone staircase and instructed me to go to the second floor and wait for

"Clare." With fifteen minutes to spare, I sat outside the classroom and thumbed through the stack of paperwork. Scrolling down the teacher trainee list, one name caught my eye: "Gabi." *Good, another foreigner.*

As I read through the school's Welcome Guide, I didn't notice the presence of another likely trainee leaning against the vending machine until his smoke rings roused my nasal passages. He was wearing a camel-colored leather jacket far too bulky for his lean frame, but which matched his hair color. Well-defined thighs protruded through his ripped jeans—not Calvin Kleins, but the kind you wear when you only own one pair. *He must be Hungarian.*

I forced a smile, hoping he'd extinguish his cigarette, but he continued puffing and expelling in synchronized spurts. As I picked up a few stapled pages and began fanning away the smoke, a petite blonde beckoned us inside. The guy waited until I had grabbed my briefcase before snuffing out his cigarette and following me into the room.

"Like no one smokes in America," he exhaled softly into my ear. I wanted to respond, but he was already heading to the back of the room; I dropped my things in the first row. The four other students arrived, greeting one another with "*Szia.*"

In a distinct British accent and a meticulous bob, Clare introduced herself as our trainer and explained that we would be engaging in an icebreaker exercise, "Find Someone Who." The curly-haired guy next to me rolled his droopy brown eyes and closed his notebook. "Here's a list of ten questions for you to ask one another," Clare continued. "Now circulate until all your blanks are filled in. The first person who gets all ten wins."

"What do we say when that happens?" the smoker uttered from behind. "Bingo?"

"No. For fun, let's say '*csíz*,'" Clare suggested.

I turned to Curlytop and shrugged.

In a thick Irish brogue, he introduced himself as "Charles"

and explained that the Hungarian word, which sounded like "cheese," was used when taking someone's photograph, as in, "Say cheese!"

Clare handed out the questions and clapped her hands to mobilize us. Soon we were all standing up and mingling while she paced around the sidelines, taking notes.

Sára, a beautiful Botticelli blonde with sapphire eyes and alabaster skin, was the first to greet me. Her wavy mane extended to the waist of her flowing Bohemian-style black skirt. Despite her Hungarian lineage, she looked very different from other Magyar women her age, who exhibited darker features and wore skintight clothing.

Dóra was a lustier version on the goddess theme, flaunting full lashes and hips, silky black hair, and penetrating brown eyes. Her English was as flawless as her porcelain skin and sparkling white teeth. *Is everyone here so good-looking?*

I turned to find the smoker watching me interact with the others while he chatted with a guy who shared his same olive skin and bewitching sky-blue eyes, but was taller and more heavy-set. Suddenly, the taller one walked over to me.

"I saw you staring and thought I'd better end the suspense," he said. "I'm Béla, and that over there is my brother." He pointed to the smoker; I scrunched up my nose. As we breezed through the remaining questions, Béla told me they had lived abroad for many years, including several in America. Before I could probe, Clare signaled that only five minutes of the exercise remained. I left Béla to track down Charles when the smoker intercepted.

"Gabi," he said, extending a yellow-tinged hand.

"No way!" I blurted. "*You* are Gabi?" I started giggling.

"I don't see what's so funny."

"Well, Gabi, when I saw the list of trainees, I thought you were a French or American female. Where I come from, Gabi is a girl's name."

"Here it's short for 'Gabriel.' You *have* heard of that name, haven't you?" He pushed his chest forward and lifted the ends of his moth-eaten rag sweater to reveal a chiseled six-pack. "As you can see, I'm hardly a girl." *Boy, I'll say!* I hadn't been up close and personal with such a sinewy physique since a few post-college romps.

Goosebumps popped up under my black cashmere sweater as Gabi's eyes wandered from my black lace-up boots and gray wool skirt to my silver hoop earrings. "Yup, just as I thought. One hundred percent American," he uttered under his breath. Before I could respond, Charles shouted "*Csíz!*" and we all returned to our seats.

Clare went around the room and asked us to share what we had learned about one another. When Gabi's turn came to talk about me, a big grin leapt to his face. "Like most Americans, Linda's a bit gender-confused," he said.

The room erupted in laughter; my cheeks turned beet red. Fortunately, Clare excused us for a fifteen-minute break. I bolted for the bathroom, doused my face with cold water, and patted the springs gushing from my armpits. Sára joined me by the sink, reapplying mascara and eye shadow. "What was all that about?" she said.

"I think I hit a nerve," I said, explaining how I'd mistaken Gabi for a female.

"Looks like he did, too," she said, winking.

Back in the classroom, I sat down and pretended to make notes on my pad when Gabi leaned over my chair, a smug look on his youthful face. "Cheer up, Miss America. In a few months you'll be back in the smoke-free zone."

His nicotine-laced breath brushed against my neck, and I quivered. It wasn't so much the comment as the realization that he looked like Brad Pitt. Well, an Eastern European double of the hunky actor, minus his millions and Hollywood glamour. Gabi would need a whole new wardrobe and a handful of stardust to be in the same league.

Still, he exuded a strong sex appeal and playful edginess I found attractive, maybe too much so for a woman about ten years his senior.

"What do you have against us Americans, anyway?" I asked. "It's not my fault they elected George Bush."

"Oh, a Democrat, too." He pushed some flaxen strands away from his forehead. "Next thing you know, you'll tell me you went to Yale."

"Harvard-Radcliffe, if you must know."

"Well, excuse me, Miss Ivy League!" He smirked and threw down his pen.

While our fellow trainees stared in confusion at Gabi's histrionics, Clare bounced around our chairs, handing out the course timetables and teaching assignments. We would be divided into two teams, she explained, with the Team A teacher trainees presenting their debut lessons to the guinea pig students the following evening. I held my breath, hoping to be on Team B, without Gabi.

"Linda, you're up first tomorrow; Gabi follows," Clare continued. Noting my pained expression, she encouraged us to pick simple, familiar topics that would generate interest among the students. Then she dismissed us on the early side.

I walked with Dóra down to the tram stop on Margit Street, where she showed me how to buy a *jegy* from the bright orange vending machine, a throwback to the forty years Hungary had spent under Communist rule. As suspected, it ate my coin and didn't produce a ticket.

"Can you help me out?" I asked her. "It seems I'm having another *nem működik* moment."

She laughed. "Now that's a phrase that'll come in handy in Hungary." After giving me a spare ticket, she left, and I boarded the tram. My eyes struggled to stay open until I noticed a big poster for *Ocean's Eleven* starring Mr. Pitt. Despite my exhaustion, my tantalized mind and body found it hard to simmer down that night.

Chapter 7

Never Neverland

Rather than explore the Castle District the next day as originally planned, I fussed over my lesson plan, opting for the topic "homesick." To put my best foot forward, I borrowed some of Heléna's Avon products and attempted to shower, but the patches of tape on the tiles became wet and unleashed clumps of plaster into the tub. As I struggled to prevent an avalanche, the hose dropped, spraying the stucco walls and bath towels. I dried off with a couple of unused dishrags and prayed I wouldn't electrocute myself while using the blow dryer. Then I slipped into my olive-green Jones New York suit and rushed to IH.

When the time for my lesson came, I strode into the center of the classroom and faced Clare, my fellow trainees, and a dozen Hungarian students, whose eyes were glued to me. Before Gabi could utter a snide remark from the sidelines, I introduced myself and wrote "HOMESICK" on the board. A few men giggled, and one put his finger into his mouth and uttered, "After night at bar."

"Can anyone tell me what this word means?" Pens clicked, throats cleared. I whipped out a few photos of

Wendy's wedding and wrote the words "sister," "bride," and "groom" on the board. The students perked up; some let out "ahs" and "oohs." As the pictures circulated, Gabi examined them carefully. "I miss my family," I said, walking toward them. "I am homesick." The students shrugged at one another. Realizing I wasn't getting through, I drew a simple map of the United States and showed where Hungary was roughly located in relation to America's East Coast. "So many miles," I said, folding my hands over my heart and pouting.

Eventually, one young student waved her hand and shouted, "*Hazavágyódó!*" I recognized "*haza*" for "home" and looked over at Clare, who nodded. The students wrote the word in their notebooks.

"Do you ever get homesick when traveling abroad?" I asked them.

"Missing my Pick," an older gent, Sándor, said, referring to Hungary's most popular sausage brand.

"Need my Sopianae," said Rafael, holding up a pack of cigarettes.

Other students blurted out words and short sentences, but before I could address each one, the thirty-minute session was over.

After a round of applause, Clare stood up. "Overall, Linda, you did well for your first lesson. You were confident, warm, and friendly, but spoke way too fast. When addressing the students, you need to slow down. And not just verbally, but in terms of staging." She pointed to a metal chair on the parquet floor. "Sit down once in a while and pace yourself."

From the corner of my eye, I caught Gabi grinning and shaking his head. "How the mighty have fallen," he muttered, just loud enough for me to hear.

"Also, you talked solely about yourself, not engaging the students by asking about their own families. We call this too much 'Teacher Talking Time.'" My face crimsoned; I stared down at my notes. "Anything else?" she asked, directing the comment to my peers.

"This isn't your home in the States, is it?" Gabi remarked, holding up a photo of Mom and Dad embracing in front of their Amherst garden.

My cheeks now aflame, I wanted to snap back, but instead I smiled and said, "Yes, my parents live there." I walked over and snatched the photos, flashing him a cold stare.

"It's just that the size of their yard looks like some palatial grounds here in Hungary." I hoped the students wouldn't understand "palatial grounds."

"It's only a standard one-acre plot in the suburbs," I explained.

Gabi scanned the room and addressed his fellow Magyars: "Why does everything have to be so much bigger in America?"

I hoped he was talking about the photograph and not my backside, which I'd squeezed into a size ten skirt. "Do you Hungarians have an issue with size?" I wiped my brow and looked pleadingly at Clare.

She clasped her hands together. "Okay, everyone, time for a break!"

I headed for the bathroom, shut myself in one of the stalls, and suppressed a sob. *Why does this person have it out for me?* As if reading my mind, I heard Dóra say, "I think Gabi likes you."

I flushed the toilet and joined her by the sink. "What makes you say that? He does nothing but taunt me."

She glanced at me in the mirror and smiled. "But the way he stares at you is different from how he looks at me and the other females," she said in the frank, open way that reminded me of Heléna. "He also teases you a lot."

"It feels more like he's trying to insult or humiliate me in front of the group."

She reached for the towel dispenser. "He's young and immature. Maybe he doesn't realize what he's doing."

"How young do you think he is?" I asked, immediately embarrassed I'd shown interest.

"About our age." I looked at Dóra's Dove-white, unlined skin and laughed.

"I'm at least ten years older than you are," I told her, pointing to my scalp. I pulled away some chestnut strands aside to reveal the gray beneath. "Here, take a look."

She examined my hair closely. "Okay, so you're older than Gabi and me, what does that matter? If I were available, I'd go after him."

Despite Gabi's dishy looks, I'd not thought of him as an entrée, or even a starter. But now that Dóra had put him into a romantic context, I thought to pay more attention to our interactions. "He probably has scores of girlfriends," I said with a wave of my hand.

"I don't think so. I can tell by his body language and the way he speaks Hungarian that he's not comfortable with our mother tongue. Perhaps because he lived abroad, English comes more naturally to him."

When we arrived back at the classroom, it was Gabi's turn to face the students. I rubbed my hands together, eager to pounce on his first grammatical error, but when he began handing out small cups of popcorn, I soon realized it was futile.

"Tonight we're going to the cinema," he told the cheering students. His well-planned lesson led to a discussion about their favorite movies and Hollywood stars. Everyone was riveted, including me.

"Well done, Gabi," Clare said, before mentioning a few minor points she would have done differently. "Have you taught before?" She asked for feedback from the other trainees, but rather than criticize, we clapped as Gabi bowed and reached for his leather jacket. While he and the others filed out into the stairwells after class, Béla took the opportunity to sidle up to me.

"Don't let my brother get to you," he said. "He's a bit on the socially immature side."

"Boy, I'll say." I shoved my photos into the briefcase and struggled to close its zipper. "Like that comment about everything being bigger in America. Why'd he have to say that?"

Béla laughed. "Well, I guess he jumped to that conclusion because Americans *are* known for liking things on a grand scale. You know—McMansions, Big Macs, SUVs." I thought of White Beauty and winced. "Not to mention this bulging briefcase." Béla reached for my bag and insisted on carrying it outside, where Gabi was lurking next to the Fondue Bár across the street. I quickly turned the corner; Béla followed. "Please don't let this influence your impressions of us Hungarians," he continued. "With Gabi, you have to understand that our mother's death has been particularly hard on him. He nursed her for two years before she died from bone marrow cancer."

"Oh, Béla, I'm so sorry about your mom."

He struck a match against the graffitied bricks of the flower shop and huddled his fingers over the flame. "He's also the baby of the family, which is why he seems young for his age." Béla inhaled deeply, held his breath, and then added, "Think of him as Peter Pan."

I imagined Brad Pitt flying around in green tights and burst out laughing. Béla arched his faint eyebrows. "I just got a strange visual," I told him. *If only he knew.* "Listen, I need to pass this course so I can teach ESL in the fall. I don't care if your brother is Peter Pan or Peter Rabbit, but his comments make it uncomfortable for me and maybe the others as well."

Béla nodded and handed over my briefcase. After wishing him "*Jó éjszakát*," I fled toward the waiting tram. From the stop on Margit Bridge, Fisherman's Bastion glistened from Buda's Castle District, its seven turrets extending heavenward toward the late neo-Gothic, gargoyled Mátyás Church. Below, the illuminated Eye of God symbol between the twin spires of St. Anne's Church pierced the darkness along the banks of the Danube.

Upon returning home, I sought out comfort across the hall, but it was already lights out at Heléna's. I thought she might be waterlogged from another roll in the surf with István, but the next morning learned she had other preoccupations. At ten o'clock, she appeared at my door, disheveled in her patchwork robe and threadbare slippers. Before I could ask where she'd been the night before, she came inside and wobbled toward the sofa. "I feel terrible," she said, looking quite pale. "I have visitor."

"István?"

She forced a laugh. "No, my period." She rubbed her midsection with one hand and clutched her coffee mug with the other.

"Can I help in some way?"

"Yes. My son coming home from school at one and wants go ice-skating. Since I am sick, can you take?"

"You mean . . . *him* . . . skating?" I wondered how I could manage a fifteen-year-old Hungarian boy, let alone the ice. It had been at least a decade since I'd had been anywhere near a rink. "But I don't have any skates," I said, hoping to get out of it.

She reassured me that I'd be able to rent skates there and emphasized that this would be no ordinary skating experience, as I'd be twirling under the magical spell of the magnificent Vajdahunyad Castle. She had a street map ready and pointed to its location, writing down directions from our building. I was disappointed about having to

reorganize my day, but the new itinerary did sound alluring, except for the teenager part.

"He meet you there two o'clock by *kassza*. Of course,
he pay. He's wearing T-shirt that says the 'Iron Maiden.'" I
wondered aloud how Róbert and I could communicate, but
Heléna reminded me that he was already studying English;
I hoped not as a guinea pig at IH.

She handed me a recent photo of her darling. I took it,
realizing I had no choice but to accompany him. "Okay,
sounds like fun," I lied. "I can't bring him back here afterward, though. My class starts at five."

"No problem. He's okay on Metró. I'm just nervous
when he's with friends." *Friends?* "Some are bad influence."

I wanted to pry and was also hoping to confide in
Heléna about Gabi, but she shuffled back toward the door.
"Good luck with Róbert," she said, "and please report
back any strange behaviors."

After lunch, I headed to Heroes' Square. Exiting the
subway, I pulled out my guidebook and examined the
statues of Hungary's most prominent rulers and warriors
located in the niches of two semicircles. A statue of Angel
Gabriel hovered above, holding the Crown of St. Stephen
with its lopsided cross in a nod to the legendary dream in
which Gabriel had offered him, Hungary's first king, the
Crown of Hungary.

Gabriel . . . Gabi . . .

I wasn't aware of the skateboarders zooming past at
breakneck speeds until one of them nearly knocked me
over. From the corner of my eye, I thought he looked like
Heléna's son. I stopped reading and crossed the street to
the rink, where I waited for him and his friends on a bench.

Minutes later, the same kids approached, clutching their
skateboards and puffing on cigarettes. The Iron Maiden
T-shirt tipped me off to Róbert, who was taller and more

acned than the image in my pocket. When he saw me, he quickly stomped out the smoke and popped a piece of gum in his mouth.

"You must be the *American*," he said, flashing me a syrupy smile through his braces.

"Yes, I'm Linda, your neighbor." I extended my hand, feeling like a party crasher.

He shoved his hand into his jeans. "Listen lady, I don't need no babysitter, all right?" Two boys with pierced tongues and gothic hairstyles snickered; their bouncy blonde dates giggled.

"I understand. Your mom only thought I'd like to check out the skating scene."

Róbert spit on the ground. In between eruptions of "*Szar!*" and other obscenities, he uttered Hungarian mouthfuls to a friend wearing a sweatshirt with the words "*Baszd meg.*"

"Who's Meg?" I asked.

They keeled over in laughter. "It means 'Fuck you!'" Róbert pointed to the lettering.

Lovely. I ignored them and looked for the skate rental area. By the time I figured out my European shoe size, Róbert and his pals had disappeared. I wondered if they were up to whatever mischief Heléna suspected.

I laced up and clung to the railings, looking for a spot to enter the frenzy of skaters. The man-made frozen lake was full of kids whizzing by at high speeds; I kept to the edges, afraid to travel at their pace. When I eventually looked up, the fairy-tale Vajdahunyad Castle beckoned me like a mirage. It wasn't really a castle, but a variety of stone and brick buildings showcasing an array of Hungarian architectural styles. Inspired by the romantic surroundings and the abundance of amorous couples, I started daydreaming about Gabi. He certainly was no Angel Gabriel, nor did he meet the description of the "tall man with glasses," but did it hurt to harbor these fantasies until I met him? *Of course not. My Odyssey is only beginning!* As I envisioned Gabi and I gliding across the ice, his sculpted arm wound tightly around my waist, I stumbled and fell on my knees.

"What's wrong?" Róbert shouted, zipping by. "Forgot how to skate?" He grabbed one of his girlfriends and twirled her around.

I stood up slowly and wiped a dusting of ice shavings from my pants. Undeterred, I forced my wobbly legs to move. As Ricky Martin belted out "Livin' la Vida Loca," I swayed to the beat, keeping a distant eye on Róbert.

Under one of the light towers, he and his friends sat in a haze of smoke. I assumed the legal age was eighteen but didn't feel right chastising him and his buddies, especially in English. Instead, I skated by, and upon making eye contact, nodded with a knowing smile. A medley of "*Baszd meg!*" and "*Szar!*" rang out from the teenybopper crowd. By the time I returned to their area on the next lap, they were nursing Fanta sodas.

When they finally got off the ice and returned their skates, I yanked off mine and ran over toward the *kassza* where they were standing. Róbert left his friends and walked over.

"You're not going to tell my mother, are you?" he asked, reverting to the gangly youngster he was and not the macho Magyar he aspired to become.

"That depends, Róbert." I sized him up, my eyes stopping at the half-eaten Milka bar in his right hand. "Personally, I don't care if you smoke or not. But I do care about how your behavior affects your mother, so I'm a bit confused about what to do."

"Here, take this," he said, dislodging the chocolate. I remembered that Dad had started smoking at age thirteen with his handball buddies on the Bronx streets and that some of my high-school pals had also flirted with tobacco.

Maybe Róbert was going through a cool phase. I decided to give him the benefit of the doubt and promised not to say anything to his mom later that night. Then I rushed to IH.

∞

"If you think the Vajdahunyad is amazing, wait until you see the Castle District lit up at night," Sára told me during class break that night. "That whole area is a protected World Heritage site." As she flipped her gorgeous creamy locks over a delicate bare shoulder, I thought she could be, too.

Gabi was in his favorite position by the vending machine, watching us from across the room. If I was still smarting from his comments the night before, I refused to show it.

Minutes later, Clare came out and motioned us back inside the classroom, where we dozed off while she described the differences between past continuous and past perfect continuous verb tenses. When the lesson was over, we all expelled a sigh of relief.

Béla caught up with me as we stepped into the late winter chill. His brother lagged behind, accompanied by Charles, whose brogue was as thick as the gooey Gruyère served up at the Fondue Bár across the street. Gabi hadn't addressed me at all, leading me to conclude that his older brother had put an end to his classroom antics.

"What happened to you?" Béla asked me. "You're walking with a bit of a hobble."

"I took a tumble with Róbert on the ice earlier today." *While fantasizing about your brother.*

"Sounds promising." He moved in closer and nudged my elbow. "Do tell."

"No, nothing like that. My neighbor asked me to keep

an eye on her fifteen-year-old. I was dreading it but haven't had so much fun on the ice since I was his age."

"And how long ago would that be?"

"My, what a personal question," I said. "Don't you know that American women never reveal their age or weight?"

"Sorry if I offended you. It's just that Hungarians are fascinated with foreigners, especially Americans, and want to know everything about them."

I sized up Béla, from his dusty cowboy boots to buzz-styled scalp, and estimated he was in his mid-thirties. "Let's just say I'm older than you are."

"Fair enough. I turned thirty last December." *Thirty?* He definitely looked older than my sister Wendy, who was about the same age. I immediately wondered how old that made Gabi, whom I'd taken to be in his early thirties.

"And your brother?"

"He'll be twenty-six in November."

"That makes him twenty-five," I muttered toward the ground, trying to conceal my surprise.

"I told you Gabi was immature. He's young, even though he thinks he's more sophisticated than most Hungarians his age."

"You don't have to share all this with me," I said. "I'm just happy Gabi has backed off." The headlights of my tram approached, and I wished Béla luck in preparing his initial lesson the next week. As we waved goodbye, I hoped he couldn't see the disappointment etched on my face. At sixteen years my junior, Gabi really was in Never Never-land.

Get On Up

Ibolted up Bimbó Street, already one hour late for class. What I'd thought would be a simple trip to the mall had turned into an intricate affair: the salesclerk at Mammut Mall in nearby Moscow Square hadn't allowed me to purchase a mobile phone without a residence permit. At my request, Heléna had been called in to vouch for me and co-signed the contract.

Upon entering IH, I heard the unmistakable beat of James Brown echoing through the corridors and wondered if a dance party had taken over the building. *Have I come on the wrong evening?* I peeked inside the classroom, where Clare was sitting at the back, tapping her foot and trying to suppress a wide grin.

"*Bocsánat,*" I apologized to the group before explaining my tardiness to Clare.

"*Nem probléma,*" she said, waving her hand. "You'll soon get used to all this red tape." I snuck over to the only available seat, next to Gabi.

Béla stood in front of the class with a boom box and lowered the volume. "This was only a preview," he told the students. "Today we're going to learn about 'to get.' Most of you are familiar with phrases such as 'to get on a bus.'" They scribbled in their notebooks. "Now for the fun part," Béla continued. "I think you'll know this song, but listen carefully for the phrasal verb that James Brown keeps repeating." He hit the play button.

Gabi wrote on a piece of paper and handed it to me. *Get on up!* it said. *I'm a Sex Machine!* My eyes widened. He grabbed the paper back, adding, *Title of song, not modest confession or statement of fact.*

I fumbled for Gabi's pen. *How about "Let's Get It On" by Marvin Gaye?*

I could go for some "Sexual Healing," he wrote back. I tugged at my purple turtleneck and wished Clare would open a window.

Suddenly, Sándor, one of the older students, asked me to dance. At first, I resisted, then quickly realized it was probably impolite, and joined him and the others in a boogie session while Béla clapped from the sidelines. As the brasses squealed and James scatted toward the climax, everyone was grooving on the floor except Gabi. I caught him staring at me a few times and wondered why he didn't pay more attention to the young, attractive female students. After James wound down, I returned to my seat, breathless.

Béla ejected the CD and asked the students for the phrasal verb. "Get on up!" they all shouted, except for Sándor.

"No, I'm a sex machine," he insisted. Squeals of laughter bounced off the walls.

"Yes, those words are in the song," Béla said. "But what does 'get on up' mean?"

"Maybe 'let's party,'" Rafael suggested. "Let's have fun, or—"

"Let's do the nasty," Gabi chimed in. The students didn't understand, but Clare winced.

"Use your imaginations," she said, looking at the clock. "See you next week!"

As we left the classroom, Béla motioned his brother over. After they volleyed the word "Papa" back and forth, Gabi made a quick phone call, and then approached me.

"Everything okay?" I asked.

"Yup. I just needed to run something by my father." He pulled a cigarette from his pack and dangled it from his lower lip. "Listen, I know I've been a bit of an asshole."

"Yes, you have been getting to me."

"But I'd like to make it up to you."

"And how do you propose to do that?"

"I thought maybe we could *get together.*" He used his fingers as quotation marks around the phrasal verb.

I fidgeted inside my bag, avoiding his enticing gaze. "When did you have in mind?"

We walked out into the lobby, where he lit up. "Tonight, perhaps?"

"You mean *now?*" It was already past nine.

"Well, I just thought . . . it being Women's Day and all."

Earlier that morning, an unusual abundance of flower vendors sprouting up on the sidewalks of St. Stephen's Boulevard had led me to believe it was a special Hungarian holiday for honoring women. But did it have any romantic connotation? *Szar!* I needed to call Heléna for the lowdown, but my new Vodafone wasn't charged up yet.

"You don't have to answer now," Gabi said, glancing at the clock. "You have another fifteen minutes to decide." He pulled at his wool sweater, which was a few snags away from unraveling, and pushed out his stomach. *Those abs again!* Then he lit his cigarette and whispered, "Unless, of course, you have a better offer."

"It's not that." To stall, I slowly buttoned up my black ankle-length coat.

"Aren't you homesick for McDonald's yet?" he asked. I

hadn't eaten in over eight hours, and my stomach growled at the thought of a greasy cheeseburger.

"Is that where you want to take me?" He nodded. *Sounds harmless enough.* "Okay."

We left Béla and the others and walked to Moscow Square, where the Golden Arches beckoned, along with other neon lights flashing atop drab concrete buildings. Late-night commuters bustled to and from the Metró, dodging an avalanche of salespeople who, despite the chilly air, continued to sell underwear, "designer" bags, and cosmetics. Pages of the *Magyar Nemzet* blew away from the kiosk, adding to the mounds of candy wrappers and transport ticket stubs already strewn on the seedy streets. No one seemed to notice or care.

Gabi ordered us each a double cheeseburger, large Coke, and medium fries, then picked up the tab, which I sensed was a big splurge. With his tray, he led me to an available table near a large picture window. Despite the late hour, the place was teeming with small children devouring Happy Meals. After we sat down on the bright orange stools, he tapped my hand. "Okay, Miss America . . . it is *Miss*, isn't it?" I nodded. "Tell me why you ditched your Cliffie diploma and, I presume, some high-level job to come here." He unwrapped his burger. "There's a guy involved, right?"

"Was."

"So, I suspected. What happened?"

"Let's just say he wasn't ready to settle down and have kids. I doubt he ever will be."

"It's incredible to me that a man wouldn't want to have a child."

"There were other issues as well, which I won't go into." Angelica's predictions and my parents' generosity sprang to mind.

"Fair enough. Good for you for not settling, though."

I smiled, thinking of Jenni's insistence that I settle *down*, not settle *for*. Eager to change the subject, I asked Gabi about his family's former life in America. He explained that his father's expertise as a medical researcher had allowed them to live in Buffalo for two years when he was a child, a time he called the happiest of his life. After that, they had moved to London, where he and Béla were educated in English.

"Why did you leave America if you were so happy there?"

"My father was eager to return to Hungary, but my mother begged him to apply for American citizenship for all of us so we could stay. It would be nice to have the option of living in the U.S. now." He swished the ice cubes around his paper cup and shared his fascination with the New World. "I've even been told I speak English with an American accent!"

"Yes, you do." I scraped the mayo off my burger. "It's interesting to hear you so smitten with the States because it's been a dream of mine to live in Eastern Europe."

"That's what I don't get. You're American and can stay in America. Why on earth would you ever want to come *here*?"

"Curiosity. My father's parents were from Poland and Russia. After I get certified at IH, I hope to teach in one of those countries next semester."

"Ugh!" Gabi wiped mustard from his mouth with the back of his hand. "Do you have any idea what the Russians did to this country?" He scanned the room, as if looking for Communists lurking among us. "My grandfather was a minister and couldn't practice his religion; people weren't allowed to congregate; they forced everyone to learn their language; they raped our land and our women, too." He took out the last cigarette from his pack and tapped it against his wrist. After lighting it and inhaling deeply, he let out small spirals of smoke rings that danced up toward the neon lights. "Maybe now you can see why Russians aren't very popular around here."

"I understand those sentiments, Gabi. But my grandmother was only a poor potato picker who hoped for a better life. I want to learn more about her and visit my homeland."

"America's your homeland!" he said, pounding his fist onto the marble tabletop. "You don't know how lucky you are."

I stared out the window at a homeless-looking *babushka* selling daffodils by the Metró. *That could have been Nana.* "Yes, it's true that as an American, I've had certain advantages, but that doesn't mean I don't want to travel or live elsewhere."

"Then why not stay longer in Hungary? I mean, you barely got here, and already you want to leave."

He does have a point. After an awkward silence, I asked Gabi where he'd moved to after his mother had died. He described a Baroque village, Vác, a thirty-minute train ride away in the countryside.

"It must get kind of lonely for you out there."

"Not really." I wondered if Gabi had a live-in girlfriend but didn't want to pry. As if reading my mind, he quickly added, "I live with my father."

That possibility hadn't crossed my mind. "Nice for your father," I blurted out, not quite sure how to respond.

"Speaking of which," Gabi said, "I need to check the time because he's fetching me from the train station soon." He reached into the pocket of his leather jacket, which he had placed on the seat behind him, and tossed its contents onto the table. "Am I going crazy? I thought my watch was in here." He slapped his jeans pockets and rummaged through his knapsack. "It was my grandfather's, a family heirloom." He got down on his knees and searched the area around the table. "*Szar!* My mobile phone's missing, too." He threw his cigarette down and stomped on it. "Did you see anyone suspicious sitting behind me?"

"Sorry, no."

Gabi found a pay phone and went to call his father. "I'll have to stay and file a police report," he said. "What a frickin' drag. These *Hungarians*."

I thanked him for dinner and gathered my belongings, feeling guilty that Gabi had gotten more than he'd bargained for. As I heard him discuss the night's events with "Papa," I wondered if I had, too.

Linduska

On Sunday afternoon, Heléna invited me over for home-made *gulyás*, a much spicier version of goulash than I was used to. After greeting me at the door, she returned to the stovetop and continued to field customer service calls on her supposed day off. Her once-copper curls, now burgundy spikes, poked out from a Russian-style headscarf. Obviously, she'd been back to the hairdresser; I dared not pry.

After switching off her phone, she ladled pieces of meat, potatoes, and carrots swimming in blood red paprika broth into my ceramic bowl. "I'm impressed," Heléna said, after I filled her in on the evening with Gabi. "You here only short time and already had date."

"It was hardly a date, especially after the weird ending."

"Yes, unfortunate. Those gypsy stealers!"

"Well, we don't really know who took the phone or watch now, do we?" I helped myself to a thick slice of homemade bread. "I mean, it could've been anyone, including me."

"Oh, come now—rich American or gypsy man?"

Heléna chortled and wagged her middle finger at me. "I'm sure it gypsy man, not you, Linduska."

"Linduska?"

"Yes, that's you." She explained that changing the ending of my name made it a term of endearment, like "Marci" for "Márton." "When you hear, it means person likes you."

"*Linduska.* That does have a certain flair."

Róbert zoomed in with his dinner bowl, and after spotting me, tried to make a quick getaway.

"Your son was an absolute angel last week," I told Heléna in a slightly sarcastic tone. "So considerate, so helpful on the ice." Heléna chastised him for ignoring me, their guest; Róbert rolled his eyes and fled back to his bedroom.

"Oh, thanks be to the God," Heléna said, crossing herself. "I was worried that he and his friends are smoking the grass." I was sure the cigarettes had been of the legal variety. She uncorked a bottle of Bikavér, or "Bull's Blood," from Eger's wine region and poured two glasses of the red wine. "And now a toast. In Hungary, we say '*Egészségedre.*'"

"*Eggeshegg,*" I sputtered, clinking my crystal against hers.

"Linduska," she said, brushing my knuckles, "never say that. Hungarians think you mean 'ass.'" She put down her glass and leaned forward. "It's *Eg-ész-ség-e-dre.*" She pointed to her mouth, enunciating the "sz" sound, like "s" in English.

I tried again.

"Perfect," she said. "Now here's toast to you and your new boyfriend."

"I wouldn't call him a boyfriend, although it seems he is a boy." I mentioned how I had miscalculated Gabi's age by about six years.

"My dear, here in Hungary, age not important when

doing sex. Look at me—I'm fortysomething and the István ten years younger."

"Ten years is a lot different than sixteen."

"Only in brain it is." She went into the kitchen nook and returned with a cold salad of diced eggs, pickles, and mushrooms smothered in mayo. "Your last boyfriend was old man. Now time for young one."

I reached over the embroidered tablecloth to spoon out the salad. "Another problem is that Gabi lives with his father. Is that common here in Hungary?"

"Absolutely." Heléna sat down and placed a linen napkin on her lap. "Young people can't afford to have own flat until married or inherit from family." I thought of Heléna's long haul with Róbert and shuddered. "My dear Linduska, stop worrying where Gabi live, his age, and have fun. 'Go for it!' as you Americans say."

Suddenly, the overhead lights flickered on and off, and Heléna bustled about the room, lighting several candles. *There goes the electrical system again.* She eventually sat down and took out a few Post-it notes and a pen. "Now I'm going to learn you some useful Hungarian words. The first thing you need know when you alone with Gabi again is '*Veled akarok lenni.*'"

"And that would mean?"

"I want to lay with you."

"That's quite an icebreaker," I said, grinning. "I think I prefer 'Find Someone Who.'"

"It's nice way, not pervo way," she insisted, writing the words down.

"More importantly, I need to know how to discuss safe sex. You know, condoms."

"*Nem, nem,*" Heléna said, waving her fork at me. "Most Magyar men don't use. Instead, they say, '*Nem szeretek zokniban szeretkezni.*'"

"And that translates to?"

"I don't make love in socks."

I thought back to what Heléna had told me about István, giving me the impression that Hungarian men were spoiled by their doting partners. "Well, that's that then," I said, wiping imaginary crumbs from my hands. She pushed the Post-its into my palms, which I reluctantly slid into my bag and imagined sticking onto my headboard. *Who knows? I may need to refer to them in a pinch.*

After clearing the table, Heléna excused herself and poked into her son's room. A heated exchange of "*Szar!*" and "*Baszd meg!*" was followed by her return to the living room with an offer of fifteen minutes on their computer. "Sorry, Linduska, that's the limit because we pay for Internet connection by the minute."

Heléna understood that I hadn't brought a laptop with me to Hungary because the IH flats were not wired for Internet access. Grateful for the chance to check messages from concerned loved ones, I squeezed into Róbert's room, which he shared with a full-sized refrigerator, and sat at the wobbly computer workstation. Since there was no time to read through or respond to every email, I wrote a group one to family and friends:

My dears,

Having a great time so far. At my neighbor's eating goulash and other treats. Flat isn't great, electrical system dubious, but hopefully moving soon. School seems promising. Beautiful city! Enjoying swimming in spas, ice skating at castle, Art Nouveau architecture, friendly people. Soon concerts at the Franz Liszt Music Academy.

Love and miss you,

Linduska

I reread what I'd written; something wasn't right. I was having way too much fun to be homesick. I moved the cursor over to "and miss" and deleted it.

Guardian Angel

As much as I enjoyed the perks of living across from Heléna, the long commute to IH was getting to me, as were the building's temperamental utility systems. After surviving yet another electrical power outage, I spoke with Vali about moving to a more convenient location; she claimed to have the perfect place in mind. An hour later, she drove me up the very steep hills surrounding IH to the new neighborhood, where once elegant, crumbling mansions stood behind wrought iron fences. Near the top, she turned left onto a dead-end street and turned off the ignition. The sign read "Tulipán utca." Tulip Street.

"There it is, on the first floor," Vali said, pointing through the fence. "You even have a balcony."

I glanced around at the peaceful, bucolic surroundings and the upscale villa next door. Having a balcony overlooking a large yard lined with birch trees and forsythia bushes more than made up for whatever the interior might lack.

"This must be much more expensive than what I'm already paying." In my eagerness to move, I'd forgotten to ask Vali about the monthly rent and utility fees.

"No, the price is the same, about 300 US dollars."

"Really?" I marveled at the low overhead and my good fortune.

Vali guided me to the apartment's entrance at the back of the building. As soon as she opened the door, light burst through the windows and bounced off the parquet floors and high ceilings. A small but clean kitchen overlooked the spacious backyard. The long, narrow hallway was lined with Persian rugs and led into a large living room decorated with wooden antiques, including a huge hand-carved desk and mirrored teak bar lined with crystal apéritif glasses. An enormous marble tub filled the spotless, modernized bathroom. I thought of the dreaded hose back in the shower of my drab apartment and almost jumped for joy. The bedroom boasted a massive Art Deco armoire and matching dresser; all the bed coverings were handcrafted in silk and lace. I'd never seen such romantic sleeping quarters and already felt tucked in.

"Well, what do you think?" said Vali.

"It's heavenly."

"Let me show you how to operate the heating system." We walked back to the living room and over to a large object enclosed in shiny green ceramic. As we got closer, Vali pointed to the pilot light; I noticed various images of male warriors etched into the ceramic cover. In one motif, two identical men were standing shoulder to shoulder, protecting themselves with frontal shields. Another ancient Greek figure stood alone atop a sailboat, his arms outstretched, a single word carved beneath his feet: ODYSSEUS.

A familiar tingly feeling shot up my limbs to the crown of my head. I grasped the top of the heater and pulled myself up eye level with Vali. "How soon can I move in?"

∞

In celebration of moving to my new digs, Gabi and Béla promised to take me out to dinner after Friday's class. I chose the small, mysterious eatery we often passed en route to IH, intrigued by its boarded-up look, the bright yellow "FONDUE BÁR" sign the only indication that diners were welcome. Fortunately, Béla had done some sleuthing and nabbed a reservation. I was happy for the opportunity to spend time with my friends outside the classroom, without Béla rushing home to his wife Ágnes, or Gabi to Papa in Vác.

We entered a space the size of my new bedroom and squeezed into a picnic table with two others. After translating the menu, Béla motioned to the bartender, who nodded to one of his patrons, a middle-aged woman wearing a black business suit. She slid down from a bar stool and almost landed in my lap. "*Bocs,*" she apologized, her eyes glazed over, her breath reeking of Bailey's. *No wonder the blinds are always drawn here.* She fumbled for a pen and scribbled down our order for drinks and three *Svájci* meals. When she tottered away, Béla explained that she was filling in for the regular waitress, who had phoned in sick.

The bar was stacked with as many old jazz LPs as bottles of booze. Ella Fitzgerald's velvety voice mingled with the tempting aroma of Gruyère and garlic wafting in from the kitchen. Photos of celebrity guests, framed comic strips, and Route 66 license plates covered the shiny, knotty pine-paneled walls.

Before the first round of drinks was finished, our fondue pots arrived, and we dipped pieces of dried bread and apple into the thick, greasy vats of cheese.

"Your new place sounds incredible," Béla said. "But why not get a roommate? Your rent will be cheaper." I didn't want to tell him and Gabi that the monthly rent of 300 US dollars was a bargain; for most Hungarian professionals, it was one month's salary.

"I guess I like my privacy, so I'm willing to tighten my belt elsewhere."

"If she's not concerned about the money, Béla, let her have the place to herself."

"I'll drink to that," I said, raising my glass of Bikavér to the ceiling. "*Egészségedre!*"

"Not bad pronunciation," Gabi said, leaning over to clink my glass.

Béla seemed preoccupied and lit a cigarette from the sterno can. "What a relief that we're halfway through the course," he said. "Soon I'll have time for more important matters."

"Like what?" I wanted to know.

"Like making a baby. Ágnes and I have been trying to get pregnant."

"Obviously not hard enough," Gabi said, shooting me a furtive wink.

Béla blew smoke rings up to the inverted straw baskets that doubled as lampshades. "When I get home from IH, I'm so pooped, all I can do is sit in front of the TV."

"Haven't you guys heard of multitasking, or is that an American concept?"

"I think it's a gal thing," Gabi said. "Men can only focus on one thing at a time." He glanced up at the clock. "Which reminds me, I have to get going."

"What about your dinner?" I pointed to the remaining apples and tiny pickles waiting to be dipped into his fondue pot. *Is he slipping out early to meet a date?*

"I'm too excited to eat. I need to get home to *The Philosopher's Stone*. Harry is about to play his first Quidditch match, and the suspense is killing me." Gabi downed his Dreher beer and threw a few coins on the table. "I'll call over the weekend, Linda, and let you know how it turns out."

"Great," I said, forcing a smile. Although I hadn't seen

much of Gabi socially since our visit to McDonald's, he had been calling almost every night with a *Harry Potter* update. While I wasn't a big fan of the book, I looked forward to our magical pillow talk.

"Gabi only has eyes for *Harry* these days," Béla commented after his brother had left. "That's not normal for a guy his age. Instead of being interested in this . . ." he cupped his hands by his chest, ". . . he's interested in wizards and warlocks."

"Seems like a waste," I muttered.

"What did you say?" Béla cocked an eye at me.

"I mean, Gabi *is* quite attractive—Hogwarts and all."

"You think my brother's good-looking?"

"Doesn't everybody? You see the way the female students swoon over him in class." *Not to mention me.*

"Hmm . . ."

After more wine and one last *"Egészségedre,"* Béla offered to walk me to my new home. Sensing that Ágnes was counting the minutes until her husband's return, I declined. As soon as he left, I eyed Lövőház Street and the steep climb up to Tulip Street. Since moving to the neighborhood two weeks earlier, I walked from Moscow Square daily but hadn't attempted the hill so late at night. Aside from a few dozen moviegoers leaving Mammut Cineplex, the road was desolate. I crossed over to the well-lit tennis club and walked to Marczibányi Square, where an abandoned mansion dominated one corner and a boarded-up convenience store another. The only sound was the swishing of treetops swaying in the breeze. Goosebumps popped up beneath my black wool jacket, and I quickly turned onto the main road for the last leg of the trek.

As I crossed the intersection, a man emerged from the shadows of the mansion and brushed against my shoulder as he passed. He was young—about thirty, small frame, outdated clothes—and didn't strike me as drunk or homeless. I kept walking and felt his eyes boring into my back. Sensing trouble, I turned around and headed back down toward the better-lit square. He followed.

Most of the homes were nestled far from the road, situated behind concrete walls or steel fences, making it impossible to seek help. I rummaged in my bag for my new mobile phone and the piece of paper with Béla's number, actions which only encouraged the stranger to come closer. He mumbled some indecipherable Hungarian mouthfuls in a strange accent; I recognized the word "*táska*" for "bag."

"Get away!" I shouted, running toward the nearest store in the hope of flagging down an oncoming car. When I turned around, he had vanished, although I sensed he was lurking close by. I struggled to catch my breath, legs shaking from the adrenaline rush. They wobbled me back down Lövőház Street, where I stopped in front of a large institutional building with a façade of white-yellow stone and sleek glass. Unfortunately, it was locked behind a metal gate. A nearby telephone booth offered refuge; I ducked inside and fumbled again for Béla's number. When I looked up, the stalker was approaching. My heart pumped as if it might shatter the glass. I quickly opened the door and stood facing the gate, not knowing what to do.

Suddenly, a young woman in a wheelchair zoomed up in front of him and came toward me. She looked about twenty years old and had long, wavy honey-colored hair.

I pointed to the man a few yards behind her and said, "*Férfi nem jó.*" The girl wasn't able to turn her head but smiled at my attempt to describe the "bad man." "*Férfi* want *táska*," I added, tugging on my bag and enacting the scene I was sure would follow. The man stopped behind the girl, his devious plans thwarted.

"Come," she said, leaning forward to change speeds on her wheelchair. She directed me with a slow arm toward the gate and pushed down on a navigational panel that magically opened it. As soon as we got inside, it closed on the stranger a few footsteps behind. He sped around and slithered down Lövőház Street.

We passed a security checkpoint and soon were safely inside the building's blue and white concrete walls. I unbuttoned my coat and gasped the stuffy air. "What's your name?" I asked the girl.

"Beatrix," she said in a sweet voice. "But everyone call me Bea."

I introduced myself and clasped her warm hands in mine. "*Köszi*, Bea. You are my Guardian Angel."

She looked at me with large blue saucers that lit up the skies. "Sorry, I no understand. I call Gyöngyi, and we visit her. She speak better English."

As we entered the brightly lit lobby, I wondered if the heat was on full force or if I was experiencing the aftermath of a panic attack. I took off my coat and aired out my armpits. Despite the late hour, several residents of what appeared to be a home for disabled youth whizzed by in their wheelchairs. One young man with short reddish hair lay face down on a stretcher, using a pencil in his mouth to press a device that allowed it to move. Although his twisted hands were where his elbows should have been, and his legs knotted up behind his back, he was undeterred and zipped about gracefully.

A collection of colorful, whimsical paintings adorned the otherwise cheerless walls. One piece suggested a Chagall-esque landscape, where animals levitated over a thatched roof barn and a field full of red poppies. Nearby, a large replica of a ship had been created with thousands of toothpicks. The name "Lajos" was scrawled on a plaque.

"Who is Lajos?" I asked Bea. "He's very talented."

She looked around and nodded toward the man in the stretcher, who was now busy conversing with another resident. "That's him." My eyes widened. "He does using only his mouth."

"Amazing!" I would have liked to meet him, but Bea swiveled into the elevator and motioned for me to join her.

Gyöngyi was waiting for us in the dormitory-style room she and Bea shared. Glancing around, I recalled the home for young women with similar limitations I'd often visited as a volunteer during my undergraduate years at Bard. Although I was now on a different continent, the rooms here looked much the same as those of their American counterparts. Life-sized posters of pop stars lined the walls, dressers bulged with makeup and candy, and dirty linens were strewn on the industrial carpeting. As memories of former decades gushed back in warm waves, I wondered what had become of those young women of whom I'd been so fond.

"Welcome," Gyöngyi whispered. Bea's friend had jet-black hair and snow-white skin, which captured the essence of her translated name, "Pearl." Her luminous almond-shaped eyes appeared crossed, but it was too dark to be certain. "Tell us what happened, Linda."

"I moved to Tulipán Street recently, and this was my first late night out," I began. I described how the stalker had followed me and how Bea had intercepted him just when I thought he would attack.

"Good that Bea was there," Gyöngyi said, smiling at her friend.

I was curious as to what Bea had been doing out at that late hour but didn't pry. As our conversation continued, I learned that Gyöngyi came from a large, loving family, whereas Bea had been orphaned by a mother, who had died a few years earlier, and a father "who don't want me like this." She tapped the sides of her wheelchair with her elbows.

"I'm sorry," I said, at a loss for words as to why any father would abandon his child, especially one like Bea.

"I accept," she said, tears in her eyes. I fought hard not to let mine show.

The girls told me that they spent their days in the workshop next door, weaving straw placemats, which were sold to local retailers, and attended on-site high school classes, where they learned English.

"You both speak very well." They giggled and conversed in their native tongue. "Listen, it's late, and we all need some sleep. Could you please call me a taxi? I'm still too shaken up to walk home alone." I offered my phone, but Gyöngyi was already on hers, dialing a cab service. The three of us squeezed into the elevator and returned to the lobby.

A honking sound alerted me to the taxi; I leaned over and whispered to Gyöngyi. "Earlier I told Bea that she's my Guardian Angel. Do you know what that means?" She nodded. "Please explain to her. I promise to visit you soon." They followed me outside and waited until I was safely in the car. From my window, I waved and shouted, "*Köszi, Köszi!*"

As their angelic smiles faded in the distance, I settled into my seat and relished the full weight of my arms and legs. Then I marveled at the evening's series of events, which had put Bea serendipitously in my path.

The Trouble With Harry

Béla shook a finger at me during our coffee break in class the next day. "Why didn't you call me first thing? You have my number."

"Yes, but I hadn't yet programmed it into my new phone."

He rolled his sleepy blue eyes, pushed his palm through his spiky-haired scalp, and exhaled some swearwords along with his cigarette smoke. "Tell me what this guy looked like."

After I described the stalker's dark features and frumpy fashion style, Béla remarked that he was most likely a Roma gypsy looking for a way to finance a new mobile phone or to permanently borrow mine. "But lucky you escaped. If that ever happens again, scream '*Fasz kivan!*' and the guy will run away so fast with his tail between his legs, he won't know what hit him."

Gabi, who was engaged with some of the guinea pig students across the room, suddenly gasped and looked down at his jeans zipper. Then he threw his hands up in his brother's direction; Béla waved him off.

"What does that expression mean?" I asked Béla. "Is it like the F-word in English?"

He grinned. "Something like that, only stronger. Here, repeat after me: *Fasz kivan, fasz kivan.*" As he continued drilling me, the students stared in confusion.

"She's brushing up on her Hungarian," Gabi told them before strutting over in his poured-on, ripped jeans, affording me a peek at the toned physique underneath. "Enough about gerunds," he said. "This conversation sounds far more interesting."

"You have to walk Linda home after class, Gabi. Linda was stalked the other night. I'll clear it with Papa."

"Okey dokey." Gabi raised his eyebrows many times, which inspired me to fantasize about what might happen once we got to my place.

After the teaching session was over, he and I began the slow ascent to my apartment in the waning dusk, past once-grand homes now overrun with weeds. The last few days had been warm, hinting at spring, with crocuses poking up through cracks in the asphalt. Gabi stopped every few minutes to catch his breath. Finally, he gripped the metal grating outside a bakery and bent over.

"You okay, Gabi?"

"Yup. Just these cigarettes."

"You really should quit, you know."

"Yes, *Mom.* Like I don't already know that."

"It's just that you're so young and . . ." *I've such a crush on you.*

"I'm not quitting, at least not now. I'll do that after I become a dad."

"That could be years."

"I hope not. I intend to be a father fairly soon, actually."

"Sounds serious." I hoped he'd elaborate, but he did

not. "If Ms. Rowling keeps cranking out more *Harry Potter* novels, you might be permanently out of circulation."

He smiled long enough to keep a cigarette out of his mouth.

Approaching the darkened intersection at Marczibányi Tér, where I'd been stalked, Gabi asked for a recap of the incident. He listened intently as I described how lovingly Bea and Gyöngyi had taken care of me. "It's like magic the way Bea suddenly appeared," he said. "You should do something to show your appreciation."

"Like what?" I had already visited the girls twice and brought them chocolates and flowers. They had seemed happy to see me and eager to practice English with a native speaker.

"Slip them a wad of greenbacks. You are a rich American, after all."

"I knew you'd say that. But money isn't the answer. I prefer to spoil them on occasion and spend time with them."

"Hey, I've got it!" Gabi said as we arrived at Tulip Street. "You're a fundraiser, right? Why not volunteer for a local organization that helps the disabled?" The idea had crossed my mind, but I'd wanted to wait until our course was over. "I'm sure many agencies would appreciate your American expertise."

"I'll think about it. Especially since I don't want to lose my fundraising chops."

"You won't." He took out another Sopianae and let it dangle from his lips. "It's like riding a bicycle. You never forget how to *do it*."

I stopped, and we stood facing each other in front of my building gate. Except for the lone light shining from the neighboring villa, it was pitch dark. A few days earlier at IH, when Gabi had discreetly draped an arm around my waist in the hallway, I'd been tempted to pull him into an empty classroom for a quick kiss. Unfortunately, Béla had been close behind. Now I desperately wished he'd reel me in close enough so I could feel his smooth olive skin against mine.

Gabi locked eyes with mine in a seductive way that sent sparks dancing down my torso. I quickly turned away before I found myself doing a cougar-sized pounce in his direction.

He pulled the cigarette from his mouth. "Sorry if I offended you. I was only trying to impress you with my vast knowledge of English expressions now that you're so well-versed in the Hungarian ones."

"It's not that." *Veled akarok lenni. I want to lay with you.*

"Then?" He touched my shoulder gently; I turned around to meet his smoldering gaze.

"It's been a while," I said, glancing up at my flat. "Since I've been on a bicycle, I mean."

"I hear you." He ran his fingers through his slightly disheveled, flaxen-colored locks and moved in closer, facing the building. "I'd love to come in, but . . ."

"I know, your father's waiting. *Harry,* too." I fumbled in my bag for the keys.

"A rain check, perhaps?"

"Sure."

I poked around with the key, but in the dim light couldn't find the keyhole; Gabi had more luck. After I walked through the gate and closed it quietly behind, he leaned against it in push-up position and pointed his index fingers at me through the wires. "In the near future, there's something important I'd like to share with you."

After he fled down the hill, I spent much of the night imagining what it might be.

Maribel

A few weeks later, I noticed an advertisement on the IH events board for the International Women's Club Spring Ball. Intrigued that it was exactly what Gabi had mentioned—a fundraiser for local charities that supported disabled youth—I phoned the organization for more details and was invited to attend their April meeting at the Marriott Hotel.

The venue was a short walk from the Pest side of Margit Bridge. I exited the tram in favor of a stroll along the banks of the Danube and passed the sprawling Parliament Building that had been modeled after its counterpart on the Thames. Nearby, the bullet-ridden Ministry of Agriculture Building bore testimony to the ravages of the failed Uprising of 1956, when thousands of Hungarian students had protested USSR oppression. Their attempts to broadcast demands for political reform were crushed by Soviet tanks and the State Security Police, who threw tear gas and opened fire, killing thousands. It had taken Hungary over thirty years to become liberated from the Soviet Union.

The concrete-terraced façade of the Marriott contrasted

with its swanky interior. I followed signs for the meeting registration up to the spacious mezzanine. Through the panoramic windows, Hungary's version of the Statue of Liberty held an enormous olive leaf in her outstretched arms atop Gellért Hill. Below, traffic buzzed on Elizabeth Bridge as riverboats glided up and down the Danube.

After checking in, I entered the Buda Ballroom, where the red-gold carpeting was as loud as the makeup on the professionally attired, perfectly coiffed women. Then I made my way through the numerous booths set up by local restaurants, gyms, and other businesses on the lookout for the almighty American dollar.

At the table promoting the Friends of the Franz Liszt Music Academy, I spoke with Aiko, a young Japanese woman who studied piano there. After sharing our love of the Master's work, she invited me to become a member of their organization; I eagerly signed up.

The International Women's Club (IWC) charity booth was a few tables away. Janice, a volunteer from America, informed me that the group was desperate to find a fund-raising chair. I told her about my professional background and desire to help people like Bea and Gyönyi. She scribbled down a phone number and encouraged me to meet as soon as possible with the group's President, Maribel, who did the "hiring."

When I returned home, I contacted Maribel, who invited me to breakfast at the posh Le Méridien Hotel in Deák Square. Her choice seemed extravagant for a nonprofit organization and made me a bit wary. Nonetheless, the next morning I donned my gray power pantsuit, draped a silk Japanese scarf from Jenni around my neck, and went downtown to meet her.

Upon arriving at Le Méridien, an attractive male attendant greeted me in English and motioned toward the revolving glass door. Inside, a long Oriental carpet cut a path toward an inviting plush velvet sofa. Exactly on time, I sat down and glanced around the sumptuous lobby for someone from the Far East, as I'd detected an accent in Maribel's voice. I noted an attractive fiftyish woman of Asian descent standing by the window, talking on her mobile phone. Her clingy, silver mesh dress showed off a graceful physique and delicate features; large diamond ear studs gleamed against her shiny black hair. She caught my reflection and turned, then nodded slightly before resuming her conversation. It took ten more minutes for her to acknowledge me again.

"Linda, I presume?" She swaggered over to greet me, one hand extended, the other holding a tightly rolled ciga-rette, definitely not of the Sopianae variety. Despite the smoke clouding her pretty but reserved face, an aroma of gardenias enveloped her. "This way, please." She studied me from head to toe as we walked into Le Bourbon restau-rant, whose rotunda had most likely been chiseled out of several tons of white marble.

"You must excuse," she said, waving her cigarette in a circular motion. "I just finished one meeting, now this." She pushed a stack of paperwork away from my side of the table and pointed to the menu. "I don't have much time," she continued, glancing down at her diamond-encrusted watch. Her perfectly manicured fingers snapped three times, and the same number of tuxed waiters appeared before I had a chance to decide what to order.

"A pot of Earl Grey tea," I told them, suddenly feeling quite full.

"Another espresso," Maribel said, tossing her thick mane as she turned toward me. "Janice told me a little about your background," she began, blowing smoke toward the crystal chandelier dangling from the stained-glass ceiling. "Why do you want to fundraise for the IWC and not another group?"

Other than my interest in helping people with physical challenges, I hadn't thought of pitting one organization against another. "I like the idea of fundraising for various charities under the auspices of one international group," I fudged. "Plus, it's a fun way to meet women from other cultures."

"Fun? Did you say *fun*?"

"Why, yes."

"I wouldn't call fundraising *fun*. That's why we can't find anyone for the position."

"It can be—that's why the word 'fun' is in 'fundraising.'"

Maribel pursed her magenta-stained lips. "Listen, miss," she said, snapping her fingers again. "It *is* miss, isn't it?"

"Yes," I said, feeling like a seventy-year-old spinster. "Please just call me Linda."

All three waiters glided back across the spotless marble floor: one with my porcelain tea service, another with Maribel's coffee, and the third carrying a milk pitcher.

"Well, Linda. Ours is an organization of housewives, get it? *Housewives*. Women who meet once a month to discuss these pesky fundraising issues." Her cool brown eyes pierced mine; sweat dripped down my armpits, staining my suit jacket. "In a nutshell, we are housewives who have time for these projects, and believe me, they are *quite* demanding."

"Yes, Janice was telling me—"

"Let me cut to the chase, miss, er, um—"

"Linda."

"Precisely. We are looking for a fundraising chair with lots of time on her hands." Maribel motioned one of the waiters over and indicated her ashtray was full. He quickly scooped up a clean one from a neighboring table and placed it in front of her. "I take it that you're working?"

"Not yet, but I hope to teach ESL starting this fall." I

shifted in my silk-covered seat and mentioned the certification program at IH; her blank stare spoke volumes about what she thought of the teaching profession. "I have extra time and thought I might help with special events, such as your upcoming Spring Ball."

Maribel exhaled abruptly and leaned her petite frame over the ashtray to dispense with the ashes dangling from her cigarette tip. "My dear, you have no idea how much work is involved in this type of gala."

"Actually, I do." I told her about the AIDS fundraising dinner with honorary guest Goldie Hawn that I'd once helped organize for over one thousand attendees in Boston.

"Good. Then you'll agree it really is a full-time job. We're looking for someone who can devote thirty or more hours per week to the task."

I sipped the last of my tea and firmly put down the gold-rimmed cup. Janice hadn't mentioned this type of commitment; I sensed Maribel was looking for a way out of "hiring" me because I was a miss and not a missus. In case I hadn't yet fully understood her point, she added, "Tell me, what are your diplomatic connections here in Budapest?"

I wiped my mouth with a white linen napkin. "I've only been here about two months."

"My husband is a 56er. Do you know what that means?"

"Yes." I couldn't imagine why Maribel would bring up the Hungarian Revolution of that year, other than to stress her superiority in having married a national hero. I leaned over for my bag and slid the equivalent of three dollars in forints across the table. "This is to cover the cost of the tea," I said. "Money that could be helping people who really need it." I slung the satchel over my shoulder. "Sorry, but this doesn't seem to be a good fit for either of us. Good luck finding this fantasy person."

Maribel's ignored my comment and mashed her cigarette stub into the ashtray. I escaped through the lobby and exited via the revolving glass door. Rather than hire one of the shiny black Mercedes taxis waiting outside, I walked and seethed my way back to Tulip Street. As much as Maribel's comments stung, the worst part was having her squash my enthusiasm.

Once at home, I slipped into my comfy robe, poured a shot of Unicum liqueur, and flipped through a handful of classical CDs on the balcony. Beethoven's Ninth Symphony always lifted my spirits, especially the heavenly choral movement, "Ode to Joy." I placed it on the dinky Sony player and sang along in German, inhaling the sweet scent of lilacs arching over the driveway.

As the tenor and alto soloists wove their voices together, the landline rang. I debated answering it but thought it might be an emergency call from the States.

"Hello, Linda?" a woman with a perky, unfamiliar voice asked.

"Yes."

"This is Adél Simon. I'm on the Board of the Friends of the Franz Liszt Music Academy. Aiko tells me you're a devoted Liszt fan." I put Ludwig on pause and dashed over to the desk, pen and notebook in hand.

"Yes, big time."

I could hear Adél smile. "She also told me you're a fundraiser. I'm hoping you'll be interested in helping the Academy with our upcoming special events. Will you still be in Budapest next term?"

I sensed that this opportunity was somehow a pivotal part of my Odyssey, and felt a lump rising in my throat. "Yes, I'll be here," I said. And for the first time, I truly meant it.

Lisztomania

The day before my interview at the Music Academy, I bought a few Liszt biographies and brushed up on the history of my musical idol. Although Adél's warm and welcoming tone had reassured me that she wasn't Maribel's alter ego, I wanted to be super prepared for our first meeting.

I knew that Liszt had grown up in the small Hungarian village of Doborján, now known as Raiding in Austria. However, I was surprised to learn that his father, who had taught him the piano and considered him a child prodigy, had whisked him away to Vienna when he was only eleven. The boy then studied with Carl Czerny and played for the much-impressed Beethoven. Years later, inspired by a performance by Paganini, Liszt vowed to match the Italian violinist's skill with his prowess on the piano. After achieving this goal, he embarked on extensive European tours, dazzling audiences with his stupendous talent.

As a musician, I was fascinated to read that Liszt often gave the illusion of playing with a third hand and used his nose to compensate for missing notes beyond the range of his fingers. As the foremost pianist of his time, he created the concept of the solo recital and was the first to perform in profile position, drawing attention to his handsome features and driving rapt females in the audience into a frenzy. Many swooned, others fainted. One is said to have carried the remnants of the Master's extinguished cigar next to her bosom until death.

"Lisztomania" reached new heights in Paris, where Franz quickly became the darling of the crème de la crème, soaking up their language and culture while courting and bedding rich aristocratic women. One, Countess Marie d'Agoult, scandalized her husband by leaving him to travel with Liszt and bearing her lover's three children.

While performing in Kiev in 1847, Liszt met Princess Carolyne von Sayn-Wittgenstein, who became his instant soul mate and long-time mistress. After she encouraged him to give up the concert stage in favor of composition, they left for Weimar, where he wrote most of his one thousand-plus opuses for piano and taught aspiring musicians free of charge.

I hadn't realized that Liszt never properly learned Hungarian, as his parents' mother tongue was German, and he'd resided most of his adult life abroad. Despite the language barrier, he considered himself a patriot, often performing charity concerts to raise funds for flood and hunger relief in Hungary. Later in life, he returned to Budapest, where he was hailed a national hero and helped found the renowned musical institution bearing his name.

The next morning, I approached the palatial Franz Liszt Music Academy, clad in a new deep purple suit from Marks & Spencer and armed with a polished fundraising resume. High above the neat rows of chestnut trees, nightclubs, and trendy restaurants, an enthroned statue of the Master, surrounded by ornate limestone columns, dominated the square. In awe, I looked up. *If only I can give back some of what you've given me, Franz.*

A few steps later, I inhaled deeply and entered the Academy's Art Nouveau interior. Adél had promised to meet me at nine o'clock, and with ten minutes to spare, I strolled through the exquisite lobby, gravitating toward frescoes of angels and semi-nude nymphs. Young music students from all over the world bustled about the cavernous foyer, carrying oboes, French horns, and violins. Light seeped in through stained-glass windows and danced upon shiny black marble columns adorned with gold swirls offset by malachite Zsolnay tiles. *Am I really here, or did I sleep through the alarms?*

As I basked in the Jugendstil splendor, a pretty thirty-something woman approached, wearing a gorgeous beige silk coat and carrying a briefcase. Her shiny dark brown bob matched the color of her luminous eyes, which smiled above plum-colored lips. Adél spotted me at once and greeted me with kisses. Before I could respond, she led me up the sweeping, ornamental staircase to an oak-paneled room lined with portraits of former directors and teachers of the Music Academy, including composers Bartók and Kodály. A painting of Liszt, circa 1876, hung at the head of the conference table. Two Yamaha grands had been pushed into a faraway corner. My fingertips tingled; it had been five months since I'd touched a keyboard.

"I was so pleased to hear from Aiko that you're a pianist, as well as a Liszt lover," Adél said, motioning me toward a wooden chair. "Tell me, which Liszt piece is your favorite?"

"That would be his third *Liebestraum*."

"I prefer his choral works, although they're not quite as well-known." She told me she sang with a chorus that often performed in the Great Hall downstairs, and invited me to hear them in the fall. I noted the concert date in my planner.

Before Adél uttered one word about fundraising for the Friends, I had already decided I would do anything, schedule permitting, to help her and the Academy. Still, I listened to her pitch about the importance of maintaining the building, or "shrine," the need to support gifted musicians, the ability to attract the most prominent instructors. After an hour, during which I gazed up at Franz's picture and fought the urge to pinch myself, I told Adél I'd be honored to help out.

She exhaled a blissful sigh. "You have no idea how difficult it is to find someone with your experience in Hungary. Fundraising is still a new concept here."

"You have no idea how much I've enjoyed meeting *you*." We agreed to be in touch over the summer and meet in September for a brainstorming session.

Back on Franz Liszt Square, I spotted a bronze statue of the older Master wearing a traditional cassock of his time. His telltale facial moles were quite pronounced, as was the still-full head of hair, which swung toward his outstretched right hand. I gave it a squeeze. "*Köszönöm*, Franz," I whispered in gratitude before rushing to IH.

∞

"Yippee!" Gabi shouted, throwing his pack of cigarettes into the air on Bimbó Street after I'd told him about the meeting with Adél. "This means you're staying in Budapest beyond the summer?"

"Assuming I can line up a teaching job for the fall semester."

"You just made my day . . . no, make that my whole year." We passed a kebab stand and turned into the IH courtyard. "Although I don't quite understand your obsession with Liszt."

"How can you say that about your famous national treasure?"

"Linda, the guy was barely Hungarian." He took my elbow and led me up the marble staircase. "Do you know that his name means 'flour'?"

"Oh, flower. How lovely."

"No, flour as in baking."

My idol, a biscuit ingredient? I tried to hide my disappointment. "That's probably why he was discouraged from learning your language."

Inside the classroom, we found two seats in the corner. Clare introduced yet another icebreaker based on the question: "What one thing would you bring to a desert island?"

"That's easy," Gabi told the group. "Cindy Crawford." Charles nodded furiously; Béla rolled his eyes. Gabi turned to me, adding, "I'm partial to those dark-looking types."

"Me, too," I said, eyeing his light brown locks.

"Guess I'll have to dye my hair black and spend more time in the sun." He pulled at his fair strands and arched his eyebrows. "What do you think, Linduska?"

I'll make an exception for you! As I took in his sculpted, yet graceful arms, I conspired to move our relationship from a fun flirtation to a fling. I'd never had a casual relationship without the object of my desire quickly becoming a steady boyfriend, nor had I dated anyone so much younger. Perhaps now was the time to rendezvous with someone sixteen years my junior. I again reminded myself that Angelica had said the "tall man with glasses" wouldn't be coming into my life for a while.

As the others continued with the exercise, I leaned over Gabi's shoulder. "Gabi, I was wondering if . . . if you have time, that is . . . if you have time this weekend?"

"Yes."

"Yes, what? You don't even know the question."

Gabi looked up from his notebook and smiled. "It doesn't matter. The answer is yes." *Wow, that was easy.*

"Seriously, I could use help with renting a piano, now that I'm feeling so inspired."

After class, Gabi accompanied me to the bottom of the hill and promised to line up piano rental shops for Saturday. Then he leaned over and very deliberately kissed me once on each cheek. "*Szép álmokat.*"

"Sweet dreams to you, too." I didn't mind facing the climb home alone; I floated up the steep street.

∞

On Saturday, Gabi escorted me to the Fellegi Piano Salon, where the manager, Rudolf, invited me to sample the upright rentals. I didn't recognize any of the brand names, but the *zongora* selection sounded decent enough for my modest price range. After settling on a Czech model, Gabi negotiated the terms with Rudolf, who then translated them into English and asked for my approval.

"A steal," I whispered to Gabi, who co-signed the contract. Rudolf informed us that the piano would be delivered early the next week.

Outside the shop, I jumped up and down. "Now I can play again, thanks to you, my Angel Gabriel." I planted a big kiss on his cheek. He stopped abruptly and covered his face in a failed attempt to hide his crimsoned cheeks. I waltzed to the end of the oak-lined street while he staggered behind. "Are you okay?"

"Yup, I'm fine," he stammered, seeming to have lost his balance. *What's with the sudden shyness?* Gabi fidgeted with the buttons on his shirt and reached for a cigarette from his jeans pocket. "Can we sit down for a while?" *Now it's coming—the talk I've been waiting for.* He motioned to a park bench, where he then removed papers from his bag and spread them over the grass.

"Is this another ESL icebreaker, or are we going to play charades?"

"No. Remember I told you there was something important I wanted to share with you?" I nodded. "Well, lean over and take a look."

The image was unclear, but with my meager history knowledge, I pieced together that the area on the map was the former Austro-Hungarian Empire.

"Are you showing me this to prove that Liszt was really an Austrian?"

"*Nem.*" Gabi lit up and got down on his knees and pointed to the map's borders. "Do you see any difference between this map and Hungary today?" He pulled out another map and placed them side by side.

"Well, for starters, Old Hungary looks a lot bigger," I said.

"Correct."

I squinted my eyes. "The countries that are now Croatia, Romania, and Slovakia were once part of Austria-Hungary. Romania was a lot smaller, too."

"True. We lost over two-thirds of our territory in 1920 after World War I."

I didn't know where the conversation was going; I wasn't sure I wanted to. All I knew was that any inkling I had toward setting a seduction scene wasn't going as planned.

"Are you one of those nationalists who wants to take back the borders?"

"Not exactly. But my family and I are members of a group that holds conferences on the topic." He threw down his cigarette and stomped on it with his sneaker. "Under the Treaty of Trianon, countless Hungarians became citizens of other nations overnight. In Romania alone, over one and a half million Hungarians were forced to learn another language, lost their homes, churches, and jobs." He pointed to Transylvania, once part of Eastern Hungary.

While I could understand Gabi's fury at the past, I didn't know what he hoped could be achieved over eighty years later. "What do you plan to do about this?" I asked him.

"In two weeks, I'm attending a conference in Romania that's addressing this blight on our history." Gabi bent over the map and started dissecting Old Hungary, much like Russia and her Allies had years before.

"Two weeks, huh?" I muttered under my breath.

"What's the matter? Don't tell me it's your birthday."

"Actually, it is."

"I'll make it up to you," he said, quickly gathering his things. "But now I have to run. Papa's expecting me." I smiled half-heartedly, as I'd hoped we might spend the day together, catching a movie at Mammut Cineplex or sightseeing in the Castle District. "I promised to watch a Fradi soccer game with him this afternoon."

"Whatever. Thanks for helping me out today." After he left, I rushed home to phone Jenni with the Gabi update, or lack thereof. She would be the first to agree that the carefree "fling" I'd imagined had morphed into something more confusing and complex.

∞

On the evening of our last class, I was strolling down Tulip Street en route to IH when I saw Gabi sitting on a fence post in Marczibányi Square, book in hand. "How long have you been here?" I asked him.

"Since the end of Beethoven's *Moonlight* Sonata."

"You were lurking outside my window?"

"Well, I was afraid you'd stop playing if I knocked. Next time I'll sell tickets, and we can split the proceeds."

He jumped down and joined me. As we approached the Fondue Bár, Gabi stopped. "It's been bothering me all weekend that I'm going to miss your birthday, Linda."

"It's really okay." I waved a hand toward Pest. "I already made other plans."

"You did?"

"Yes, my former neighbor Heléna is planning a surprise getaway for us that day."

Gabi contemplated the spray-painted profanities on the side of the bakery. "When I return from my trip, I'd like to take you to the opera as a birthday present." His eyes avoided my widened ones. "You don't have to agree now or anything—it's not like it's an all-Liszt program."

"It's a date." I wondered if "date" was too forward, but it did sound like one. As we walked into IH's ornate lobby one last time, I tried not to swoon as Gabi gently placed his hand on my lower back and guided me up the stairs.

In the classroom, Clare poured out glasses of Törley champagne and announced that we had all passed the course. "Bottoms up!" she toasted us.

"*Egészségedre!*" we shouted back.

I immediately downed one plastic cup and reached for another. As we went around the room recapping highlights from the course, I didn't know if I felt more tantalized by the bubbles in my glass or the prospect of an opera date with Gabi.

After class, I sought out my fellow trainees, promising to stay in touch, and then caught up with Dóra on her way to Moscow Square. "I want to let you know I accepted a date with Gabi," I told her.

"You go, girl," she said, hugging me. "Where's he taking you?"

Before I could answer, Gabi began serenading us in a mock falsetto from across the street: "*Figaro, Figaro, Figaro!*"

Part Three

Liebestraum (Love Dream)

That Love is all there is,
Is all we know of Love . . .

Emily Dickinson

The Master's House

On the morning of my forty-second birthday, I slipped into my new teal spaghetti strap dress and took the tram to Nyugati station, where I'd promised to meet Heléna. She had organized an outing but refused to divulge our destination. All I knew was that we were limited to a day trip and to bring my passport. I assumed we were heading west to Austria, or to Slovakia in the north—new territory for me—and was excited that the exploration part of my Odyssey was now beginning in earnest.

As the tram crossed over the Danube, I gazed at the still-astonishing view of the Buda Castle and Fisherman's Bastion, a panorama now part of my everyday commute. Life was so very different than one year before, when I was praying for a marriage proposal from the non-committal Hank. Now I had new friends, a titillating love interest, and a volunteer job at the Liszt Music Academy, something I'd never dreamed possible. Even though the previous year had gotten off to a shaky start, it had become the happiest of my adult life.

Heléna was already waiting at the train station when I

arrived, looking fashionable and foxy in the clingy fuchsia pantsuit she'd scored at a secondhand shop. *We must be going to Vienna! Good thing I got dressed up.*

After we boarded the graffiti-ridden Sopron-bound train, four teenagers squished into our compartment and began gobbling Pick sausage sandwiches smeared with the overpowering smell of paprika. Heléna and I hightailed it into the windswept corridor and reveled in the sun-drenched views. As we rounded the Danube Bend, ruins of once glorious fortresses and old palaces dotted the riverbanks. I hummed a few bars of a Strauss waltz and turned to my friend. "Austria?"

She nodded. "But the rest is surprise."

The train turned inland, and for the next few hours, we were treated to fields of sunflowers and traditional countryside homes with thatched straw roofs. When we arrived in Sopron, Hungary's western-most city, Heléna immediately hailed a taxicab, and after a long, heated discussion with the driver, directed him to the "Casino."

"Are we spending the day gambling?" I asked, half-joking, half-mortified that we might have to do a bit of fundraising before celebrating.

"No, we're driving to town center, but not staying." Heléna explained that from there we were going on an excursion and would return in time to catch the evening train home.

The taxi wove past quaint pastel-colored buildings suggesting a dainty assortment of petits fours. As we approached the Casino, Heléna mumbled to the driver, who screeched to a halt on the curb. Then she led me to the side of that landmark building and ordered me to stand under a large commemorative plaque. "This is the first place Liszt play in public, in 1820," she said. "He was only nine years old. Look!" She snapped my photo as I gazed in awe at the Master's youthful face.

Our next destination was Storno House, a palatial Baroque jewel, where Liszt had played on several occasions. Heléna stopped the driver, whisked me out of the vehicle, and posed me under another etched memorial. "Say *csíz!*"

Remembering the Hungarian word from my first class at International House, I smiled as she took another picture. "I'm sensing a theme here."

"You shall see," Heléna said, wagging a middle finger at me.

After leaving Sopron, we arrived shortly at "*Passkontrolle,*" which I knew from three years of German studies meant "Passport control." Entering Austria, the driver sped through miles of rolling verdant farmland, gleaming white cement homes with orange-tiled roofs, and an occasional Walmart-type store. Thirty minutes later, we approached Raiding, where banners announcing the upcoming Liszt Music Festival decorated the few lampposts on the main road. I surmised that the tiny town, birthplace of the famous composer-pianist, could not have more than a thousand inhabitants.

Reaching our destination, the taxi pulled up to the Liszt family home, which had once been part of the royal Eszterházy estate. As Heléna continued her conversation with the driver in strained tones, I walked reverently toward an arched gate that guarded the Master's childhood house. A statue of Mother Mary greeted visitors from a peaceful perch above the walkway. Since my vision of Mary, I'd been drawn to all likenesses of her.

"*Guten Tag,* Maria," I now whispered under my breath. "What a wonderful birthday gift to find you here."

I knew that Liszt had been raised a devout Catholic, and as a teenager had begged his father, an employee of the wealthy Eszterházy family, to allow him to enter the priesthood. But Ádám, convinced of his son's divine musical talents, had refused. Liszt's youthful wish came true decades later, but not in the way he might have expected.

I thought back a few years to my visit to San Carlo al Corso Church in Rome, where Liszt had planned to marry his Polish-Catholic fiancée, Princess Carolyne von Sayn-Wittgenstein, on his fiftieth birthday. Although Carolyne had been granted a divorce from Russian Prince Nikolaus, there was one last hitch: he was refusing to acknowledge an annulment, which would deem their daughter illegitimate and seriously affect her marital prospects.

As I'd stood by the church altar, listening to the tour guide describe the fate of the star-crossed lovers, I envisioned it ablaze with votive candles and covered in cascades of delicate white roses in preparation for Franz and Carolyne's nuptials. I imagined their joyful anticipation as the wedding day approached. But it wasn't meant to be. The couple's hopes were dashed by the Pope, who called off the ceremony the night before.

Having waged an exhausting battle against the Catholic Church, Carolyne finally conceded defeat. Heartbroken, Liszt went into seclusion for a few years in Rome's Madonna del Rosario Monastery. After taking minor orders of the priesthood, he emerged as Abbé Liszt, and from then on divided his time between the Eternal City, Budapest, and Weimar. He and Carolyne corresponded faithfully after the wedding fiasco, but their relationship remained platonic until his death in 1886. She died less than a year later.

Such a sad story, I thought as Heléna and I passed through the gate and approached the charming white stone house where Franz had grown up. Its sloping wooden shingle roof was shaded by ancient oak trees and surrounded by lush, manicured lawns. I picked a few pink rose petals from a nearby bush and pressed them into my diary.

When we arrived at the cashier, Heléna pulled out two identification cards and handed me one. "Who's this?" I asked, pointing to the photo of a woman named Balácz Anna.

"That's you." Heléna showed me a picture of herself with the Hungarian word *tanár* printed on the top. "Teachers go free here. See—this is me."

"But you're not a teacher anymore."

"I was."

"How many years ago was that? Twenty?" Heléna scrunched up her nose. "And I'm not a teacher, at least not yet."

"But studying to be." She snatched the photo and held it up to the sun. "That's my friend, Anna. You looks a little like her, no?"

I stared at the fair-skinned instructor, who had a short black bob and hook nose. "She's at least ten years older than me." The birth date on the back of the laminated card offered proof.

"Okay, Linduska, so there's little difference. You cover photo with finger and who knows?"

"*I* know. It bothers me to cheat the system—and at this sacred site, no less."

Heléna chortled and grabbed the card from my hand. "Okay, I'll see if they take Hungarian forints." The cashier spoke Magyarul and accepted Heléna's payment.

We made our way through the former living quarters of the Liszt family, taking information sheets in our respective native languages. Portraits of the Master and his family lined the walls, along with original music scores, personal correspondence, and framed images of the family tree. A death mask from 1886 stood next to a bronze cast of Liszt's virtuosic right hand. When no one was looking, I placed mine atop his, and then slipped it away when a security guard walked in.

Heléna motioned for me to follow her into the adjoining room, where one of Liszt's Erard pianos stood in the middle. I pictured the Master composing one of his nineteen *Hungarian Rhapsodies* or performing a Chopin Nocturne on that very instrument. As I walked around the seven-foot rosewood marvel, I thought I might levitate through the chimney. I desperately wanted to touch the keyboard, to place my fingers where Franz's had been, but the sign "*Bitte nicht berühren!*" warned against it.

I waved Heléna over and poked my head into the next room to ensure the security guard was out of sight. "Can you watch in the doorway while I check out the piano?"

Heléna stood in the archway fanning herself, eyes moving between me and the security guard two rooms away. I wiped the sweat from my palms on my dress and placed them over the ivories, closing my eyes while pretending to play a Liszt Etude. When my accomplice coughed, I jumped up and over to the side window, feigning interest in the view. After the guard left, Heléna snapped her fingers, and I returned to the velvety surface of the Erard, lingering over a few minor dents and scrapes. Had they resulted from late-night scuffles with jealous lovers or after hours of indulgence at a pub with Frédéric?

A sign in the next room informed us that the infant Franz was born there on October 22, 1811. A large urn filled with coins stood amid another bust of the Maestro draped with ribbons. Dozens of floral arrangements from fans vied for space with ivy wreaths bearing the red, white, and green of the Hungarian flag. I imagined Anna Liszt lulling her baby to sleep with a melodious *Wiegenlied*. In awe, I leaned over and placed one thousand forints (three American dollars) into the receptacle. Heléna's mouth snapped open, but before she could chastise me for supporting an Austrian institution that "don't need the money," I grabbed her by the wrist and escorted her to the exit. "Now what about that picnic you mentioned?"

We meandered to a nearby bench, where she arranged

paper plates full of Pick sausage, cheese, and chunks of freshly baked bread. As we began to make sandwiches, Heléna's mobile phone rang. She repeated *"Igen"* several times to the caller and walked over toward the church to continue what seemed a tense discussion. When she returned, her pale complexion was all blotchy.

"That was István. He orders we speak immediately in person."

"Sounds serious." I draped a piece of sausage over a slice of bread.

"Yes, I never heard him so upset."

As we discussed our options—linger longer or leave ASAP—it was clear that Heléna's frazzled nerves couldn't stand the suspense. After deciding on an earlier train, she called the same taxi driver, who was at a nearby pub. "He'll be here fifteen minutes later."

"He's been waiting this whole time?" I cringed to think of how much schnapps he might have downed since then.

"Yes, it's only way I can pay in forints. Don't worry, I gave him lunch." I chuckled at her ingenuity.

She sat down again and lit a candle on a big piece of Eszterházy torta, my favorite Hungarian dessert, and sang "Happy Birthday," or *"Boldog szülinapot."* After we devoured the crème fraîche and walnut cake, she handed me a small plastic bag. "Here's gift for hot date with Gabi."

I opened it and fingered a few pieces of black elastic attached to a triangular piece of fabric adorned with rhinestone specks. "What on earth is this?" I contorted the item into various forms, like a cat's cradle.

"No!" She slapped my hands down toward my buttocks. "You wear that. It's called G-string."

"You must be joking." I imagined its limited possibilities on my physique. "I'm flattered you think I could even put my right arm through this thing."

"Well, it's thought that matters."

I leaned over and pecked her cheeks. "You didn't have to get me anything, Heléna." I pinched two seams of the gift together. "This heartfelt pilgrimage is gift enough." She smiled, but seemed preoccupied.

On the train ride back to Budapest, I asked her if there was any reason why István might be mad at her. She mentioned their most recent romp at his house, during which, unknown to the heated lovers, the waterbed had sprung a leak and emptied onto the floor.

"Maybe his wife didn't like cleaning up the mess," I suggested.

"That's what I think, too."

During the rest of the trip, Heléna stared mutely out the window. When our train pulled into Nyugati Station, I wished my friend good luck with István and watched her reapply makeup using her compact mirror. I didn't think any amount of lipstick could win him back.

Speechless

Mammut was very quiet for a Saturday afternoon. Usually, the multilevel mall was teeming with noisy teenagers and well-heeled tourists on the lookout for Louis Vuitton luggage, elegant Herend china, and pricey Pinot Noir. I went there a few times a week to check emails at Libri Bookstore's Internet café, but today I was on a different mission.

The night before, my college friend Eve had phoned and invited me on a tour of Turkey and Greece during her summer vacation. As an art therapist for a nursing home in Chicago, she had all of July off. It didn't take the burned-out tone in Eve's voice to convince me to join her, as Heléna had already warned of the sweltering summers in landlocked Budapest. I was excited; Eve was a fun and adventurous travel companion. Like me, she was also single with eyes wide open. She offered to organize logistics while I searched for a teaching job for fall.

I gravitated to a *Lonely Planet* guidebook on Turkey and marveled at a photo of the beautiful former home of Mother Mary, now a chapel, located on Nightingale Hill near Ephesus. As I began reading up on how to travel there, my phone rang.

Gyöngyi was frantic. "Bea didn't speak for one week!" she told me. "She doesn't eat much, either. I'm worried."

I quickly returned the guidebook to the shelf. "Is she sick?"

"No. I think boy troubles."

"I'll be right there." I bought a Milka bar from the kiosk and headed up Lövőház Street. Gyöngyi met me at the security gate. The piercing early summer sun reflected off the rows of wheelchairs parked on the front yard. "Gyöngyi, tell me, what's the matter with Bea?"

"Bea likes Kristóf, who works in kitchen here. I think something happened."

My maternal instincts kicked in. *Has Bea been taken advantage of or abused?* She and the other female residents confined to wheelchairs were such vulnerable targets. "I'll see what I can find out," I promised Bea's worried friend.

Once inside the building, Gyöngyi swiveled into the elevator and pushed the third-floor button. We parted ways outside their room, where I knocked. Not hearing a response, I crept inside. The curtains were drawn; the only sound emanated from a lone gerbil spinning on a rotating wheel inside his cage. Bea appeared to be sleeping, but as I stood at the foot of her bed, her eyes opened.

"*Szia*, Bea." I reached over the metal railing and squeezed her hand. "Gyöngyi told me you're not feeling well." A few dewdrops moistened Bea's smooth skin. "I was eager to see you." She sniffled and used the bedsheet to dry away her tears.

With the language, age, and cultural barriers, I didn't know where to begin, other than to reassure Bea that her feelings were normal and universal. During our visits, she had often shared her deep frustrations of living with Cerebral Palsy and the way she was treated as an asexual person, even though she had feelings like any other young woman. While I hadn't experienced Bea's physical limitations, I certainly knew the pain of unrequited love and during my weekly visits, always listened with sympathy.

I bent over the bed and brushed a few wet strands of honey-colored hair from her kind face. "Did someone hurt you, Bea?" She shook her head and with great effort, took her hands out from under the blanket and clutched her chest. "Someone broke your heart?" She burst into tears and reached for a tissue from under her pillow.

I moved to the foot of the bed, where the railing ended, and sat down. "I've had my share of heartbreaks, Bea. Shortly after graduating college, my boyfriend Steve broke up with me because, as he put it: 'You'll never be Einstein.' Imagine! As if I wanted to be Einstein. *Rubenstein*, maybe." Bea bobbed her head up and down. I thought of how Steve, a doctor, had discouraged me from pursuing a master's degree in social work because he "dare not marry someone in that type of occupation." I wondered how many Beas I could have helped if I had ignored his advice and followed my twenty-three-year-old heart.

I glanced at the posters of Hungarian pop stars and soccer players over Bea's bed. She also liked tall, dark, and handsome types. "Yes, it hurts when we love someone who doesn't feel the same about us," I continued. "I'm still getting over my breakup with Hank. Last week he sent me a tape recording of our cat meowing 'Happy Birthday.'" Bea pouted. "Hearing Squeak again really pulled on my heartstrings. I was a mess and didn't leave my flat for days." I dabbed my eyes with tissues from her nightstand. "I know I did the right thing by ending the relationship, but I miss the company. Seven years is a long time."

Bea patted my hand, her childlike touch triggering a stream of maternal tears. I thought how lovely it would be to have a daughter like Bea to share secrets with and to comfort one another, the way Mom and I had when I was young. I let out a loud groan; Bea made soft sounds but did not speak. Instead, she reached under her sheet and pulled out the small blackboard she used to convey messages. *I glad you here,* she wrote, slowly.

"Me, too. I never would have met you if I'd stayed with Hank in America." I pulled out the Milka chocolate bar, Bea's favorite. Her sky-blue eyes lit up, even more so when I told her I planned to stay in Hungary for one more year.

You marry and stay? she wrote.

I'm working on it.

And Gabi? she spelled out.

I glanced at my watch and explained that he was soon picking me up for our opera date. Then I got up and kissed Bea on the forehead; she closed her eyes and smiled. "You're a big blessing in my life, Bea." I promised to visit soon and started to leave, hoping she wouldn't see my blotchy face. As I opened the door, a metallic sound commanded me to turn around. Bea pointed to the blackboard; I walked back.

"*Szeretlek*," she'd written.

"I love you too, my precious girl."

∞

Once at home, I applied frozen pea packages to my swollen eyelids. Gabi was coming in less than an hour; it was obviously time for a Maybelline moment. I modeled a few seductive outfits in the full-length mirror, including the G-string gift from Heléna, which better served as a slingshot. Then I tugged on a lacy purple teddy and slinked into a shimmery black dress with a not-too-plunging V-neck that showed off my tan. *Voilá!* Soon the buzzer rang.

From his neatly pressed beige pants and navy blazer to his shiny yellow tie, Gabi was a knockout. *Brad in formal attire.* My flagging spirits quickly soared.

"You look so . . . different," I muttered.

Jiggling the car keys with one hand and firmly supporting my lower back with his other, Gabi escorted me through the lilac-lined path out the front gate. "I'm parked a bit down the street," he told me. As we approached the brown Volvo I knew was his father's, I noticed how packed it seemed.

"Here we are," he said, guiding me into the well-worn leather passenger seat.

"And here *we* are!" Béla shouted from behind. "Surprise!" I turned to find him, a woman I assumed to be his wife Ágnes, and Papa all squeezed into the back seat.

My jaw dropped, along with any romantic expectations. *Good thing I skipped the G-string.*

"We wanted to do something special for your birthday," Béla said. "Especially since Gabi wasn't able to be here on the actual day." While struggling to compose a response, I fidgeted with my purse. "Well, say something, Linduska!"

"This is indeed a surprise," I muttered, trying to mask my disappointment.

"I hear you're a classical pianist," Papa said, leaning over to touch my shoulder in his one-size-too-small russet brown jacket. A few tufts of gray-blond hair fell onto his high furrowed forehead. "I hope you'll enjoy tonight's performance."

Whose, mine? I smiled into his kind, dark eyes, which squinted from behind round horn-rimmed glasses, hoping I'd have the stamina to keep that expression plastered on my face for the next few hours. Was Gabi's family really so gung-ho about celebrating my birthday, or had Gabi invited them along as a buffer? It was difficult to concentrate on *Figaro* with these thoughts racing through my muddled mind.

During the Overture, my eyes drifted up to the domed

ceiling, where the Nine Muses frolicked on Mount Olympus, oblivious to the dramas being played out below. When the red velvet stage curtains opened, I looked down from the nosebleed section at the sensuous carvings of Egyptian goddesses, which appeared to hold up three tiers of ornately decorated loges. In the dim light, the golden interior sparkled; surely, King Midas had been among the first guests of the Hungarian State Opera House. So sumptuous was the Renaissance building both inside and out that Emperor Franz Joseph later regretted having commissioned it because it "upstaged" its rival in Vienna.

During intermission, I freshened up in the women's room; Béla was lurking by the door as I exited. "I hope you won't mind my asking, but it looks like you've been crying," he said. I glimpsed into the mirror in the reception area and cringed. He steered us toward the café, where his family was waiting. "What's going on?"

I told him about Hank's recent tug on my heartstrings with the recording of Squeak and how my visit to Bea's had stoked maternal feelings.

"But you want to have a child, right?"

"Ideally. If it's not too late."

"And from what you've told me, Hank wasn't interested." I nodded. "Then you were wise to leave him. At your age, whatever that is—wink, wink—you should seriously consider having a child."

"Yeah, exactly. At my age."

"No, really. Many women in their late thirties and even forties are becoming first-time mothers."

"Like Madonna and movie stars who can afford magical medical interventions."

"You never know." He led me to a plush red sofa, where the rest of his clan was savoring an assortment of *sütemény* and had saved two dainty cakes for me. You might have a baby with someone already in your life." *Are Béla's eye movements in Gabi's direction intentional?* While my attraction toward his brother had grown over the semester, I'd not thought of Gabi in terms of fathering my child, no matter how hot he looked in a suit.

"And here's the lovely Ágnes," I said, eager to change the subject. "I'm so glad we finally get to meet properly." I leaned over to kiss Béla's wife, who hadn't spoken to me during the car ride to the Opera House. Her fair, high-boned cheeks instantly turned the color of the scarlet red sofa. *Oops, have I made a cultural gaffe?*

"Ágnes is from the Hortobágy Plains," Béla said, which probably explained her colorful embroidered blouse. "She doesn't speak English, so I'm afraid you'll have to learn Hungarian." He translated what I'd said to his wife, who broke into a shy smile.

As the French horn blared out the end of intermission, I followed my hosts back to the uppermost balcony. Minutes later, Gabi leaned over for a peek at my wristwatch. *That's the third time you've looked in five minutes,* I jotted down on the libretto. *There's still one more Act.* He squirmed in his seat. *I thought you were a die-hard Mozart fan.*

Yes, but the Requiem, he wrote back.

If you're bored, why not wait for us by the coat check? I penned.

He leaned over, his flushed cheek close to mine, and whispered, "And deprive myself of the pleasure of sitting next to you in the dark?" Inhaling the lingering aroma of chocolate and cigarettes on his breath, I fervently wished Gabi would kiss me, but that was a little challenging with Papa two seats over.

"Are you following the story?" Béla interrupted. "This plot has more twists and turns than the Danube."

"And just as dirty," Gabi added, grinning. "There seems to be a lot of cross-dressing and coming in and out of closets."

As the six main characters harmonized the aria "*Rico-nosci in questo amplesso*," I followed along with the libretto. "If this English translation of 'Recognize in this embrace' is to be believed," I told my friends, "I think Figaro narrowly escaped marrying his mother."

"Gross!" Gabi said a little too loudly.

"Imagine not knowing which is your wife or mother," Papa joined in.

An elderly man behind us heard the comment and leaned over. "When you're married as long as I've been, it can be difficult to tell the difference," he said. He gave Papa a knowing clap on the back, and we all burst out laughing. The other opera attendees sitting nearby shushed us.

After the last note resonated throughout the packed hall, Gabi jumped up, impatient to leave before curtain call. Soon we squished back into the car and headed up the Buda Hills. When we arrived at Tulip Street, Gabi turned into my driveway and let the car idle.

"A very romantic place you've got here," Papa said in a semi-suggestive manner.

"Yes, I think so," I said.

My date helped me out and led me behind the car trunk, from where I caught Papa stealing a peek at us through the side-view mirror.

"Thanks for a lovely evening," I told Gabi, meaning it. Despite my initial shock at having been chaperoned by his whole family, I was touched that they had accompanied us, even if it was probably an opportunity for Papa to check me out. In that case, it appeared I'd passed muster.

Gabi took my hands and pecked me once on each cheek. "Talk soon," he promised, before taking off in the car. I entered my apartment, thinking I must be having the most chaste love affair in all of Budapest.

Chapter 16

Attila the Hung-arian

By early July, I landed the first teaching job I had interviewed for at The Bell School, located five minutes away from my flat at the other end of Tulip Street. To celebrate my good fortune, I planned a day at Dagály Strand, the *fürdő* in my former neighborhood. Despite having moved, I continued traveling to the spa three times a week, swimming in the clear, thermally heated waters even during heavy rains and snowstorms. Over the course of four months, my exercise routine had led to a twenty-pound weight loss. I was also more toned and energetic than I'd been in years.

Dagály was tucked away in a neighborhood awash with package stores, abandoned buildings, and Communist-era blockhouses. Most tourists were turned off by the dodgy commute through streets strewn with broken beer bottle shards and unlucky scratch tickets, preferring to swim beneath the ornamental fountains of naked nymphs spouting from the Széchenyi Baths or ride the wave machine at the posh Gellért Hotel. Their loss, my gain: Dagály Strand boasted the best outdoor Olympic-sized pool in the city.

The spa was a favorite meeting place for pensioners,

who shared bulky Pick sausage sandwiches and Fanta sodas while soaking with friends for hours despite the thirty-minute time limit. Aging belles squeezed into ultra-tight tiger print bikinis and strutted their cellulite and sagging tits and tummies, but were careful to cover their heads with '70s-style flowered caps. As they clucked and gossiped, the men engaged in their favorite pastime—chess—while submerged in skimpy skivvies that exposed their manatee-sized bellies.

After logging twenty-five laps in the pool, I clutched my sports bag and towel close to my thighs and buttocks and entered the soothing spa waters. The large inflatable chess set floating near the entrance made it impossible to slip in unnoticed. I waded past the all-male players and immersed my achy, Speedo-clad body in the bubbly elixir, bathing cap and goggles still intact. Floating in the shallow end, all muscle stiffness melted away as the summer breeze caressed my cool face. As sounds of children giggling in the surrounding pools faded, my mind drifted off to the elegant Európa Café, where I'd soon be sipping a piping hot cup of Earl Grey and devouring a hard-earned slice of Eszterházy torta.

This delightful image was suddenly doused by the sensation of someone's overly friendly thighs pushing against mine. "Hello! Do I *know* you?" I said, pulling away—no small feat given this man's size and ego. For a moment, I considered that he might be one of IH's students, but they would never treat me so rudely.

"Oh, you speak English. You American?" the interloper said without waiting for an answer. He grabbed me by the wrists and pulled me toward him. Soon I was up close and personal with his furry chest. "My name's Attila," he stated in a deep, throaty voice. "Come swim with me."

"Sorry, but I already went swimming and am trying to relax—*alone*—if you don't mind." I struggled to pull the goggles from my face, which Attila took as a cue to pin my arms behind my back.

"Then come take shower with me," he said, shifting my buttocks toward the bulge in his groin.

"Excuse me! I don't know you, and even if I did, I'm not about to—"

My protests were drowned out by Attila's attempts at small talk. He cooed questions into my ear, asking if I liked Hungarian men (*"Nem!"*), was an English teacher (*"Igen"*), and what I thought of his country (*"%&$#"*). All between nibbles on my earlobe. *Yuck!*

I tried shoving him away with all my strength, but I was no match for this robust Magyar. "Get off me, you brute!" I snapped. "You're too heavy and you're hurting my ribs."

"You saying I'm fat? Here, feel this!" Attila pulled my right arm toward his left bicep, and then moved it down his chiseled chest. I yanked it away, leaned against a mosaic-tiled pillar, and tried pushing him away with my legs; he only reeled me in closer. It dawned on me that Attila probably thought I was a stereotypical "easy" American woman, which might explain why he wasn't taking *"Nem!"* for an answer. *Clearly, this isn't working, Linda. Time to change strategies.*

I considered screaming, but in what language? My knowledge of Hungarian was still very limited, and most older Hungarians did not speak English. When I'd entered the spa, real couples were making out and engaging in other amorous behavior. Would they break away from their embraces to help me, a foreigner? It might look to them as if Attila and I were having a lover's spat. On the other hand, maybe this was a time-tested way for singles to meet in Hungary's longstanding spa culture. *I wouldn't be surprised.*

As Attila shifted to place me on his lap, I splashed water in his face. Rather than backing off, he opted for another tactic. "Come home with me and drink champagne," he spouted, stroking my still-capped head.

"Sorry, I don't like champagne," I lied. Through misty goggles, I made out dozens of striped vinyl bags hanging from the hooks above. A swift upward kick would send a handful of them down onto Attila's head, affording me a quick getaway.

Sensing my scheme, Attila moved us out of harm's way. While repositioning, I struggled to remember the two-word expression that Béla had taught me after I'd been stalked. I knew the first word was *fasz*, but the second didn't jump to mind. *Shit! I need that word! Fasz . . . what?* As Attila moved in for a kiss, I kicked him in the groin and yelled: "*Fasz! Fasz!*"

He immediately fell backwards and covered his crotch. The whole spa fell silent. I grabbed my bag, tore off my glasses, and sped toward the double glass doors, sending a few knights, pawns, and kings overboard for an unexpected dip. Checkmating Magyars flashed icy stares as Attila disappeared under the waters to the other side of the *fürdő*.

Once inside the safe harbor of the women's dressing room, I peeled off my Speedo and tried to calm down in the steamy sulfur showers. While drying off, I phoned Heléna, who was still stewing over the unexpected breakup with István. She agreed to meet me outside the building and accompany me down Dagály's dimly lit streets en route to the Európa Café.

∞

"I warned you about Hungarian men," she said twenty minutes later, wagging her middle finger at me, which I'd told her numerous times not to do. "Were you wearing bikini?"

"Hell no!" I snapped back. "I was wearing a Speedo swimsuit and bathing cap—not exactly the image of a *Baywatch* star."

"You think the Attila cares what you wearing?" Heléna laughed. "It's because you're American. He wants to do sex with American. All Hungarians want try sex with American, even me. Is that so wrong?" She shrugged her shoulders up to her back-to-copper curls. "It's high time you try Magyar man, Linduska," she said, again urging this apparent solution to all my problems. Sometimes it felt as if Heléna was on a personal crusade to get me laid, my celibacy within Hungarian borders an affront to her national pride. "Would it hurt to give him some *puszi?*"

My mouth dropped open. "*Pussy?* Heléna, you can't be serious!" To my relief, she explained that the word meant "kiss." *Figures.*

"Well, was he at least good-looking, this Attila?" Heléna shouted over the roar of traffic on St. Stephen's Boulevard after we had arrived at Nyugati Station. She searched my face for a glimmer of heightened sexual interest.

"How would I know? I couldn't see him clearly through my swimming goggles." Actually, I had gotten a glimpse of the handsome Hungarian as I'd bounded up the pool steps, but I wasn't about to share that with matchmaker Heléna. "If you're so interested, maybe *you* should start spending more time at Dagály," I told her.

"No, no," Heléna said, shaking her head. "You know I'm scared drowning in pool."

I grinned. "Otherwise you'd go?"

Heléna rolled her eyes. "How you finally get Attila to go away?"

"I kicked him in the you-know-what and shouted the F-word."

"You mean, fuck?"

"No, *fasz.*"

"What?" Heléna stopped and covered her mouth. "Did you shout that to the Attila?"

"Yes, and the whole spa."

"Oh, my Gods," she said, crossing herself.

"What's the matter? I was trying to say something Béla taught me, but I could only remember the first word."

"Linduska, *fasz* means penis." *Uh-oh.* "I think you wanted to say '*fasz kivan.*'"

"Yes, that's it!" I said, raising an index finger. "But if it's not like the American F-word, then what does it mean?"

Heléna started to giggle. "Let's just say you announce Attila's penis."

That explained the abrupt silence at the spa. "Well, whatever. It worked, and that's the main thing."

"Wow! You very brave," she said, linking her arm in mine.

As we strolled past the Vígszínház, Budapest's oldest theater, a cream puff of a building poised on its own city block, I wondered aloud why I couldn't find an attractive, available gentleman around my age to accompany me there.

"You too fussy is problem," Heléna said, eyeing a lingerie shop window featuring fairy queens and candy cane-thin mannequins posing seductively as Cat Woman. "We're in forties now, can't be so choosy." She arched her plucked eyebrows and nodded toward the windows. "What's so wrong with the Attila, anyhow?"

While some choice words sprang to mind, I had to be careful not to insult any time-honored Magyar mating rituals. "He was way too aggressive. That's a big turnoff for me."

"I see . . . Attila too aggressive, Gabi not enough aggressive." *Gabi.* He had been away on a family vacation, and we hadn't seen each other since *Figaro.* I missed him and Béla. Even *Harry Potter.*

"It's a little complicated," I told my friend.

"The only thing complicate is *you*, Miss America."

Suddenly, a familiar buzzing sound like Bea's wheel-chair closed in on us. I spun around, half-expecting to find her, but instead, a dark-skinned, middle-aged man was navigating the sidewalk outside the Európa. Despite the heat, a ragged blanket rested atop his stubbed kneecaps; a paper cup with a few coins jiggled in his right hand. He zoomed up to me, his chocolate-colored eyes staring into mine with a sorrowful kindness. My skin tingled with the sensation that we somehow knew one other, but that didn't seem possible. I gave him all my spare change and beamed a bright smile his way.

"Complicate, yes," I said, turning back to my friend and wrapping my arm around her slender waist. I decided it was high time to tell Heléna about Angelica's predictions and why it was important for me to be more "complicate" than "easy" while waiting for the "tall man with glasses."

As we dove under the purple canopies of the Európa into the café for that long-overdue chat, I counted the days—three—until the Turkish-Greek adventure with Eve began, grateful to have a break from Hungarian men for a couple of months.

Chapter 17

Mary's House

The overworked charter bus sputtered up Nightingale Hill, its rear dangling perilously over steep vine-covered cliffs. Eve and I squeezed our hands together and gazed down at the ancient city of Ephesus, located on the west coast of Turkey. Earlier in the day, our tour group had visited the double-columned, monumental Library of Celsus and the magnificent 25,000-seat amphitheater where Saint Paul had once preached, and more recently, Elton John had sung "Rocket Man." Our eyes strained through the darkened glass to the oasis of the azure Aegean on the horizon—anything to take attention away from the religious memorials to traffic victims dotting the hairpin turns.

At the back of the bus, the relief driver mouthed supplications to Allah and fingered his string of beads, adding to my silent prayers. During the last two weeks, we had traveled hundreds of miles via bus from Istanbul's Blue Mosque and the "fairy chimney" rock formations of Cappadocia, to Konya and the pristine Turquoise Coast. Now we were capping off the last leg of our Turkish tour with a visit to

Panaya Kapulu, Mother Mary's House, on Nightingale Hill.

As we approached our destination, Eve and I took turns reading aloud from our guidebooks. Both referenced historical records indicating that Mary had come to live in Ephesus with John the Evangelist, "the Disciple whom Jesus loved," after her Son, while dying on the Cross, had entrusted them to one another's care. It was here, four centuries later, that she was officially declared *Theotokos,* or "Mother of God," by the Third Ecumenical Council.

Our group might never have seen the tiny, modest stone house had it not been for Anne Catherine Emmerich, an eighteenth-century Augustinian nun and mystic, who had lived in poverty and was confined to a sickbed much of her adulthood. Her visions detailing the precise descriptions and location of Mary's House in Ephesus, a place she'd never visited, were recorded by the poet Clemens Brentano, who published them years later as *The Life of the Blessed Virgin Mary.* The book became a guide for those explorers seeking the house where Mary had lived out her final years.

As Eve and I continued reading, we learned that in 1891, two Lazarist priests had set out to excavate the area around Nightingale Hill. When they grew thirsty and asked the locals for water, they were directed to the "monastery." Next to a spring they found a small T-shaped stone building partially obscured by a grove of trees. It had three arches with rectangular stones and was situated on a rocky hill from which one could see over the trees and hills to Ephesus and the sea, exactly as Sister Emmerich had envisioned.

The priests' findings were subjected to a rigorous investigation and confirmed by the Vatican the following year. Eventually, the house was converted into a chapel and quickly became a pilgrimage spot for millions of Catholics, Orthodox Christians, and Muslims. I was surprised to read that followers of Islam also worshipped Maryam, the only woman to have a chapter of the *Quran* dedicated to her.

"What an amazing history," Eve said. I agreed.

As we arrived at Nightingale Hill, she and I filed out of the air-conditioned bus with our travel companions, mostly Americans, Australians, and Brits. A delicate bronze statue of Mother Mary greeted us along the path, her outstretched arms full of eucalyptus leaves. A wreath of rocks wound around her sculpted head; her eyes gazed downward.

The entrance to the chapel was overshadowed by olive trees and a canopy of sun visors blocking the arched doorway. We followed a stream of pilgrims and drew near the altar, which was sparsely decorated with wildflowers and burning votive candles. A small statue of Mary in the archway watched over the worshippers squeezed together in four rows of pews. Handwoven Persian rugs graced the stone floor. With only a moment of privacy, I lit a candle and thanked God for the opportunity to walk in Mary's footsteps, but was soon forced outside by a group of over-zealous Italians and lost sight of Eve.

While other tourists battled the intense heat with small battery-operated fans, I sought refuge under a fig tree. I glanced over at the statue by the entrance, which reminded me of the image of Mother Mary I had witnessed that night in Somerville one year before. Since then, I'd kept my vision a secret, thinking it too precious to divulge. I was also afraid of being ridiculed, or worse—treated like the three poor shepherd children of Fatima in Portugal, who'd seen Mary on several occasions. The townspeople had made life miserable for them and their families; even the local police threatened to boil them in a vat of oil if they didn't retract their story. Luckily, they were spared after they refused to cooperate.

Our tour guide, Turgay, had explained that there had been over twenty thousand reported apparitions of Mary over the centuries—from La Vang in Vietnam to Knock, Ireland and Guadalupe—as well as one witnessed by hundreds of thousands of Egyptians in the 1960s, when a self-luminous Mary appeared atop a Coptic church in Cairo. As I watched hordes of Mary lovers of all ages, faiths, and backgrounds waiting in the queue for a glimpse of her former abode, it dawned on me that I was not alone. It made sense that Mary, in her role as Intercessor between Heaven and Earth, would reach out to those in need of comfort, as she had to me during a time of despair. Surely, there were others who'd had memorable encounters with her and were also keeping mum. It was time to stop analyzing *why* or *how* and accept Mary's visit for what it was: a mystical gift I couldn't possibly fathom or explain.

I relaxed into the trunk of the tree, allowing the sweet scent of jasmine to caress the tip of my nose and coax a smile from my sunburnt face. Lizards rustled in the overgrown bushes while pairs of yellow butterflies flitted by, interlocked in mating rituals. Birds darted over the ravines, harmonizing ethereal melodies. The abundance of natural beauty lulled me into a blissful state; I closed my eyes and reveled in the sensations. *I wonder if Eve is also experiencing this . . . Eve!* I jumped up, realizing I had strayed from her and our group.

I followed a handful of older Germans laden with fancy photography equipment down a trail leading to several sinks, where hordes of visitors were filling bottles with the supposed holy water spouting from the natural spring below. Others released the taps and splashed their necks, faces, and chests. I aired out my white cotton dress before joining in the dousing, and then wiped up with the headscarf that had become a permanent fixture on my sweaty scalp.

Turgay had stressed the curative powers of the waters, as well as the granting of wishes to those who left written requests for Mary at the Wall of Wishes. In the distance, I saw Eve putting a crumpled piece of paper into a crevice between boulders around the spring. Feeling inspired, I pulled out the title page of my still-unopened Dickens novel and penned my wish:

Dearest Mary,

I am overwhelmed by the joy and peacefulness I feel at your beautiful, humble home on Nightingale Hill. This reverie can only come from your presence, which is everywhere here and which I felt once before—that night in Somerville.

Please bless all the people here today, especially those in wheelchairs and others who are suffering, as well as dear Eve and our travel companions.

As for me, please guide me to the 'tall man with glasses,' so that I'll have someone to share my secret with, someone who will understand. A kindred spirit. If this grace is bestowed on me, I promise to return to Ephesus with him and pay tribute to you.

With heartfelt thanks and love,

Linda

I folded the paper neatly and added it to the thousands of other messages written on small pieces of cloth tied to poles on the stone walls. With clasped hands, I prayed for my wish to float up to the heavens, as the faithful believed Mary had from the same spot about two thousand years earlier.

After I raised my bowed head, Eve tapped my shoulder and pointed to the parking lot. Shrouded in reverent silence, we strolled arm in arm back to the idling bus, where the others were waiting. Moments later, we bounced around the back seats as the vehicle swerved toward the ruins of Aphrodite, Goddess of Love. I didn't think anyone could feel the presence of love more deeply than at Mother Mary's House.

Chapter 18

Dutch Treats

Tinos was slowly waking up as our ferry approached port after the overnight cruise from Kuşadasi. Eve and I had left the tour soon after Ephesus and were continuing on our own in Greece. After traveling hundreds of miles and visiting countless tourist sites, we'd chosen this Cycladic island for its laid-back atmosphere in lieu of the vibrant nightlife of nearby trendy Mykonos.

The crystalline azure waters around us contrasted sharply with the arid mountains, dotted with hundreds of intricately designed centuries-old dovecotes and a sprinkling of windmills. However, what caught my eye was the bell tower hovering over an expansive marble cathedral, Our Lady of Tinos, situated above the town. I was excited to visit this most holy of Marian shrines, which my guidebook claimed had been built over the spot where a miraculous icon depicting the Annunciation had been discovered in 1823. Ever since, Greeks have flocked to their country's most popular pilgrimage site to venerate this sacred Orthodox treasure. From the boat, I marveled at the bright red carpeting that had been installed from the harbor to the cathedral doors, as many worshippers preferred to approach the church on their knees.

I gazed up at the dazzling white façade and remembered Angelica's prophetic words about how a "Russian icon" would lead me to the "tall man with glasses." *Obviously, I am in the wrong country, but perhaps another Orthodox icon will do.* Eve knew about Angelica's predictions and agreed that after logging some serious beach time, the cathedral was our top destination. We decided to visit after Mass on Sunday, as our flight to Athens left very early the next morning.

After our boat docked, we disembarked and dragged our bulging suitcases full of Turkish delight and hourglass-shaped teacups from Istanbul's Grand Bazaar across the pavement. Waiters and waitresses bustled about, opening taverna umbrellas that almost obscured the sunrise; menus boasting the best *moussaka* and *pastitsio* swayed on the tabletops. Famished from not having eaten breakfast, Eve and I found a bakery and ordered take-out *spanakopitas*.

A quick taxi ride brought us to the Agali Bay Hotel, where we checked in and enjoyed the spinach pies on our sun-drenched third-floor terrace. After lunch, we changed into sundresses and returned to reception, where the concierge suggested we begin our Greek adventure at Fokas Beach, a fifteen-minute walk away.

Soon after, we claimed two empty lounge chairs and straw umbrellas on the horseshoe-shaped beach. I dropped my towel and bag, and with beads of perspiration streaming down my neck, stripped down to a metallic gold one-piece bathing suit.

"Whoa! About time that saw the light of day," Eve said. "I thought you were forever poured into that Speedo."

I gave my padded bra-breasts a carefree jiggle in her direction, grabbed the swimming goggles, and lunged toward the sea. Inspired by the shimmery waters, I pushed back and performed a somersault. Then I dove forward, touched the bottom of the sea, and filtered a handful of sand through my wiggly fingers. Catching a deep breath while floating, my mind drifted to the sweetness I'd experienced on Nightingale Hill; my body, meanwhile, yearned for more earthly pleasures. I rolled the top of my bathing suit down and released the ladies to be massaged by the sun.

As my limp body undulated in the ripples, I drifted toward the shore, oblivious to the strengthening current, and landed on a shallow patch of sandbar. Through misty goggles, I spotted numerous sun worshippers and ripped the glasses from my face to get a better look. Directly in front of me were two drop-dead gorgeous Adonises, sitting erect on their chairs and staring at my topless body. I exited the surf on hands and knees and crawled over the damp sand while struggling to hoist up my top. Eyeing Eve in the distance, I made a beeline for our sun beds.

"Did you see those guys?" she asked after I'd gotten horizontal.

"Yes, I saw them," I said, gasping for air. "And I'm afraid they saw a bit too much of me." I explained my semi skinny-dipping spree to Eve, who shrugged it off.

"We're in Europe now—not a big deal," she said, looking at my chest. She shook her towel and positioned her chair for a better view of the Adonises. "I wonder where they're from. The one in the purple Speedo looks quite dark. Italian maybe? The blond, definitely Germanic." I ran a comb through my tangled hair and had to agree. They sure were hot—even more so than Gabi. "How can we get them to notice us?" Eve continued, lowering her black bikini bra straps to her elbows.

I reapplied sunscreen to my face and arms and reached for the *International Herald Tribune* that I'd stashed in my bag at the port.

"Hey, I've got an idea!" Eve pointed to the newspaper's masthead and spread its pages across my seat. "If those guys speak English, we can use this as bait." I wasn't so sure but agreed it was our best strategy, short of going over and introducing ourselves, which she knew wasn't my modus operandi.

I slouched into my seat and continued the crossword while trying to make the paper as visible as possible from across the beach. Eve curled up with Sue Grafton's latest mystery and peeled our hastily-packed lunch—an orange. Ten minutes later, she threw her book, along with the fruit rinds, under her seat.

"Oh. My. God!" she shrieked, as quietly as she could. "I think they're coming this way." We looked around to see if the two were heading toward others, but the nearby chairs were empty. I quickly covered the cellulite on my upper thighs with the newspaper.

"Good day!" said the tall, sandy-blond Adonis, who introduced himself as "Sven." Golden syrupy skin pulled tightly against his hairless, chiseled chest. Sapphire eyes gleamed through rectangular tortoise shell-rimmed glasses perched atop a perfectly shaped nose.

Pinch me! This must be the 'tall man with glasses.' Wow, Mary, that was fast!

"And this here is my friend Marten," he continued. We all nodded at one another. "It seems you ladies speak English?"

"Why, yes," I said, still shy from my frolic in the water.

"We haven't seen you before," said Marten, a slightly shorter, more muscular Adonis with olive skin and dark, close-cropped hair barely noticeable on his well-formed scalp. "When did you arrive?"

"Today," Eve and I said in unison.

"Where are you from?" Sven asked.

"The States," said Eve. "I live in Chicago, and my friend Linda recently left Boston for—"

"You're both American?" Marten said, squinting fiery green eyes. We nodded. "I would have thought you were French." *Oui!*

"We're from Amsterdam," Sven told us.

"Lucky you . . ." I've always wanted to go there," Eve said wistfully. "The tulips, bicycles, moonlit canals . . ."

"Anne Frank's House, the Van Gogh collection . . ." I added.

"Don't forget the Rijksmuseum," Sven said.

"Oh, I know all about the Dutch collections from my studies at the Art Institute," Eve said with a toss of her thick red ginger mane in a sexy maneuver I'd not witnessed since our escapades in college.

"Yes, Amsterdam's a beautiful city," Marten shared. "But take a look around . . . this is quite extraordinary, too." He pointed to an enclave of condos in the distance, where they had already spent half of a two-week vacation.

Eve got up and strutted over to shake their hands, the bows on her black bikini bottom swaying back and forth; I played it safe on the recliner.

"How far did you get with the crossword, Linda?" Sven asked, sitting down next to me. He eyed the mostly filled-in spaces. "Now that's one I didn't get," he said, referring to 58 Down.

"Don't be too hard on yourself. English isn't your native language. Plus, it's from *The New York Times*."

"*Au contraire*, I've been speaking English—Marten, too—since we were small kids growing up together." He got up and glanced furtively at his friend, who nodded. "Well, Linda and Eve, we thought we'd come over and invite you to our little party tonight."

"A party?" we both said, starry-eyed.

"Yes, we're inviting a few people we met this last week,

and since you're new here, we thought you'd be interested in joining us."

"Sounds great," Eve said. "Where is it?"

"Over there." Sven pointed to a sandy area below jagged cliffs on the other side of the beach.

"I see," I said. "What time?"

He uttered something to Marten in Dutch, and then turned to us. "Eleven would be good." *Eleven?* I hadn't been to any late-night parties since my college days. This effort would require a nap of at least two hours.

"That's kind of late. Do the buses even run then?" I inquired. Eve shot me one of her "Let's not worry about that now" glances.

"Yes, until midnight," Marten answered, adding, "Of course, afterward we can give you a ride to your hotel in our Jeep."

Sven kicked some sand around with his bare feet. "Just think—your first night in Tinos and already you have a party invitation. Lucky you!"

Then why am I not excited? Despite the dynamic duo's dishy looks, my mind wandered off to the distant shore, and I wondered if we'd be attending an orgy or a bona fide party.

"No worries then?" Sven asked, as if reading my thoughts. Before we could respond, they had begun walking back toward the waterfront.

Eve stared dreamily in their direction. "Is it my imagination or did they invite us to a party tonight?"

"Would seem that way." As we watched them return to their beach chairs, we agreed that they were the best-looking male specimens we'd seen in our entire lives.

"And that Marten—the way he was eyeing you," Eve said, wagging a pointed finger at me. "Better be careful."

"*Au contraire,*" I said, mocking Sven. "I didn't sense any interest from him at all."

"Oh, yes. From the corner of my eye, I saw him giving you the once-over."

"If anything, Sven was more attentive."

"No, I'd say it was the other way around." Eve's feelings were now clear; she had the hots for Sven, which was why she was putting a bug in my ear about Marten. "Plus, he has those dark, intense brooder looks you tend to go for."

"True. In any event, you're putting the olive way before the martini." I patted her arm. "And no worries, Eve. I'll stay away from Sven."

"Whatever do you mean?" She averted my gaze as she shook sand from her towel.

"Oh, come now—with his toned physique, perfect teeth, and wide smile, he's exactly the knockout you drool over. A little too Hollywood-handsome for my taste." From the gaga look on Eve's face, I could see she was a goner.

She suggested we return to the hotel to eat a real lunch and prepare for the evening's festivities. After a fortifying meal of lamb kebab with rice and salad on the veranda, we napped, and then took turns primping in the shower. We Naired, plucked, and scoured until our suntans nearly peeled off.

I opted for black drawstring pants and a T-shirt with a flowing turquoise linen jacket. To my dismay, a sun blister was festering under my lower lip. While it hurt, I was more concerned with how it looked and tried covering it up with light copper-colored lipstick, but without success.

Primped and ready to go, Eve and I took a taxi back to Fokas Beach. We slipped out of our sandals, hiked up our pants, and tried to find our way in the sand to the cliffs. Without a flashlight, we didn't make much headway and almost turned back, when a voice beckoned from a distance. Soon our hosts approached, kissing us alternately on our cheeks, Dutch style—one-two-three—before escorting us to a row of beach recliners.

"You finally made it!" Marten said, which seemed odd, as it was only a few minutes after eleven. Like Eve, he was decked out in casual black; only his tasseled leather loafers looked out of place.

Sven glided over to some guests hovering over the makeshift bar and returned with white wine for Eve and me. He held up his beer can. "*Yamas!*" he said, toasting us.

From what I could see in the low light, he was wearing beige linen pants, which snapped at the knee, a flowing white top, and brown clogs. *He could truly be a supermodel.* Sven motioned for the other guests—a Whitman's sampler of attractive women—to greet us. The few lone males looked at least ten years younger than the four of us.

"Hi! I'm Tanya," a middle-aged Croatian woman said, wrapping her tattooed arms around Sven's neck.

"And I'm Fiona from Ireland," said a petite younger woman with pixie-styled purple hair, extending a hand to us before walking back to the designated booze area.

Marten cozied up to Eve on her chair, and together they looked up at the blanket of stars, pointing out their astrological constellations. Sven slinked over next to me and talked about his latest assignment as a journalist for a popular women's magazine.

"My ex-wife and I divorced a year ago," he explained, "and I'm writing about the single man's reentry into bachelor life."

"Sorry about the divorce."

Sven dismissed my concern with a toss of his perfectly coiffed head. "I'll be fine . . . my female readers are so sympathetic. I get lots of emails and phone calls of support, so I don't feel like I'm going through this alone." *I doubt you're ever alone.*

"It must be healing for you to be on this singles journey

with your friend," I said, hoping he'd reveal his friend's romantic status.

"Marten's not exactly single. Well, I guess by American standards he is."

"What do you mean?"

"He and his girlfriend have been living together for about ten years, but they aren't actually married—at least from a legal perspective."

"I see," I said, trying not to show my disappointment.

During the next two hours, Sven rambled on and on, much like the crickets in the surrounding bushes, about his ex-wife and their divorce. Eventually, he asked me about Budapest and seemed to be fishing for an invitation to visit me there, although that could have been the Heineken talking.

Around three in the morning, I noticed that Eve and I were the only guests left on the beach and suggested we go back to our hotel. Marten got up and shook the sand from his clothes as Sven downed another beer and announced that he wasn't ready to leave quite yet. "I have a better idea. Let's all go for a swim!" A certain four-letter word sprang to mind again.

"Oh, I don't think so," I said in a firm voice.

"Come on!" he insisted, lightly touching my thigh.

"Well?" Eve turned toward me. "What do you think?" I shook my head and reached for my bag. Eve told Sven, "We're really tired. It's been a long day and—"

"We don't have our swimming things with us," I added.

"That's not a problem," Sven said. "We have towels up at our condo."

"Sorry, another time," I said more firmly. As handsome as Sven was, he was also getting drunker by the minute.

Marten had left us and was already straightening up the beach chairs, ensuring that the fire was sufficiently doused, all party evidence in the garbage bins. Afterward, he waved us over to the Jeep and revved up the engine. Eve and I moved to the back seat, allowing the soft breeze to caress our sun-kissed skin and blow sand from our hair. Soon we heard muffled Dutch words in the front seat; Eve looked at me and shrugged. Moments later, Marten turned around and invited us to join them for dinner the following evening at Ankyra Taverna, a traditional Greek fish restaurant in Tinos Town.

"Yes, we'd love to go." Eve said, nudging me with her elbow. "Count us in."

"Okay, we'll pick you up at eight," he said.

After dropping us off outside our hotel and an exchange of phone numbers, they waved "*Tot ziens!*" and sped away in their Jeep into the misty hills. Except for the gentle rolling of the surf, Agali Bay was very quiet. Then again, it was probably four in the morning.

"Yippee!" Eve shouted, tossing her sandals into the air. "We have a double date tomorrow night with two hot Dutch tidbits." We compared notes and once we got to our room, undressed, and eased our tired, sunburnt bodies under the sheets. Our efforts to stay awake were futile, and within minutes, we were sound asleep.

∾

Hours later, Joni Mitchell lyrics emanated from the shower and slipped into my semiconscious mind, rousing me from peaceful slumbers. I was shocked to see it was noon. After spending what seemed an eternity in the bathroom, Eve emerged wearing a ruby and black batik sarong. Her hair was in an upsweep, à la Rita Hayworth; she'd caked on emerald eye shadow and darkened her pale eyebrows.

"But our date isn't until tonight," I said. "Plus, the beach is right across the street."

"This is only a preview. I'm getting in the mood."

A few footsteps later, I staked my claim on a cushy recliner and opened my new book: "*It was the best of times, it was the worst of times.*" I read Dickens's words over and over. "*It was the best of times, it was . . .*"

Not able to focus past the first sentence, I opted for a nap, using the book as a sun shield over my lip blister, which was nearing eruption. I tossed and turned while my titillated mind replayed scenes from the previous day: Sven sitting next to me, his long frame bending over my shoulder as we filled in the crossword together; the way he gently wrapped his arm around me as we gazed up at Orion's Belt the night before. *Obviously, Sven is the "tall man with glasses," and we're going to rewrite* A Tale of Two Cities *about Budapest and Amsterdam!*

After returning to our room a few hours later, Eve and I resumed primping, plucking, and peeling. I donned the teal spaghetti strap dress I'd worn to Liszt's home on my birthday and topped it with a lacy Japanese-style jacket. Eve got decked out in a black wraparound dress that tied behind the neck, like a glorified bikini top. Her gold shoes and silver bauble necklace shimmered in the receding light.

As I examined my enhanced image in the mirror, my eyes zoomed in on a tiny bump poking out from my chest beneath the clingy fabric of my dress—the silk bow on my bra. I enlightened Eve as to the dire situation, trying to coax it beneath the wire.

"Guys like a little feminine flourish," she advised, slipping an exotic beaded earring from Istanbul through an earlobe. "I wouldn't try fixing it, especially if you want to catch Marten's attention." *So, she's still after Sven, eh?* "Plus, they already saw your breasts and you're worried about a bow?" She fanned out her luscious red ginger curls over her pale shoulders.

She had a point; I left it in place. "How do I look now?" I asked, spinning around.

"Like you're channeling the spirit of Aphrodite."

"I was just thinking the same about you." I blew her a kiss and began to fish through a stack of clothes on the bed for my clutch bag.

"I'm sure they're going to pick up the tab," Eve said.

"Let's hope, although you know that expression 'Dutch treat.'"

"But they invited us."

I stashed the equivalent of fifty dollars in drachma into my wallet and told Eve I'd wait for her and the guys downstairs in reception. When our dates still hadn't arrived fifteen minutes later, I sank back into the leather sofa and perused the Greek tabloids. Soon after, as if choreographed, Eve and Sven emerged from opposite sides of the lobby. I nearly swooned and thought Eve did the same when he approached in a light blue pullover tucked into tan slacks. He kissed us each three times on our cheeks and said, "My, don't you ladies look lovely this evening." We nestled into his extended arms and floated outside toward the Jeep convertible.

Marten, a vision in black, welcomed us from the driver's seat; Sven pushed down the passenger one and directed me into the back. To my surprise, he joined me. Marten patted the front seat, Eve's cue to join him. If their motives hadn't been clear the night before, they were now: she was Marten's designated date; I was Sven's. Marten's "taken" status put an interesting spin on an already alluring evening. Certain that Eve was considering the same evidence, I leaned forward and gave her shoulder a simpatico squeeze.

Our table at Ankyra's cozy garden patio overlooked the harbor where Eve and I had arrived only the day before. As we politely pulled bones from our grilled cod platters and the guys dug into their fried sardine and calamari dinners, Joni Mitchell's "Carey" wafted on a breeze through the clatter of kitchen dishes and swaying wind chimes.

"Oh, Joni!" Sven cried out. "She's my favorite."

"Mine, too," I said.

"Just one more thing you both have in common," Marten added, cocking an eye at me as he reached for the olive oil. Eve kicked my knee gently under the table. "We already know you're both devoted Dickens and crossword fans."

I poured out more white wine and started singing along with the radio.

Eve leaned back in her bright blue chair and clapped. "Here's to my friend Linda, the musician."

Sven tilted his glass of Retsina at me. "Joni even mentions Amsterdam, my hometown!"

"And a grand piano!" I said. We continued weaving our voices together between sips and gazed up at the panoply of stars. I tried not to think of the inevitable "fare-thee-wells."

"Speaking of Amsterdam," Eve said, "I want to hear all about your fairy tale of a city."

"It's not all tulips and windmills," Marten shared. "Wherever we travel, the customs officials immediately assume we're up to here," he said, motioning to his waist, "in drugs. And that subjects us to very degrading searches." I couldn't help but think of Marten's skintight Speedo, which showed off his rock-solid, shapely bum. Eve kicked me again under the table; apparently, she was having the same vision.

"Many people have a romantic image of Amsterdam," Sven added, "but there's also a gritty side, like the Red-Light District." He leaned over and patted my hand. "You'll just have to get on a plane and check it all out."

A rush of hormones surged through my tipsy body; I excused myself and found the bathroom, where I blotted my neck and face with paper towels and reapplied more eye makeup. In the neon light, I discovered—to my horror—that my lip blister was now a dime-sized bump pushing up through cracked skin. I rummaged for more lip gloss and smeared on a fingerful.

After I returned to the table, Marten flagged down the waiter for the tab and addressed his friend in Dutch. I reached for my wallet. "Oh no, gals. This is Dutch treat," he said, poring over the bill with his reading glasses. "Only in this case, it means Sven and I are treating."

We thanked them, and after leaving the table, Eve pulled me aside. "You're not going to sleep with Sven, are you?"

"What gives you that idea?"

"Well, he obviously digs you. I felt him kicking your leg under the table."

"I thought that was you!"

"No!" She pursed her lips. "I'd be careful if I were you. He seems pretty drunk."

"As am I." Although I'd barely indulged compared to the others, the heat, excitement, and alcohol were going to my head. "Which is why I can't imagine anything happening. You know I'm not the type to jump into bed with somebody, Eve, especially when I feel like this. Plus, he's obviously on the rebound."

We piled back into the Jeep, and during the bumpy ride back to Agali Bay, Sven asked us to lunch at their condo the next day. Eve and I had decided to visit Our Lady of Tinos to see the miraculous icon then. *Darn!* Before I could decline the invitation, Eve agreed that we would meet them outside our hotel the next day at noon.

Marten gave her a thumbs-up and kissed her Dutch style, then me. Sven did the same to Eve. When he approached me, he planted two kisses on my cheeks, but the third on my mouth. Before I realized what was happening, he tilted my head back and caressed my hair while tenderly parting my lips with his. My whole body tingled; the hormones I'd tried to keep at bay flooded my veins, radiating shockwaves down my upper thighs.

After a few minutes, Eve's voice seeped into my consciousness. *Yikes! She and Marten are only a few steps away!* I gently broke away from Sven, who touched me lightly on the chin. As he walked away, a strange look twisted onto his face.

"Until tomorrow," he said. They boarded the Jeep and zoomed out of sight.

"Now, that was something," Eve said with a detectable smidgen of envy in her voice. It had been decades since we'd had the hots for the same guy. Usually she fell for the hunky jock, whereas I preferred the sensitive artist or stimulating conversationalist. "I'm happy for you, but I have to admit, I wish Sven had kissed me like that."

"It's been a year, Eve, but worth the wait." As we walked toward the hotel, I felt a pang of guilt about canceling our visit to the church the next day. "Only, I'd hoped to see the famous icon tomorrow, as planned," I continued. "It seems a shame—sinful, even—to travel all the way to Tinos and not see it, especially if it works miracles."

Eve wrapped her arm around my waist. "Maybe the Universe is telling you that you don't need a miracle because one is already in the works."

"That's what I love about you, Eve. You're an eternal romantic optimist." I kissed her forehead. "Let's see how things unfold."

After crouching by the concierge in reception, we glanced at our images in the lobby mirror. My makeup had been holding up, but the blister on my lip had erupted and was spouting blood. Aghast, I leaned in for a closer look. "Holy shit!"

Eve stared in disbelief and examined the unsightly protrusion. "How'd that happen? It wasn't like that even an hour ago."

I thought of the contorted expression that had flashed across Sven's face as he walked away from our embrace.

He had seen the blood on my lip. "I think I got kissed by a toad."

∞

When my blister saw no improvement the next morning, Eve bought a tube of ointment from the pharmacy to dull the throbbing. "What about our lunch date with the guys?" she said, looking at the clock. "They said they'd be here in an hour."

"I doubt they're coming, Eve."

"What do you mean?"

"I'm sure Sven is avoiding me because he thinks I have herpes."

"Oh, stop!"

"No, really." I zipped up my shorts and threw on the T-shirt from the previous day. "When we first met Sven, there was something about him that made me uneasy, although I couldn't quite put my finger on it. Call it superficiality, or arrogance. Like his comment, 'Today's your lucky day.' Are we supposed to feel privileged that someone of his stature is paying us attention? Maybe his good looks are blinding us to the fact that he's a jerk."

When they failed to show up at noon or call our mobile phones, we returned to our room in case they'd misplaced our numbers and might try the landline. Eve hunched over the bed and pretended to read her novel. She hadn't shared any sentiments regarding Marten, but I was sure she was plotting to woo him away from the monogamous clutch of his Dutch girl.

A few hours and four chapters into Dickens later, I realized that my hunch was probably correct and got more pissed off at Sven for jilting us. The worst part was that Eve and I had missed the opportunity to visit the sacred icon, instead staying at the hotel and waiting for the phone to ring. *Serves me right, Mary!*

"Let's dine at Ankyra Taverna again tonight," I told Eve. "I want to confront Sven head-on if we see him."

She laughed. "You've obviously been out of the singles scene way too long. I've met more than my share of men who say they're going to call and never do. They take your phone number, make a big fuss, and then—nada. And who knows why?"

Hours later, all dolled up, Eve and I strolled arm in arm through the windy alleys of Tinos Town, pretending to scope out menus at various tavernas, but really on the lookout for the Dutch Treats. It didn't take long for Eve to spot them at Ankyra, seated at the same table we'd shared with them the night before. "There's someone with them!" She squinted her eyes. "It doesn't look like anyone from the party the other night."

"No, it isn't." At once I understood why Sven hadn't called. Maybe it had nothing to do with my lips, but someone else's. I took Eve's hand. "Let's move in for the kill."

Marten offered a tentative smile before he got up and kissed Eve; a look of terror froze on Sven's beet red face. "Please join us," the blond Adonis said, pulling up two chairs. He introduced the mystery woman as a "friend from Geneva," whom they'd met the day before. She greeted me with an unsteady hand and looked perplexed as Sven and I sized each other up. He explained that she didn't speak English. *How perfect for you.*

"What happened to you earlier today?" I asked. "Eve and I waited for your call."

Sven downed the remainder of his beer and sprang from his seat. "Let's discuss this elsewhere," he said in a stern voice. He led me by the arm behind the restaurant, which was quite unnecessary, as I'd already figured out that he'd lined up his date with Swiss Miss before inviting us for lunch.

"I'm aware that I didn't phone you this morning," he said.

"And why not?"

He shook his head and stared down at his sandals. "You *do* speak English, don't you?" I suddenly wished I didn't. "Obviously, I didn't want to see you again."

I gazed at him with a hollow stare. His interest in bedding Swiss Miss pre-empted any need to spend chaste time with me, but why all the anger?

"Well, why not tell me? I thought we had a nice time last night."

"We did."

"Then what's the matter?"

"We kissed," he said, glaring at my blister, "and I didn't want *that* to happen again."

"It's not as if I had a choice when you pushed your tongue into my mouth." *Ugh! Let me rephrase that.* "Listen, we kissed, you were drunk, I was tipsy—let's leave it at that." He hung his head. "In the future, Sven, if you meet a woman you really like and hope to have a future with, you don't want to treat her this way. Trust me."

Sven snaked back to his friends; I motioned for Eve to join me. She reluctantly draped a black shawl over her bare arms and leaned over Marten, who jotted something on a cocktail napkin and handed it to her. Then he pulled her in for a heartfelt embrace and kissed her cheeks before she caught up with me at the taxi stand.

"Why the quick getaway?" Eve asked.

I pointed toward the taverna. "Do you have any idea what just happened over there?"

"No, but it mustn't have been very good."

"Sven is just as I thought," I said, my voice rising. "A

superficial jerk." After I filled her in, she agreed. Then she showed me her remembrance from Marten.

"He gave me his email address and phone number," she said, eyes aglow.

"You really like him, don't you?"

"It doesn't matter what I feel because he has a girl-friend."

Poor Eve. I'd been so caught up in my own search for a mate that I had forgotten my friend was also on the lookout. I knew the frustration of clicking with a guy who was off-limits and imagined the heartache she was experiencing. "If it's any consolation, Marten seemed smitten with you, too." Although the most likely scenario was that he would be reuniting with his partner, I knew Eve didn't want to hear that now. "Maybe he'll be free in the future," I continued, my face brightening. "You never know."

"Now you're the eternal optimist." She turned around for a final glimpse of Marten and sighed. "He lives half a world away, anyway."

"That doesn't mean you can't visit Amsterdam now, does it?" I stopped and looked at her tear-stained face. "Hey, why don't we meet there during your next vacation?"

"That's an idea! I have a week off in October."

"Let's make a plan. You can write Marten beforehand and see how he responds."

"And you?"

"I'm sure there are plenty of tall men with glasses in Holland, but without the attitude."

"That's the spirit!" Eve wiped off some smeared mascara from her cheeks with a tissue. "I hope you don't have to kiss too many more toads before you meet your Prince, Linda."

I hugged her close. "Me, too, Eve. Me, too."

Part Four

Nuages Gris (Gray Clouds)

*Music expresses that which cannot be said
and on which it is impossible to be silent.*

Victor Hugo

Totentanz (Dance of the Dead)

After Eve and I retreated to our respective corners of the world, one week of freedom remained before The Bell School, my new employer, kicked off another academic year. Much to my excitement, the last gasps of summer coincided with the Franz Liszt International Piano Competition at the Music Academy, where I'd started volunteering for Adél and the Friends of that institution. In between fundraising tasks and meetings, I heard as many performances as possible, often with Heléna. However, on September 11th, I attended the semifinals alone.

Inside the aptly named Great Hall, swathed in gold with green marble, the lights on the enormous crystal-brass chandeliers dimmed in anticipation of the leading favorite, Canadian pianist Li Wang. In an elegant dark black tuxedo that matched the color of his shiny hair, the twenty-seven-year-old sorcerer swept the audience away with the Master's *Dante Sonata;* I half-expected the golden statue depicting the tempo *Adagio* to start weeping. The other contestants performed various *Hungarian Rhapsodies* or *Nuages Gris* but couldn't match Mr. Wang's sensitive touch.

Around three o'clock, the stage fell silent, and the flashing lights signaled another break. In the lobby, I leaned against one of the malachite Zsolnay-tiled pillars and checked my voicemail. Heléna had tried calling three times and left one message. Although her recorded voice was drowned out by a group of Americans screaming at one another across the crowded space, I made out the words "tower" and "plane." Concerned, I slipped outside and sought refuge in Pizza Hut, where I ordered a Coke and dialed my friend.

"My dear, there's been accident in New York City," Heléna gasped into the phone. "Twin Towers are burning."

"What do you mean, *burning*?" I asked, assuming another language glitch.

"An airplane hit them."

"You mean, there was a plane crash?" Heléna revved up the volume on her TV.

"No, not certain. Could be terrorist act."

I knocked over my soda and reached for a handful of napkins. Heléna encouraged me to leave the competition and head over to her flat to watch CNN, which I didn't get at my place; I immediately rode the rails to my old neighborhood. Heléna had heard my impatient stride outside the building and was waiting at the door. "You're going to need this," she said, handing me a glass of Bikavér wine. "Terrible tragedy."

I plopped down on the sofa, trying to fathom the disturbing, repetitive images of huge aircraft crashing into the World Trade Center's North Tower. Then the South Tower. Heléna and I stared in disbelief at the gigantic balls of fire engulfing their uppermost floors. Was it possible that two aviation accidents had occurred around the same time, both colliding into neighboring buildings? It seemed too coincidental, yet I was loath to believe that a sinister attack of such magnitude had been planned and executed. As fires smoldered uncontrollably and smoke billowed from shattered glass windows, the second tower buckled.

"As you know, I have friends in New York," I told Heléna, battling waves of nausea, "and my parents often visit my uncle there." *Mom and Dad!* I wouldn't be at peace until I spoke with them and knew they were safe. After several failed attempts because "all circuits are busy now," I rejoiced at the sound of my mother's voice. Heléna crossed herself and mouthed, "Thanks be to the God."

Mom ended the call abruptly so that she and Dad could stay glued to CNN. I missed them terribly and longed to be watching TV with them in Amherst. I drifted back over to Heléna, who was still riveted to the images of the raging inferno. "I cannot believe this happening," she said, poking her middle fingers at the TV set. "Why? Why? Why?" I had the same question. "Maybe like the Nostradamus predict, world coming to end." She refilled my wine glass multiple times while we stared at the screen over the next few hours. I finally left at midnight and wove my way back to Tulip Street through a haze of tears.

∞

For the next two weeks, I hibernated inside my apartment, transfixed by the images on BBC News or distracted by the detective novels Eve had given me when we parted ways in Athens. I returned a call from Béla after he'd sent a text message wondering how I was "handling all the shit happening in New York."

"Gabi and I are at Mammut and would like to buy you a drink," he said, sounding relieved to hear my voice. "Can you meet us now?" I hadn't seen the brothers since *Figaro*, and unable to resist the invitation, I threw on the fire engine red batik dress I'd bought in Tinos and headed down Lövőház Street.

Leroy Café was dimly lit, except for the electrically charged aura of the curvaceous blonde sitting between the two brothers. Her pretty face was as round as her breasts, which dipped perilously close to the nachos appetizer. A skimpy black Lycra top crisscrossed in front of her chest, drawing the room's attention to her God-given attributes. I immediately felt a pang of jealousy, although I had no right to. Gabi had never been my boyfriend.

"This is Laura," Béla said, introducing their guest, who got up to peck my cheeks.

"I'm so sorry about what's happening in your country," she said, wiping a mascara-stained tear from her cheek. "I'm Gabi's colleague." Gabi had also found a job as an ESL instructor and was already teaching at an adult ed school. *He's not wasting any time.*

Before I could gauge Gabi's interest in Laura, he and Béla asked for my take on recent events. Amid the clashing of bowling balls and pins at the alley next door, we discussed where we'd been on September 11th, President Bush's reaction to the attack, and the plans to capture Osama bin Laden. Despite Gabi's complaints that Bush wasn't doing enough to catch the suspected mastermind, I reminded him that he'd been a big fan of the American President only months before.

"That was then, this is now," he said, digging into his potato skins. Whether it was the continual rehashing of the distressing subject or the lack of crow's feet around Laura's luminous eyes, I desperately wanted to hightail it out of there and reached for my bag.

"But you just got here," Béla said. "You haven't even touched your margarita."

"Not thirsty," I lied. I threw the equivalent of three dollars in forints on the table and told them I'd be in touch. But Béla couldn't wait; two hours later he phoned me at home.

"Everything okay, Linduska?"

"No, of course not. I'm very disturbed by what's going on in New York."

"Yes, I know. But I don't mean that. I'm talking about my brother."

I put down *Time* magazine. "What about him?"

"You weren't your usual warm, friendly self. It's Laura, isn't it?" I heard Béla exhale deeply from his cigarette. "Laura's not Gabi's girlfriend."

"She's not?" I tried not to sound too relieved and opened the door to my balcony, unleashing a humid breeze.

"No. When Gabi learned that her family once belonged to the Communist Party, he lost interest."

"Could've fooled me. They looked pretty chummy."

"I've been encouraging him to date Laura, or anyone for that matter. He's so shy and still stays with Papa in Vác most of the time. If only someone would take the initiative."

"You know I've tried getting closer to Gabi, but he doesn't seem all that interested. And I can't possibly compete with *Harry Potter*."

Béla laughed. "Isn't that pathetic?" He paused as Ágnes shouted in the background. "By the way, Linduska, I have some happy news in light of so much tragedy."

"Ágnes is pregnant?"

"You guessed it. We're expecting twins in early March."

"Congratulations to you both, Béla."

"Listen, let's be in touch, okay? In the meantime, it wouldn't hurt to turn up the heat."

Flustered, I hung up and decided to shelve the whole Gabi issue, at least temporarily. It was such a small concern compared to the chaos wracking the world, not to mention the fate of pianist Li Wang.

The day before, Heléna had surprised me with two tickets to the Gala Concert as a way of prying me out of my apartment. We entered the Great Hall certain that Mr. Wang had won top prize but were stunned to learn none had been awarded. Instead, a young Hungarian prodigy, Péter Tóth, had snatched second prize, with three third-prize winners. "It doesn't make any sense," I told my friend. "Our favorite hasn't placed at all."

"Nothing now makes sense," Heléna said.

After taking our seats, the lights dimmed, and conductor András Ligeti walked onstage with members of the Matáv Hungarian Symphony Orchestra. They first played selections from the repertoire of the runners-up. After we'd listened to various renditions of Liszt's Sonata in B Minor and the Second Piano Concerto, the curtains dropped. During intermission, Heléna and I shared a plate of pink-iced *sütemény* and caught a glimpse of our Canadian idol standing alone near the *kassza*.

"Let's go talk to him," Heléna said, quickly downing the last morsel of cake.

"What are we going to say? It's not as if he needs to be reminded that he didn't win."

She threw her hands up. "You want to end this mystery or not?" We walked gingerly toward the pianist, who was perusing the posters of upcoming concerts on the bulletin boards.

"Mr. Wang, my friend Linda is from America. She's also pianist and thinks you very great musician." My cheeks flushed the color of the wine he was sipping.

"Well, Mr. Wang," I said, finally finding my voice, "I heard you play twice during the competition and was expecting to see your name on the cover of tonight's program."

"Ah, yes," he said, placing an index finger on his chin.

"Ask him what happened," Heléna whispered a bit too loudly. Fortunately, I was spared.

"You see, back in Canada, I don't have much experience playing with an orchestra," Mr. Wang revealed. "When I performed the First Piano Concerto the other night, I was not in sync with the other musicians."

"We think you're the best," I said, impressed by his candor.

"You're too kind," he said. The flashing lights reminded us that the second half was about to start. We wished him luck in his career and slipped back inside the Great Hall.

The highlight of the evening was a repeat of Péter Tóth's winning performance of *Totentanz*, or "Dance of the Dead," a piece that had plagued the Master throughout his life. Liszt first composed this work in 1838, and then spent two decades revising it. A symphonic poem with medieval overtones, *Totentanz* was inspired by a fresco he had seen at a cathedral in Pisa.

Thunderous applause greeted the teenaged prodigy as he entered the stage, taking long strides toward the Steinway grand. Péter pulled his tux tails back, and after sitting down, flexed his long, graceful fingers. Maestro Ligeti held up his baton, waiting for Péter's hands to jump onto the ivories, which they did with an enormous thud. The brass players entered with the ominous theme, unleashing the Devil in his stomping grounds, the abyss at Ground Zero. I closed my eyes and imagined that wretched day . . .

Somewhere in the clear blue sky, a plane veers out of control. The thunder of restless chords culminates in an explosive cymbal crash—the North Tower has been struck!

Péter rips the tumultuous melody from the others, his fingers scampering up and down the ivories and dislodging shards of glass that fly through the air. A succession of rapid notes and trills follows; thousands of innocent panicky hearts thump in unison against a crescendo of havoc. Shock waves creep up and down the tower, causing it to buckle. Bodies, like meteors, litter the hellish skies.

Stone silence follows. Slowly, the melody crawls in, meanders, seeks rest. The tempo skids down. Two bassoon-

ists *weave a duet against the plucking of anxious strings.
A trumpet cries out in agony. Péter's left hand pounds out
the macabre theme; his right is lost in a series of glissandi
he creates by sliding his thumb up and down the keyboard.
He then pounces onto the piano, like a lion protecting its
young, as the brass fight back, defiant.*

*During the prayer-like variation, angels descend; their
feathers fall, along with ashes, chunks of metal, and wiring
into the abyss. While softly stroking their harps, they carry
the dying up to the Everafter on their wings. Only the
wailing of a lone clarinet reminds the victims of the earthly
suffering they've left behind.*

*Suddenly, out of the ash heap, the Devil rears up, the
snare of his voice piercing the reverie. Willowy flutes fight
to keep the peace, but Satan stokes the bonfire's flames.*

*Distant footsteps approach and race up the stairwells. Can
help be on the way? Firemen yank hoses and sirens blast, emergency vehicles screech through the soot-covered city streets.
Expressions of hope dominate, but brass players hurl fireballs
the size of ambulances; the violins struggle to douse the flames.
Finally, the cymbal's earth-shattering boom rattles the room. A
second plane crashes into the South Tower!*

*While the Orchestra catches its breath, Péter attacks
the cadenza. His right hand leaps up and down the upper
registers, desperately looking for an escape, but is overcome
by his left hand hammering the keys in the lower one. The
conductor guides the musicians as they seep back in with
the triumphant brass section blaring out the shifting theme.*

*The Devil is back, staggering between the two teetering
towers. Péter whips the keys, begging for mercy, but this
last attempt is pushed back by the full weight of the Orchestra. Together, they all spiral down into the abyss, the last
gasp of chords striking nails into the coffin of Humanity.*

I stifled a sob and exhaled a loud "Bravo," grateful to
be back among the living.

Teacher's Pets

I was greatly relieved when The Bell School officially kicked off its fall term. In preparation for my first teaching assignment at Right Angles Inc., an architectural firm, I spent several hours at the school's resource room flipping through the intermediate level reference books. Unable to concentrate on anything other than Ground Zero, my eyes wandered to the breathtaking views of the school's verdant yard, which sloped down toward a cherry tree orchard. A seemingly stray tabby noticed my restlessness and leapt onto the table, demanding full attention. I patted the cat's vibrating black, gray, and white fur and discovered his favorite scratch points.

"Well, hello there, cutie. Can you sing 'Happy Birthday' like Squeak, or do you only purr?" He curled up into a big fluffy ball, and for the first time in weeks, a wave of calm flowed over me. Soon we were breathing in relaxed sync.

The feline wore no collar; I glanced around the premises, hoping to catnap him for a quick snuggle. Perhaps if he were homeless, Ilona, Bell's Director, would let me adopt him. Before I could ask, she walked into the room, her petite frame weighed down by armfuls of gardening tools. I appreciated my boss's down-to-earth supervisory style, which she had more likely cultivated in these bucolic surroundings than during her years of study in the UK.

"Looks like you've made a friend," she said as I stroked the tabby's luxurious mane.

I told her about Squeak, withholding details of my former cat's musical abilities. She put down the hand shovels, shook some stray leaves from her dark brown hair, and leaned against a hoe. "You live at the other end of Tulip Street, don't you?" I nodded. "Would you be interested in looking after him, even temporarily? That way, he can come and go between both ends of the block and have company in the evenings."

A Cheshire-like grin crept across my face. "Are you serious?"

"Absolutely. He's been hanging around here for months, and no one's claimed him."

I scooped the tabby up in my arms and rubbed my nose against his. "I'll name him Lester, an Anglo name, in honor of your English language school."

Ilona smiled and turned to me as she was about to leave. "I've been meaning to introduce you to Gretchen, another American who teaches at Bell. She's from Seattle and has been with us a few years. I think you two would hit it off." She jotted down Gretchen's phone number. "It might do you some good to call her and discuss what's going on in your country."

"Thanks, Ilona." I hadn't met another American expat since the International Women's Club meeting earlier in the year, and I'd stopped attending after the Maribel debacle.

When I left for home that afternoon, Lester followed me down Tulip Street, and after sniffing around his new digs, sprawled out on the living room sofa. As I positioned myself for a cuddle, Eve called to tell me her "fabulous" news: she had met "someone special," whom she sensed was The One. Jim was a new psychologist at the nursing home where she worked, and after three dates, they were already spending most of their free time together. As she animatedly described his sensitivity with the elder residents, his sporty, rugged good looks, and his penchant for Picasso, I knew she wouldn't be interested in meeting up in Holland one month later. While I was disappointed, I considered that traveling solo might "increase my chances of meeting someone," as Mom liked to point out.

"Jim sounds like a catch," I told Eve. "I'm happy for you."

"With all the craziness in the world right now," Eve continued, "it's reassuring to have someone's loving arms around me."

I looked at Lester and laughed. "I have someone's loving arms around me right now."

Eve gasped. "That Gabi guy you told me about is with you?"

"No, Lester."

"You're dating a Brit?"

"No, Lester is my newly adopted cat. I'm cuddling with him as we speak."

"Uh-oh! Time to send Gabi an SOS." Despite her and Béla's encouragement about my former crush, I stayed put with my furry feline and rested up for my inaugural teaching gig the next day.

∞

Csaba, one of the architects at Right Angles, shifted his massive bulk from side to side, stretching the blue buttons on his white starched shirt beyond their limits. "We're not very keen on the Jewishes," he said, matter-of-factly, his dark brown eyes narrowing to tiny marbles, which were out of proportion to the massive clean-shaven orb above.

For a moment, I thought I'd mistakenly stumbled into a neo-Nazi meeting instead of the cushy office of an architectural firm. It was day one of my teaching assignment with Csaba and his two colleagues, Viktor and Ádám, and if I passed this "audition," I'd land an eight-month contract there.

We had been discussing Budapest's major tourist attractions, but after I mentioned the stunning Byzantine Great Temple in the old Jewish Quarter, the conversation had drifted into slippery terrain. I wondered how I'd survive the next hour, let alone the rest of the course.

"There are a couple of problems with your statement, Csaba," I said. "First of all, we don't say 'Jewishes.' When referring to a group of people of the Jewish faith, we say 'Jews' or 'Jewish people.'"

"But you say 'radishes,' don't you? Then why not 'Jewishes?'" he countered, stabbing his pen into a company notepad.

Other than one word referring to a vegetable and the other a religious group, I was stumped. As usual, when I didn't know the answer, I improvised. "Each nationality or cultural group has its own unique plural ending. For example: Finns, Romanians, Chinese. You have to memorize them."

Three blank faces stared back. "Well, whatever you call them, my feelings are the same," Csaba said.

I knew from reading about Hungary's history that over half a million Jews had perished during World War II, most of them at Auschwitz. During a recent visit to the Raoul Wallenberg Holocaust Memorial Park, I'd been moved to tears by the Weeping Willow sculpture, constructed with metal leaves bearing the engraved names of Hungarian victims. I leapt to the board, marker in hand, and wrote: "RACISM." The group scribbled down the word.

"Can one of you tell me what this means?" The students glanced sideways at one another for a glimmer of recognition. "It's when someone from one country or religious group has a negative view toward another without a specific reason."

"That's not me," Csaba said, shaking his head defiantly. "I'm not racism."

"You're not a racist, is what you mean." I wrote that word on the board. "A racist is the person who exhibits feelings of racism."

"Then I'm not a racist."

"Okay, let me ask you this." I put down the marker and approached Csaba, stopping short of his chair. "How many Jewish people do you know? Four? One?" I walked over to the other two students. "What about you guys?" They stared down at their papers. "Exactly. The definition states that these negative views are based on lack of information."

Boy, am I in hot water! Ilona's going to be steaming mad if Bell loses this contract. I tried another approach. "Let's take America, where I come from. If someone who'd never met a Magyar said they hated Hungarians, would that be a fair judgment?"

"It's not individual Jews who are the problem," Viktor chimed in. He was a short, doughy man with a reddish complexion, sporting Hungarian flag cuff links and a matching tiepin. "It's when they're in a group that they bother us. They want to control our businesses, take our tax money, change our—"

"Whoa, hold on a moment!" I marched over to Viktor's spot at the table. "With such a small Jewish population in Hungary today, why do you feel threatened by them?"

Suddenly, Ádám spoke up. Until now, he'd been largely

quiet, preferring to sit back and gaze upon this bonfire of cultural clashes from the oasis of his twinkling blue eyes. "It's a complicated issue that's deeply embedded in our country's past."

"Well put, Ádám. There's a lot I don't know about your history." I poured out another glass of water. "Let's just say I won't be recommending Budapest as a tourist destination to my Jewish friends any time soon." He nodded, and I beamed a grateful smile his way. While introducing another subject, I sized him up. Unlike the other two, Ádám wore jeans and a short-sleeved cotton shirt, revealing athletic biceps. His thick head of black hair shone as brightly as the band of gold on his wedding finger.

After the lesson, he approached and apologized for his colleagues. "No worries," I said, knowing I'd never see them again. Certainly, Right Angles would request another, less controversial teacher, and Ilona would have no choice other than to cancel all my other contracts, leaving me jobless. My fears, however, were unfounded.

"The architects really liked you," she congratulated me the next morning by phone.

"You're joking."

"No. They said you were 'provocative.' I hope that doesn't mean you were showing your boobies." She laughed.

"Fat chance of that," I said, glancing down my pajama top.

By the end of our conversation, I had committed to returning to Right Angles and signed on with nearby St. László's School, where a group of teenagers was preparing to become English-speaking tour guides. During classes at that trade school, it was obvious that the mostly male students were more interested in the features of their mobile phones than in their ability to describe local attractions. They put their "handys" on vibrate mode and watched them wiggle on their desks while my voice strained to attract their attention; I was no match for Vodafone.

In November, the administrators at St. László's planned an excursion to Gödöllő Royal Palace, the double U-shaped summer residence of Emperor Franz Joseph and Empress Elisabeth, whom the Hungarians still lovingly referred to as Sissi. Once there, the aim was for the students to become acquainted with the mansion, and then deliver their commentary to me in English.

As I walked with the teens through a small section of the building's cavernous staterooms and Baroque bedchambers, I urged them to listen carefully to the guide and take notes. They grunted and turned away. When it came time for them to translate various facts into English, they flashed icy stares. "We have to leave now," or "We'll miss the train," several shouted as others slipped out the side doors. A snowstorm had hit Budapest, and they were anxious to get back.

I trudged through rows of snow-laden trees, struggling to catch up with the students in my L.L. Bean boots. Approaching the train station, I noticed the worst offenders, Luca and Dániel, throwing snowballs at one other. When I raised my voice in protest, they hurled them at me, turning my black wool coat white. I instinctively covered my hands over my head and screamed, "*Baszd meg!*" They howled at my odd pronunciation.

As soon as I got home, I peeled off the soggy layers and slid into my gargantuan tub for a long hot soak. Obviously, I wasn't getting through to these young adults and doubted I ever would. After toweling off and pondering this dilemma with Lester, I phoned Ilona for advice.

"They were throwing snowballs at you, eh?" she said. "That means they like you."

"They didn't just throw them; they pounded me." I patted my sore shoulder. "I'm still recovering."

"Then they must *really* like you."

"Listen, Ilona, I would appreciate it, and sense the teenagers would too, if you'd find them a more gender and age-appropriate instructor," I said, struggling to hide my exasperation.

I heard her flipping through the personnel cards, and with each *"Nem"* she uttered, realized I would be facing Luca and company again. "Sorry, but I don't have a replacement. You'll have to stick it out until the end of the academic year."

"You mean semester."

"No, until the end of May."

I expelled a huge sigh.

"Linda, why not lay off the tour guide curriculum for a while and discuss subjects they're more interested in?"

"Like sex, drugs, and rock 'n' roll?"

"No, like movies, food, and shopping." She explained that activating their oral language skills was the primary goal, regardless of the topic. After hanging up with my boss, I reluctantly phoned the only Hungarian teenager I knew for advice.

American Pie

"Those guys sound bored," Róbert told me. "They're only waiting around until they get into university. They're not really serious about becoming tour guides."

"Then how can I capture their interest three hours a week?"

I heard the sound of Róbert's fingers flying over his computer keyboard. After a few moments of silence, he said: "*American Pie.*"

"You mean the song?" I hummed a few bars from the golden oldie by Don McLean.

Róbert shushed me. "No, granny! *American Pie*, the *movie*. You do have access to a TV and video player at the school, don't you?"

"Yes."

"In that case, I recommend watching that with them. It's sure to break the ice."

"How do you mean?"

"Trust me. It's an American classic."

I remembered having seen ads for *American Pie 2* around the city but knew nothing about the original. Before

Thursday's class at St. László, I found a copy of *American Pie* in the school's video collection. Although the description of the movie was in Hungarian, the four-star reviews led me to believe it was a classic of sorts. I took the cassette over to the librarian, who pointed to the words "Uncut Version" and flashed me a stern look. "This film is so . . . so . . . *American,*" she said.

"Exactly. I want to share a bit about my culture."

When class started, I told the students that for the next few weeks, we would be viewing American films. "After the challenging visit to Gödöllő, I thought we could all use a break. For starters, today we'll view *American Pie.*"

Luca raised his eyebrows and let out a howl; Dániel snickered and covered his mouth. A few girls cheered that it was their favorite movie. The words "*király*" and "*sirály,*" slang for "cool," echoed across the room.

"I'll be taking notes on the more difficult expressions during the movie," I told them. "Please listen closely so you'll know what they mean when I quiz you at the end of class." They glanced at one another sideways and winked; I was relieved to have chosen a subject of interest.

A few minutes into the film, I squirmed in my seat. Was *American Pie* about a bunch of nerds losing their virginity? The incessant toilet humor was gross enough, but when one of the lead characters began eyeing the apple pie on the kitchen table, I knew it was time for a break. I excused myself, breezed out into the hallway, and dialed Róbert.

"How could you?" I yelled into the phone. "The movie is totally disgusting. All the fart jokes, the diarrhea scene . . ."

"That one's my favorite!" Róbert belted out.

"I can't believe you recommended this. What are they going to think of me?"

"Probably that you're one cool teacher."

"Yuck."

"Cheer up, it can't be all that bad. The movie's only R-rated." *Oops.* The version I'd taken out was uncut. I told Róbert.

"*Sirály! Király!*" he yelled into the phone, sounding as if he had scored a date with Britney Spears.

After hanging up, I slipped back into the classroom and plopped onto a stool in the corner, where I pretended to take notes. There was no way I could eke a lesson out of the movie's featured vocabulary: "virginity," "body fluids," "jerking off."

As the credits finally rolled, the students clapped. "Great class!" they cried in unison, high fiving one another as they paraded out of the room. I stayed behind in the dimmed light, my feet floating atop an imaginary puddle. Perhaps Róbert had been right: the ice was finally melting.

∾

After the lesson, I headed to Vörösmarty Square and with thirty minutes to spare poked around the outdoor Christmas market in search of a gift for Gabi, who, to my surprise, had asked me to celebrate his birthday with him. In the frosty air, some vendors peddled handmade ceramics, beaded jewelry, and souvenirs while others served up *paprikás* chicken and a "delicacy" of rooster testicle stew. I disappeared into a side street and gravitated toward the festively decorated windows of Írománia bookshop and its appealing display of handcrafted diaries. Each unique piece was bound in goat leather and tied with a colorful silk bow. I bought a medium-sized tan one that matched the color of Gabi's hair.

He was already waiting at the upscale Café Gerbeaud when I arrived. "Before we indulge, there's something I want to show you," Gabi said, holding my hand and escorting me through the alleys off Váci Street back to Írománia. *Déjà vu!* "This is my favorite shop in all of Budapest." We ducked inside. "Of course, I can't possibly afford to buy anything here, but sometimes there are those special occasions." He directed my attention toward the showcase of diaries. "Take that journal, for example. It's beautiful and of the highest quality." Gabi reached for the exact model I'd bought him and lovingly fingered its pages. "Have you ever seen such a perfect gift?"

"As a matter of fact, yes." I handed him his present. "*Boldog szülinapot*, Gabi!"

He tore off the gift wrap from the journal and clutched it toward his chest. "How's it possible you knew what to buy me?"

"I was here a few minutes ago and felt especially drawn to this one. I started keeping a journal after reading *The Diary of a Young Girl* by Anne Frank when I was eleven. It made such a strong impression on me." Gabi tried to stifle a sob with the sleeve of his leather jacket. "I had a premonition you'd like this one." As soon as I uttered the word "premonition," I wondered if there were a cosmic meaning in what had happened, perhaps a sign to give our relationship more its due.

"Thank you ever so much," he said, in between sniffles as we left the shop. "You have no idea how much this means to me."

We strolled along the Danube past the Vígadó, a neoclassical concert hall decorated with the country's coat of arms and lined with statues of prominent Hungarians, where many great pianists—from Liszt to Rubenstein—had performed. Across the river, the vertiginous Sikló funicular transported tourists up to a panoramic spot outside the Buda Castle. After settling into an empty bench along the promenade, Gabi asked me to inscribe the gift. I wrote: *For Gabi, on the happy occasion of his twenty-sixth birthday. May you have many adventures to record in this diary. Love, Linda.*

He read the words carefully. "I'm not sure about adventures, but hopefully I'll have something to write about."

"Oh, you will." I touched his arm and smiled. "I know you will."

Sensing his unease at having revealed too much emotion, I told him about the Gödöllő fiasco and my horror at having viewed *American Pie* with my students.

"Wow! From Sissi to the gutter. You have quite a teaching repertoire."

I smirked and suggested we walk back to Gerbeaud, where we could indulge in some decadent birthday cake; Gabi said he preferred to watch the sun setting over the Buda Hills. "Gerbeaud is a bit stuffy anyway. Remember, I'm more of a McD's kind of guy."

I glanced over at the red, white, and green Hungarian flags flapping in the brisk breeze on the Chain Bridge and sensed another Gabi Moment, in which he'd start brooding about life in Hungary or deliver another earful about the Treaty of Trianon. Instead, his eyes fixated on the handful of young mothers and their children parading by the statue of *Kiskirálylány*, or the "Little Princess," perched on the iron balustrade in front of us. Without lifting his gaze, he took the unlit cigarette from his mouth and turned toward me.

"Doesn't it bother you, Linda, that you don't have a family of your own?"

Whoa. My eyes spun cartwheels.

"What I mean to say is, I'm twenty-six today, and I feel like a failure because I don't have a child—let alone a wife—and that makes me sad. I'm eager to start a family."

"What's the rush? You still have a few decades—"

"Yes, but I'm thinking more about you. If I'm twenty-six, you must be at least . . ." He tried to pry the number out of me, but I wasn't sharing. ". . . Thirty . . . or forty-something?" He winked.

"Something like that." I winked back.

"Don't you ever think about it?"

I reminded Gabi of the conversation we'd had at McDonald's about why I'd left Hank to come to Budapest.

"You've been here nine months already. You could've had a baby in that time."

"Gimme a break, Gabi. I don't even have a partner."

"That could change." He lit up the Sopianae and blew smoke rings toward the Danube, adding to the twilight haze settling over the Buda Hills. "Plus, that's immaterial, don't you think? If you really wanted a child, you'd have one."

My eyes darted to the moms bouncing newborns on their laps as their doting partners captured these magical encounters on camera with the bronze princess, who looked more like a pixie wearing a whimsical crown and tomboy attire. "Yes, I've thought of that. But for me, the love relationship is primary, the kid thing secondary. I can't imagine having a baby with someone I'm not utterly in love with."

Gabi held the cigarette to his lips and tilted his head to gaze into my eyes. "It's just that I think you'd make a fantastic mother."

"Thanks, Gabi." Not many men had paid me that compliment; a tear trickled down my plaid purple scarf. "That doesn't mean it will happen, though."

He threw down the Sopianae, squished it with his sneaker, and draped an arm around the bench. "Imagine for a moment there was someone you cared for . . . let's say a friend." He shifted toward me; I locked eyes with the Little Princess. "Let's say the guy sitting next to you." My heart leapt toward the river. *Is this Gabi's version of a proposal?*

"What about it?" I said, not sure how to respond.

"Well, for example, if we got married and moved to the States . . ."

Ah, yes. I quickly realized that Gabi's eagerness to board the Baby Bandwagon was really a way to hitch a ride on the Green Card Express. "Listen, I appreciate your concern for me and my chances of motherhood, but I've not been thinking along those lines lately."

"I guess what I'm saying is that I'd like you to." He rested a gentle hand on my arm. "It's a win-win situation: I'll get to be back in the States, and you'll get the child you want."

"Who, *you*?" I gazed across the Danube at the statue of a Turul falcon perched on a pillar, its enormous wings poised for takeoff from the Buda Castle. In Hungarian mythology, the Turul was a divine messenger who hovered over the Tree of Life and the spirits of unborn children. I closed my eyes, tightly. *Gabi isn't The One.* He was too immature and wasn't truly in love with me. On the other hand, I wasn't getting any younger and his could be the final offer of marriage and babymaking I would receive.

Gabi encouraged me to take some time to consider his idea. I promised to let him know upon my return from America after Christmas. We sat in silence until a tram roared into the platform below. I stood up and wound my scarf around my neck; he shuffled in place and pulled me in for a hug. His leather jacket was open, allowing his body heat to penetrate through my thin wool coat. I wondered what it would be like to have this waiting for me at home on a nightly basis. Before my imagination ran wild, I tapped him on the chest and slowly moved away. "Happy Birthday, Gabi, you old fogey."

He smiled so delicately, I thought his handsome face might break. "Bye, bye, Miss American Pie."

As I walked toward the Deák Square Metró, I marveled at how easily Gabi was able to speak about his longing for a child, when Hank had never uttered a single word in our seven years together.

Gábor

After celebrating Christmas in Amherst with my parents, I returned to Budapest with three weeks to spare before The Bell School's spring semester began. As I debated how best to tell Gabi my decision—over tea and cakes at the Európa or on the phone with Papa at his side—I revved up my fundraising efforts at the Liszt Academy. In addition to a long list of grant proposals, the Friends had a few special events planned at the Kempinski Hotel, and tickets needed to be sold, corporate donors wooed, logistics finalized.

One night, after the Music Academy board members had left Adél's urban home, she asked me to stay and tell her about my trip. As we unwound with glasses of *pálinka*, or "brandy," I cheerfully recounted the snowstorm that had blanketed Amherst, affording me, Mom, and Dad a white Christmas, and how we'd shared a traditional turkey dinner at the Lord Jeffrey Inn. But as I started to speak about my visit to Ground Zero on New Year's Eve, my voice broke.

As she listened, Adél's usually radiant brown eyes misted over, and she moved across the floor toward the stereo player. "If you'll indulge me, this is what I've been listening to since 9/11."

I sank back into a sofa cushion while the haunting tenor solo wafted up to the beamed cathedral ceiling, where shiny red and silver balls dangled from tinsel boughs. "*Requiem aeternam dona eis Domine*. Grant them eternal rest, Lord." I took another sip of brandy and tilted my glass upward. "Ah, yes, Fauré's *Requiem*. One of my favorite pieces."

Adél joined me on the black leather sofa and rested a warm hand on mine. "I'm glad to hear that, because now whenever I listen to this, I always think of you and your country."

I leaned forward and burst into tears. Only a few days earlier, I had joined hundreds of other curiosity seekers in a tour of what remained of the World Trade Center. Only a chain-link fence had separated us from the abyss, where trucks and cranes plucked through the wreckage of the Twin Towers, like ravenous vultures dissecting a carcass. Remembering the stench of toxic fumes piercing through the chilly Manhattan air, I suddenly felt woozy and held on to the edge of the coffee table.

"Are you okay?" Adél asked, fanning me with a napkin. "You look a bit pale."

As the Fauré receded, I conjured up the Salvation Army Band's haunting rendition of "Auld Lang Syne" at Ground Zero and thought of the thousands of innocent victims and their loved ones. How had the latter managed to survive the holiday season with empty seats at their dinner tables, piles of unopened presents, unsung carols, and unlit menorahs? I took the napkin from Adél and dabbed my eyelids. "It's still so raw and painful to describe."

Adél put down her glass and gently rubbed the back of my neck. "When words aren't enough, Linduska, we always have music."

I struggled to smile. "Yes, thank God for that."

She reached for the CD and pointed to the acronym, BACS, on its cover. "This is the ensemble I'm in, the Budapest Academic Choral Society."

"Yes, I remember from your concert in the Great Hall a few months ago." I examined the insert. "I have to confess, it's been a long-time dream of mine to sing in a chorus again."

"Which part do you sing?"

"Alto, last I checked. It's been about twenty years since I sang Mozart's *Requiem* in my college chorus."

"That's nothing to sneeze at." Adél shifted on the couch, her eyes shimmering against the silver sequins on her jacket collar. "Linda, why didn't I think of this before? You should join us! Singing is the best therapy. At the end of the year, we're performing the Fauré, as well as Bach's *Magnificat*. If you sang the Mozart, you could certainly tackle those."

I threw my head back with the last drop of *pálinka* and considered Adél's offer. While my heart leapt at the thought of singing en masse again, I wondered aloud if I were good enough for such a high-caliber chorus and how I could handle the rehearsals, which were conducted in Hungarian.

"I've heard you play Chopin," she said, motioning to the upright piano. "You can obviously read music."

"That doesn't mean I can carry a tune."

"Well, I'm no diva either," Adél confessed, slinking back into the sofa, rather looking like one. "I never formally studied music and would be thrilled to sit next to someone who did. Plus, I can translate for you." She opened the CD cover and pointed to a photo of a middle-aged man with salt-and-pepper hair and eyebrows bushier than Hank's. "This is our conductor, Gábor Hollerung."

"He's German?"

"No, trust me. He's 100% Hungarian." Her eyes glowed. I wanted to press her, but her son shouted from upstairs, begging to be read a bedtime story. Adél led me to her office, where she rummaged through the bookcases for his favorite fairy tales.

"Please consider joining us, Linda," she said as I slipped into my winter coat. "It would be great to have another foreigner in our chorus. Right now, there's only William from England. I think the two of you would hit it off."

Unsure if she was plotting to match me up with William or encourage my musical interests, I agreed to attend the next week's practice and gauge how comfortable I felt after a hiatus of two decades. Adél promised to let Gábor know about my musical background and winked a few times while speaking about him. Then she escorted me to the end of her gated driveway, and I rode the tram home.

∞

The choral rehearsal venue lived up to part of its name on Rottenbiller Street. A sleepy security guard at the front door motioned to the darkened staircase, where I walked up two flights, hoping to catch Adél along the way. As I approached the room, I heard her voice and entered. Styrofoam panels dangled from the ceiling, exposing a frayed electrical system; chipped paint was peeling off the brown walls. Accustomed to the disarray, the singers bustled about, hugging and kissing one another affectionately after the long Christmas break.

"There she is!" Adél shouted from the crowded alto section, where at least two dozen young women were passing around potato chips and lipstick. Fortunately, she'd saved me a seat, and I tiptoed over. "Do you want me to introduce you to everyone?"

"Heavens, no!" I dropped down into the metal chair, hoping to blend in with the eighty or so others. I searched behind me in the rows of tenors for the lone Brit, whom

I assumed was the guy with shaggy brown hair and wire-rimmed glasses. When our eyes met, he nodded. I smiled, noting he looked more like Mr. Bean than Jude Law.

Adél handed me the Bach music while Gábor sat in front on a high stool, flipping through the score. He looked older than his image on the CD photo with a thick head of hair that extended down to his wrists. As the chatter around him swelled to a huge *fortissimo,* he tore his glasses from his face and shouted, "*Gyerekek!*" to shush his "children." Suddenly, the room fell very still, and his assistant Flóra approached the grand piano. As she led us through warm-up exercises, I shuddered to see how the expensive Bösendorfer had been doubling as a gigantic ashtray, its once-lustrous mahogany cover now a Rorschach test of cigarette burns.

As we sang through octaves of scales, I caught Gábor winking at a cute alto sitting a few seats away. I turned to Adél with raised brows.

"Isn't he something?" she whispered, starry-eyed.

Before I could respond, Gábor addressed us in English: "Okay, everyone, turn to page ten after the orchestral introduction." He looked my way and nodded; stunned, I returned a shy smile. Then with a long white baton, he raised his arms and inhaled deeply. When he finally exhaled "*És!*" we were off.

The sweet soprano voices rhapsodized on the word "*Magnificat*" before passing the theme to the altos and tenors in a melodious relay race. Soon all voices were fugueing in their own musical form of the word. My body vibrated against the seat; for an amateur group, they were good. *Very* good.

The euphoria was cut short by a deep-throated blooper emanating from a few rows behind me. Gábor threw his hands up, nearly dislodging a ceiling panel. "*Ki az?*" he shouted, demanding to know the culprit. When no one took responsibility, he hurled his keys into the bass section. "*Idióta!*" he cried out to the anonymous transgressor. "*Idióta!*"

My concerns about being reprimanded in a similar way were assuaged after the room erupted in laughter. Gábor was telling what sounded like a joke in Hungarian. William caught my eye and shook his head. As soon as it was break time, he introduced himself.

"Welcome, fellow foreigner," he said in a gorgeous British accent, extending a warm hand. "I'm glad there are two of us now."

"What was that diatribe all about?" I asked, my eyes darting in Gábor's direction, where a throng of gaga female fans threatened to crush him.

"I wouldn't repeat it in polite company," William said, nodding toward two male singers massaging the upper torsos of their female counterparts. "Although I'm not sure how polite this company is."

"You understand Hungarian, William?" He nodded and shared that he was fluent because his long-time girl-friend was a native. He was also an English teacher. As we watched our fellow choristers crack open their boiled egg snacks and exchange greetings in an alien language, I was grateful for his company.

Minutes later, Flóra pounded on the piano, signaling a return to our seats. We repeated the first movement of the *Magnificat* for another two hours as Gábor continually interrupted and made us go over the same measures until we knew them by heart.

At the end of rehearsal, Adél leaned over and gently pushed out her chin. "Well?"

"I survived," I said, wiping imaginary sweat from my brow.

"You did great," she said, hugging me.

"I only hope Gábor will let me join the chorus. He's

quite the perfectionist." I didn't tell her about my fear of becoming a target of thrown objects.

She dismissed my concern with a downturned hand and told me that Flóra would add my name to the roster of members. My eyes followed Adél's to where Gábor was wrapping his arms around the waists of two twentysome-things.

"Hmpf!" Adél muttered. "*That* one?"

"Who?" I asked.

"It's nothing," she said, kissing me goodbye. "See you at Thursday's rehearsal."

I thanked her for inviting me and joined William and the others filing out of the room. When we were out of earshot, he predicted that Gábor would grow on me over time. "He is considered a musical genius, not just a bit of a character."

"And chick magnet," I added.

"Yes, that would be the American way of putting it."

I wondered why so many women, especially the young ones, were fawning over him. Was Gábor really such a charmer? With the language barrier, it was impossible to tell.

William and I made our way through the maze of construction and shabby buildings around Keleti train station and descended to the Metró below. Rows of home-less men and women huddled together on ragged blan-kets, clutching adorable kittens and puppies in the hopes of arousing our sympathies. We dropped a few forints into the empty pet food dishes.

After bidding one another "Cheerio" at Nyugati five stops later, I continued via tram across Margit Bridge to the Buda side with Bach's melodious strains dancing in my head: "*Magnificat anima mea Dominum.*" I wasn't sure that my "Soul magnified the Lord," but I did wonder if my "Rejoicing spirit" would float up to Tulip Street before I reached home.

Grace

The windows of the Európa Café glistened with tantalizing tortes and dainty bonbons; in their reflections, I saw the familiar man sitting in a wheelchair. His jet-black hair was sprinkled with confectioner's sugar-like flakes, which barely hid the pockmarks furrowed on his dark-skinned forehead. He loosened his tattered wool scarf and craned his leathery neck in search of a kind soul who would drop a few forints into his tin cup.

Each time after indulging my sweet tooth at the Európa, I handed him my spare change. He gratefully nodded and stashed the coins under his fake fur seat cover, greeting me with the formal "*Csókolom*," an expression of respect reserved for women only. I learned this the hard way after telling an amused male taxi driver, "I kiss your hand."

On that January afternoon, the man was shivering against his wheelchair, exhaling into his glove-less fists. My eyes teared up as I watched passersby do exactly that: pass by without a glance. While he circled the nearby newspaper kiosk, I snuck into the Európa and ordered him a slice of Eszterházy torta and an Earl Grey tea to go. Gabi was running late, as usual, which gave me time to warm up my speech, as well as the brisk St. Stephen's sidewalks.

The man's eyes twinkled as he downed the tea and gobbled up the dessert.

"Linda *vagyok*," I introduced myself, extending a hand.

He tossed the empty paper cup into a side pocket and returned the handshake. "János *vagyok*."

"That's 'John' in America."

"*Amerikai?*" János's belly laugh confirmed Gabi's assertions that I smiled way too much to be from anywhere other than America. "What you do here?" he asked, his calloused hands motioning toward Margit Island, the direction from which I'd come.

In basic Magyarul, I shared a few details about expat life until I saw Gabi approaching from the antiquarian bookstore, his body language suggesting that of a sunken soufflé. *Uh-oh. This is going to be more difficult than I expected.*

"Hi, Gabi," I said, waving and putting on a cheerful face.

Outside the Európa door, he yanked me by the elbow and away from János. "What are you doing with that beggar?"

"Giving him tea and cake. What does it look like?"

"I was afraid of that." Before I could bid János farewell," Gabi and I were seated at a marble table by the picture window inside the balmy Európa.

"And Happy New Year to you, too," I said. Gabi shed the familiar camel-colored leather coat and threw it against his chair. Like me, he was dressed in funereal black. "What's the matter? The poor guy, who has a name by the way—János—is only trying to survive the bitter cold."

"You know I'm the first to help those down on their luck," Gabi said. "But he's a gypsy." He blew smoke from his Sopianae, which wasn't enough to hide his edginess.

"What do you have against gypsies?"

He glanced through the window at János. "Well, for starters, it was most likely a Roma who stole my wrist-watch at McD's and also stalked you that night near your flat."

"Maybe, but it definitely wasn't János."

Gabi motioned for the waitress and ordered a double espresso and Dobos torta; after eyeing the assortment of pastries and cakes in the glass display, I requested "the usual."

"The Roma are also notoriously lazy, Linda. They live off government money while people like me are working hard to make an honest living."

"It's not his fault he's in a wheelchair," I continued, watching János orbit the flower stall. "He's probably not able to work." The waitress brought our order, and I inhaled a forkful of crushed walnuts and crème fraîche for fortification. Starbucks had nothing on this place.

"Gypsies aren't very popular here," he said, "unless they play *Csárdás*. And I don't see a fiddle." He dug into the chocolate-buttercream sponge cake, dispersing bits of caramel. "Why are you defending him?"

I gazed at János's silhouette, wondering what it was like to sit and beg, day after day, persona non grata, and how he had the stamina to make ends meet, especially in the deep freeze. "But for the grace of God, I could be sitting there," I said, my eyes misting up.

Gabi stopped stirring his coffee and tilted his head toward me. "*You*, Linduska? You're a rich American. That would never happen."

It was high time to set the record straight with Gabi, whose "rich American" remarks were plucking my nerves. "Not so long ago, my father's circumstances were far different than they are now."

"How do you mean?"

"Vincent, my Polish-Lithuanian grandfather on my

dad's side, landed on Ellis Island about one hundred years ago, as did my teenaged grandmother from Russia. They were so poor when they married that they could only afford to live in a fourth-floor walk-up in Harlem. The tub was in the kitchen, and they shared a toilet with two other families."

Gabi inhaled his cigarette deeply, and then blew smoke rings that danced up to the brass railing of the balcony. "You're joking, right?"

"No. My father, his parents, and three siblings were on welfare and received food assistance." Gabi raised his eyebrows the way Gábor raised a baton. "When Dad was ten years old, he was knifed in the foyer of his family's tenement for a loaf of bread. He only survived because a Good Samaritan happened to pass by, saw my father bleeding from his wrist, and rushed him to the emergency room."

Gabi shifted in his red velvet seat cushion. He'd obviously been under the impression that Hungarians had a monopoly on heartache. "Sounds horrific."

"Because of all the crime in his neighborhood, my father was afraid to walk to school, so he commuted by leaping over the rooftops of adjoining buildings and sliding into his family's flat through the fire escape." I stirred the tea leaves in my white porcelain cup. "Eventually, the family moved to the Bronx."

"Amazing." Gabi shook his head. "How did your father manage to change his life?"

"He was drafted into the Korean War in his early twenties, and after serving, qualified for free college tuition under the G.I. Bill, a government program that helped veterans. He graduated from City University and soon started teaching high school, and then college."

"Only in America!" Gabi whooped.

I motioned to the waitress for more hot water; Gabi asked for a coffee refill. As I poured out another pitcher of milk into Earl, he leaned over and examined my hands. "What's that on your finger?"

"An image of Mary."

"I thought so." He scrunched up his nose. "I'm not so sure I want my kids to be raised Catholic."

"You know I'm not Catholic, Gabi. My mother raised us Lutheran. Plus, Mary is revered around the world by people of many faiths," I said in a defensive tone, remembering the scores of people leaving messages for Mary at her home on Nightingale Hill. "I bought this in Chinatown, if you must know." I twirled the ring around my finger. *Now is the perfect opening for the inevitable conversation. Here goes . . .* I cleared my throat multiple times. "Um . . . Gabi . . . while I was in New York . . ."

He stared into his mug and smacked his lips. "I sense what you're going to say and am wondering if I should get up and leave while I'm ahead."

I placed a jittery hand on his. "Please stay and hear me out." I pushed away the gold-rimmed dessert plate. "When I was back home, I made a trip to Ground Zero. It was an important pilgrimage because not only did I want to pay my respects to those who died on September 11th, but I wanted to go back to my roots. My grandparents settled in New York City, and I was born there." I closed my eyes and visualized standing at the edge of the abyss. "When I stared down into what's left of the World Trade Center, I thought about what it meant to be an American—an American now living abroad."

"And?" Gabi motioned with his fork for me to continue. The baby girl at the next table clapped her tiny hands; my mind flashed back to the similar scene by the *Kiskirálylány* statue on Gabi's birthday, where he had first raised the subject of marriage and motherhood.

"I thought a lot about my grandparents, Vincent and Nana, because they really struggled to make ends meet.

They had nothing to give, at least not materially." I dug an elbow into the table and leaned forward. "Here's an example. One month ago, I was celebrating Christmas with my parents in Amherst, and during the gift giving, my father got all quiet and teary-eyed. When I asked him what was wrong, he said he was thinking back to his childhood and how, if he were lucky, he would get three pennies or an orange from Santa. My point is that I feel an obligation to my ancestors. If it hadn't been for their sacrifices, I might have ended up a poor potato picker in Russia, like Nana." I tossed my head in János's direction. "Or worse."

"But what does this have to do with us?"

"My grandparents would want me to continue my Odyssey, Gabi. They didn't have a choice, but I do and with no small thanks to them." I motioned toward the ornate Vígszínház Theater across the street. "Plus, my parents are happy that by staying in Europe for now, I can immerse myself in music again, teach, and discover our ancestral roots." I thought of Angelica's visions, which I'd not shared with Gabi, as he would only pooh-pooh them.

"And you don't want to cut your adventure short is what you're saying."

"Right." According to Dad's two-year timeline, I still had another academic year left.

Gabi chuckled and flashed an expectant look. "You could do your bit to honor your ancestors by sponsoring a new immigrant to America."

"This isn't about your Odyssey, Gabi, but mine. I really appreciate your offer. It forced me to seriously think about the future and prioritize what's important."

"And that doesn't include having one of those?" He pointed to the little girl, now playing with the whipped cream in her mother's éclair.

"I'd like to think so, but I don't want to rush back to

the States. Not now. I want to continue on this journey and see where it leads."

Gabi was communing with his coffee mug and appeared not to hear me. "I really blew it, didn't I?" he kept repeating, shaking his head.

"Oh, God no." I brushed my fingers lightly against his flushed cheek. "You're a great guy, Gabi, and I lo—" *Oh, God, did I almost say that?* "I mean . . . I'm very fond of you. That's why I took your idea to heart and didn't discard it out of hand. You're smart, attractive—"

"But not enough for you?"

"I know you'll make some woman very happy." I sensed what he was thinking: *Yes, but she most likely won't be American.*

He shifted in his seat and threw his empty cigarette pack onto the table. "But I can see myself living in America . . . with you . . . and children around . . ."

"It's a lovely image, but not the ideal one for either of us. We're not in love. My goodness, we haven't even been intimate."

"Well, it wouldn't take much to straighten those few kinks out." He tapped some ashes into the dispenser and winked mischievously.

"This isn't about sex, Gabi." I held the cup to my crimsoned face, and then put it down. "The real reason we haven't become lovers is that we're both searching for our heart's desire, and deep down we realize that the other person isn't The One."

He smacked his lips a few times and gazed at me with a tinge of surrender. "I still think you'd make one helluva mother."

"Thanks. But I have to live with the consequences if that doesn't happen." I gazed wistfully at the young mother bouncing her daughter on her knee. *Oh, God, I hope I've made the right decision.*

Gabi smiled through teary eyes. "Friends, then?"

"Always." I leaned over and kissed him on the cheek; he blushed the way he had so many months ago outside the Fellegi Piano Studio.

Back on St. Stephen's, we hugged quickly and patted one another on the back. "See you soon," Gabi said, slinging his backpack over a shoulder and taking off down the street. I watched until he became a tiny white speck blending in with the snowflakes blanketing the pavement.

Eventually, I turned toward Margit Bridge for the trek home. From inside a meringue-like haze, János zoomed toward me, flashing a bright smile through cracked, bluish lips. I beamed one back—a grateful one from the depths of my heart.

Feel the Rhythm

The following month, I was checking emails at the local Internet café when a message from Eve popped up on the screen. As I opened it, my mobile phone rang.

"Where you are right now?" Béla asked.

"At Libri Bookstore in Mammut. Why?"

"Marek will be there in fifteen minutes."

"Huh? Who's Marek?"

"A friend of mine who wants to meet you."

Ignoring him, I scrolled down Eve's message, zooming in on the words "ruby ring." "Oh, my God," I blurted out, "My friend Eve got engaged to her colleague Jim on Valentine's Day!"

"Congratulations," Béla said, forcibly exhaling cigarette exhaust into his phone. "Another friend getting married."

I tuned him out and continued reading. "Listen, Béla, I need to rush home and call her before she goes to work. Your friend will have to wait."

"But Marek is fired up about meeting you. He's the lead singer in a rock band that recently put out a new CD."

"And you're suggesting I strike while the iron is hot?"

I hit "Reply" and tried typing Eve a quick congratulatory response, but multitasking proved impossible.

"Something like that. Tonight is good for Marek because he's free."

"From playing?"

"No, babysitting. He and his wife split up, and he's raising their son on his own."

With Gabi out of the picture, Béla's now my personal matchmaker? While the idea of dating someone with a young child was enticing, I didn't appreciate the sudden urgency or lack of primping time. From the muffled sounds emanating from the other end of the phone, I sensed Ágnes didn't either.

"Listen, my wife is leaking and thinks her water is breaking. Maybe tonight I'm a daddy!" I could hear him grinning. "Meanwhile, Marek will be waiting for you. Have fun!"

Disappointed for having blurted out my whereabouts, I dashed to the ladies' room, dampened my hair, and shook the chestnut strands under the dryer. A few dabs of mauve gloss brightened up my lips and cheekbones. Then I shifted my gray wool skirt back into position and brushed the lint from my black sweater. *Presentable enough.*

Back inside the shop, I was pretending to peruse "Time Out Amsterdam" when someone tapped my shoulder. I turned around and smiled at the attractive fiery-headed guy with smooth freckled skin. A shimmery silver scarf wove around the open collar of his denim shirt. From the CDs bulging out of his navy coat pocket, I knew at once he was Béla's friend.

"You must be Linda," he said, leaning down to kiss me on the cheeks. "You're just as Béla described." He squinted at me sideways with piercing emerald eyes and wove a hand through his abundance of curls. "I'm Marek. Marek Arszenik." *Ladykiller.* Without further ado, he anchored his hand against my hip and directed me toward the *kassza*, where he ordered us two double espressos.

Uh-oh. As I'd learned from pulling all-nighters at Bard, coffee was poison to my somewhat delicate nervous system and triggered an edgy sensation—one I already felt in Marek's presence. While he weeded through his coins to pay the meager tab, I glanced around the café for a place to discreetly dump the drink later, noting a potted fern next to the brown-upholstered love seat. I quickly staked my claim and directed Marek to the cushioned chair opposite. Hoping to drown out my growling stomach, I inquired about his accent, which sounded different from that of my Hungarian friends and students.

"It's because I'm Czech," he explained, adding, "but I'm also part Hungarian and Irish." He told me that he'd left his homeland five years earlier with his mother and Marek Jr. His eyes lit up when he spoke about his son; to my dismay, so did his cigarette. As I started to ask how he knew our mutual friend, he repositioned the ashtray and leaned in closer. "So, Linda, what's your deal?"

I wondered what Béla had told him about me. "Well, obviously you can hear from my voice that I'm American." He nodded. "Been here about a year. Teach ESL, play piano, and—"

"Yes, Béla told me you're a musician." He flicked the ashes from his cigarette and pulled a CD from his jacket pocket. "Then you'll be interested in my latest project," he said, grinning. "Pop tunes in English." He pointed to the bold lettering on the cover.

"*Feel the Rhythm,*" I said, reading the words.

"The title's taken from our lead song." Marek threw his head back with the last dregs of coffee and slowly moved his eyes along the curve of my hips and waist to my chest and suddenly blotchy face. "It's about sex."

"Oh?" With fidgety fingers, I opened and closed the plastic CD case multiple times.

"Maybe you'd like to finish your coffee, and we could

get going?" He smothered his Sopianae and shot me a mischievous glance. "You have a stereo player at home, don't you?"

"Why, yes."

"Great! Then we can listen to *Feel the Rhythm*."

What kind of a date has Béla organized? The only rhythm I longed to hear was the duet between my whistling teakettle and meatballs sizzling in the skillet. "If you don't mind, Marek, I worked through lunch today and need to go home and cook dinner. I'm famished."

His smile dissolved, squishing the delicate freckles around his nose. "We can pick up some takeout along the way. There's that kebab place on Bimbó Street."

Like Attila, I sensed Marek was eager to "do sex with an American" and wasn't going to let me get away so easily. While he was Béla's friend, and handsome to boot, I didn't feel comfortable inviting a near stranger to my flat, a long walk from the nearest public transport. If Marek escorted me home, he wouldn't be leaving that night.

Suddenly, Marek's phone rang, and he began speaking in an unfamiliar language. When he turned toward the *kassza,* I quickly poured out my coffee into the potted fern, but the soil was fake. I reached for a wad of paper napkins to cover up the mess. After Marek abruptly ended the call, he got up and reached for my black wool coat. While draping it around my shoulder, he again wrapped a warm hand around my waist in a seductive manner that reminded me to quickly wish him *"Jó éjszakát"* before doing something I'd later regret.

Outside in the chilly air, I pointed to the hills. "My flat's up there," I told Marek, who took this as an invitation to hold my hand. After walking a few steps in that direction, I stopped, extracted my hand, and slipped it into a green leather glove. "I appreciate your offer to escort me home, but I'm used to climbing the hill alone."

"It's really no problem at all," he said, reaching for my other hand.

I stopped and exhaled a frosty sigh. "What I'm trying to say is that I need to get home—*alone*—eat some dinner and call a girlfriend in the States who just got engaged."

"But aren't we having sex tonight?"

"Excuse me?"

"Aren't we having sex tonight?" he repeated, sounding well-versed in the phrase.

"Whatever gives you *that* idea?"

Marek removed his hand. "Well, we seem to get on like a house on fire."

"And?"

"And I find you attractive."

"As I do you."

"Then what else is there?"

I buttoned up my coat, very quickly. "Sorry, but we just met," I said, glancing at my Swatch, "less than an hour ago. I'm flattered by your comments, but that's too fast for me."

As he put a finger to his chin, it dawned on me that Béla had probably given him an earful about the pitiful state of my love life. Could I blame Marek if he had the impression that I'd jump into the sack with anyone? "Is there anything I can say to convince you?" he continued.

"I don't think so." *Boy, am I going to chew Béla out, twins or not.* "You know, Marek, if you want to feel some rhythm, you might want to slow down the tempo. You Hungarians are way too pushy."

"As I explained, I'm only part Hungarian."

I tilted my head so that my eyes fixated on his crotch. "Yeah, but which part?"

∞

I picked up the pace as I climbed up the hill, stopping occasionally to look behind me. When I got to the spot where Gabi had parked the Volvo the night that he and his family had escorted me to *Figaro*, I phoned Béla. After inquiring about Ágnes's condition and learning about "another false alarm" with the twins, I laid into him.

"An interesting thing happened to me tonight, Daddy-O. Your friend acted as if I wouldn't be able to resist him." Fortunately, Marek's mobile phone had rung again as we'd started climbing the hill, affording me a quick getaway. "Whatever—or whoever—gave him that idea?"

"I just thought you'd appreciate his musical talent and excellent English skills."

"Marek is far more interested in the universal language than in getting to know me."

"But that's exactly what you need right now—someone more on the aggressive side." I heard Béla kill the power on his TV. "I'm concerned about you, Linduska."

"How's that?"

"You've had opportunities with men, not to mention my brother, but you don't seem interested in . . . what do they say in America . . . 'closing the deal?'"

"That's unfair, Béla. Gabi was a different situation."

"But still. There are plenty of guys attracted to you, like that architect student who always drives you to Moscow Square after class."

"If you're referring to Ádám, he's married."

"Whatever. The point is that you never pursue a sexual relationship." He lowered his voice. "Have you ever thought that maybe you're climbing the fence?"

Despite the mangled expression, I knew what he meant. "No, I am *not* a lesbian. Whatever gives you that impression?"

"Gabi said you couldn't stop commenting on the gorgeous doctor you recently visited." He must have been referring to Renáta, whom I'd mentioned only because she looked like an older Cindy Crawford, and I thought Gabi should make an appointment to see for himself.

"What's wrong with admiring someone of the same sex?" By now, I had arrived at my apartment and was pouring myself a double shot of Unicum. "Does that automatically make me gay?" I grabbed the snifter and paced from room to room on the Persian area rugs.

"No, but if you are, I'll stop sending men your way."

"You can stop doing that anyway, if tonight's selection du jour is any indication."

"But you need to go to bed with someone—*anyone*—and get it over with."

"You make it sound as romantic as getting a root canal."

Béla sighed. "Listen, no hard feelings, eh? My brother and I care about you, even if it comes out in a weird way."

"I appreciate that." I took a swig of liqueur. "But please, no more pimping."

"Okay, I promise."

After ending the call with Béla, my attention turned to poor Lester, who had been rubbing up against my legs since I got home. "Are all Hungarian men like you tomcats?" I addressed him, mashing pieces of Pick sausage into his bowl of Whiskas and washing up in the kitchen. As I started making dinner, Gabi texted and asked me to phone ASAP. I thought to ignore his request but was curious and turned off the stovetop.

"Obviously, you've heard the news," I said, referring to Marek.

"Good girl for not caving."

"I'm glad someone agrees. But what's this about your lesbian theory based on an innocent comment I made?"

"Oops, sorry. I was only hoping that was the real reason you turned me down."

Sensing Gabi wanted to talk about something serious, I put on the teakettle and grabbed some salty biscuits. Lester jumped up and positioned himself for a belly scratch on the kitchen chair. "What's so important that it can't wait until tomorrow?"

There was a long pause before Gabi said, "I need to talk to you about a girl I met."

"Oh?" I tried to suppress any lingering pangs of regret. As I poured a cup of tea, he described a twenty-three-year-old Hungarian who was one of his English students. "And?" I held my breath.

"Júlia's nice, pretty enough. Wants a big family. I'd say there's chemistry there."

"Great!" I lied. I pushed Lester off my lap and put down the teacup. In the silence that ensued, I imagined Gabi's smoke rings wafting through the air at Vác along with Mozart's *Requiem*.

"Gabi, you're a wonderful, good-looking guy and should be out there dating," I continued. "I'm sure you'll be very happy with Júlia."

"It's not that we're getting married or anything. We've only gone on a few dates." *A few?* "I'm still trying to decide whether or not to pursue this."

"If she's as lovely as she sounds, you should go for it." I dropped my head into my hands, waiting for his response.

A long pause followed before he asked, "And this . . . wouldn't bother you?"

"No."

"Not at all?"

"Nope." If Gabi was asking my permission to get more involved with Júlia, I had no choice but to give him the green light. I couldn't wait for the call to end and sensed he couldn't either.

"Let's get some sleep, Linda. Thanks for listening. *Szép álmokat.*"

I fell back onto the sofa and squeezed my hands between my knees, lest I give way to temptation and call him back. While I knew I'd made the right decision, I would miss Gabi's late-night calls and flirty text messages. Instead of reaching for the phone, I repeated my mantra to "settle *down*, not settle *for*." Then I eyed the slightly dusty piano beckoning next to Odysseus. Hopefully, the neighbors would indulge my urge to commune with the cosmos at such a late hour.

My left hand glided across the keys with a rolling motion, the right hovered over the ivories; they united for the melody. Since first hearing Prokofiev's "Romance" in college, I'd imagined walking down a long church aisle on the arm of my father as a small ensemble performed selections from the *Lieutenant Kijé Suite*.

I took it slow, lingering on each beautiful note, so as not to dispel the magic before the jazzy middle section. The sultrier section followed, which I imagined played by a saxophonist, before the enchanting melody returned. Swept up by emotion, I realized that there was nothing wrong with my rhythm, or Marek's, or Gabi's. We were only three people motivated by different needs dictated by our own internal tempos. The challenge was not trying to adjust someone else's rhythm to my own, or allowing someone to do the same to me, but finding a lover whose heart beat in sync with mine. Despite my dim prospects and loneliness, the "tall man with glasses" still seemed worth waiting for.

Women's Day

"I'm a daddy! I'm a daddy!" Béla shouted over the phone a few weeks later. "Ágnes had two baby girls, Katarina and Viktoria."

"*Gratulálok!*" I said, extending my best wishes to the new family. "They sound like a couple of blue bloods." I flipped through my day planner. "How soon might I request an audience? I'm free this afternoon and would love to—"

"Gabi's visiting with Júlia later. Why not come another day?" *Ouch.*

As I cleaned up the lunch dishes in my manless abode, I thought back to one year before, when Gabi had taken me to McDonald's on Women's Day. Since then, so much had happened: Béla and Ágnes had gotten pregnant and were now enjoying their bundles of joy; Gabi had found a girlfriend and was making plans to move out of Papa's house. Over the past year, Gabi and Béla had been at the center of my social life, but now that would drastically change.

I was in desperate need of a pep talk from Jenni or Eve, but it was too early to phone the States. Heléna was spending the day at her mother's; Gretchen from Seattle, who had been joining me once a week for dinner or dancing, was traveling solo in Croatia. It had been a while since I'd seen Gyöngyi and Bea, who had finally recovered from her heartache over Kristóf and was speaking again. *What better way to celebrate Women's Day than with those dear young women?* I tossed on a denim jacket and headed down the street.

Moscow Square was teeming with flower vendors vying for customers like me, on the lookout for the freshest, most fragrant blooms. Hunchbacked *babushkas* pleaded with us to buy purple lilacs and forsythias shorn from their gardens. The sweet smell of lilies of the valley overpowered the exhaust fumes rising from the street traffic, reminding me of the perfume Nana had used on special occasions. I eventually settled on a bouquet of daffodils and yellow roses for Bea and pink lilies and carnations for Gyöngyi. Overwhelmed by images of amorous couples necking on the square and new mothers juggling babies and flower baskets, I left and ascended Lövőház Street.

My friends were sitting outside near the small shed where they spent their weekdays working. Bea was the first to see me and chucked her magazine aside before maneuvering as quickly as possible to the gate. Gyöngyi followed.

"*Boldog nőnapot!*" they said, acknowledging the holiday.

"The same to you!" I kissed their cheeks and handed them their bouquets. They inhaled the luscious aromas and invited me to a terraced area, where we sunbathed on what was an exceptionally warm March afternoon. In the distance, Lajos, artiste extraordinaire, cruised by, chasing a female resident in a wheelchair. Yes, spring was in the air.

"Gyöngyi has big news," Bea said, pointing to her friend's right hand.

Gyöngyi glanced over the premises and whispered, "I have a boyfriend. His name is Artúr." She ducked down into her chair. "It's still a secret. We haven't told no one, only Bea."

"He works with us and lives on floor below," her friend added. "Very handsome."

"Look, he gave me this ring." I reached over and took Gyöngyi's translucent white hand and examined the tiny turquoise stone surrounded by specks of pearls.

"I can see it was made just for you, *Pearl*." She smiled shyly. "You have no idea how delighted I am, Gyöngyi. Your news just made my day."

I wondered how Bea felt in light of Gyöngyi's newfound romance, given her unrequited love for Kristóf. But she was beaming; her enthusiasm for the happiness of others, despite her loneliness and limitations, knew no bounds. *A most amazing woman.*

After an hour of catching up with my friends, I continued down the street with a spring in my step and a silly smile sprawled across my face. Unsure of my ultimate destination, I strolled down St. Stephen's and window-shopped my way past the lingerie shops to the Európa Café.

Like Moscow Square, the boulevard was covered with rows of florists plying their loveliest buds and blooms. I was drawn to a colorful arrangement of tulips and thought to treat myself when a tourist tapped me on the shoulder.

"Are you Linda?" a middle-aged man asked in a distinct Scottish accent. I nodded. "Someone's calling you." He pointed down the street, where János was lingering at one of the flower kiosks. I thanked the man and turned toward János, who approached me in his wheelchair at a fast clip while others on the sidewalk looked on with concern.

"Linda! Linda!" he shouted, his hands struggling against the wheels as he rushed toward me.

"*Szia,* János," I searched my pockets for loose change but found only a fifty-forint coin. "*Bocsánat,*" I apologized, handing him half the usual amount.

"*Nem, nem, nem!*" he said, shaking his head. He politely pushed my hand away and motioned me to stand still; I obeyed. From the rucksack attached to his wheelchair, János pulled out a single-stem pink hyacinth. "Happy Woman Day!" he said, beaming. Behind him, the female employee at the flower kiosk waved and blew me a kiss.

The overwhelming fragrance of the tiny blossoms and János's thoughtfulness sent blood gushing to my cheeks. As I leaned over to embrace him, my tears trickled onto his T-shirt. At a loss for words to adequately express my appreciation, I could only utter, "*Köszönöm.*"

János tightened his lips and stared at me in a soulful manner before turning away and disappearing into the lush greenery. Somehow, I stumbled back to Tulip Street, minus the tulips but with one brilliant hyacinth.

As soon as I got home, I placed my treasure in a small ceramic vase on the desk. Then I opened the journal I'd been keeping and penned:

Dear Diary,

Today is Women's Day. I started off the day feeling sorry for myself, but someone remembered me and bought me a flower. Not anyone I expected, but a Roma beggar. This is a reminder that when you feel stuck or out of luck, life springs a wonderful surprise your way.

A few days later, I pressed the hyacinth into my diary and wrote: To commemorate March 8th, 2002. Before turning the page, I added: His name is János, and I will never forget him.

Ádám's Fib

After wrapping up the spring semester weeks later with the teenage tour guides at St. Lászlós's, I waltzed into Right Angles for my last lesson with the architects. The conference room appeared to have been taken over by baskets of flowers and platters of cheese and crackers. Two bottles of Tokaji stood, like sentinels, at my usual spot at the head of the table. Matching mugs and a small umbrella bearing the company logo made for a centerpiece.

"What's going on?" I asked Ádám, who made a grand entrance in a black suit with starched white shirt and a silver tie. "Wow!" I blurted out, taking in an eyeful of the dark-haired Hungarian hottie. "You're certainly dressed for a special occasion."

"He looks like he's going to a funeral," Csaba said.

"Well, are you?" I turned toward Ádám and pouted.

"A funeral of sorts," Ádám said, sitting down. "Because today's your last day." *Swoon.*

Earlier in the week, Ilona had notified all Bell teachers that the school, which had been having financial problems, would be permanently closing. Not only would I not be returning to Right Angles, but I'd soon have to line up another teaching job for the fall.

"Here are a few gifts, so you won't forget us," Ádám said.

As if I'd have any difficulty remembering you! For the last six months I'd practically drooled every time he opened his mouth. Unlike most Hungarian men I'd met, he was sensitive, articulate, and sweet. But like most Magyar men over thirty, Ádám was married.

Over wine and cheese, I relaxed with my three students as we discussed summer plans. My solo trip to Amsterdam was rescheduled for fall to avoid high tourist season; instead, I'd explore Hungarian cites I'd not yet visited, such as Eger and Pécs. Csaba reminded me that his family had a cottage near Eger and recommended a few vineyards worth touring. Viktor spoke of sunbathing in Bulgaria with his family; as always, Ádám was mute when discussing anything of a personal nature.

After class, Ádám offered to drive me home, which was unusual. He often gave me a lift to Moscow Square but had never offered to drive me directly to Tulipán utca. Over the past academic year, our interactions had remained strictly professional and cordial. But now, in my wine-induced semi-stupor, I wondered what, if anything, he had up his Ralph Lauren jacket sleeve.

"Here we are," I said as his Saab veered into the parking spot outside my building. "That's my place." I pointed through the lush foliage toward the balcony.

"It looks lovely. Kind of like mine."

I wished he would elaborate, but when he didn't, I reached down for the bag of treats and jiggled the door handle; Ádám put an arm out to stop me. "I know the company gave you a bunch of gifts," he said, "but I wanted to give you something just from me." He handed me a festively wrapped CD with an attached card. "Here's a small token of my appreciation."

I opened the envelope and read: *To Linda, my favorite English teacher ever. Love, Ádám.* The last two words revived my dormant hopes; for months, Ádám had been starring in my sexual fantasies. Although I'd never allowed myself to think of him as anything more, I now sat up and paid rapt attention.

"What's this?" I asked, unwrapping the CD and turning it over.

"You once told us that your father grew up in Harlem and is a big jazz fan," he said. I nodded. "Well, this is one of Hungary's best, singing your American classics."

"*Charlie.*" I read the name of the artist and title on the cover. "Yes, I've heard of him."

Ádám took the CD and asked if he could play one track. I wondered how my neighbors would feel about the impromptu serenade, but it was still early, and I'd had to endure worse from them. He hit play, closed his eyes, and sank back into his seat. "Number eight's my favorite."

Charlie's scratchy baritone voice cut through the piano introduction: "Georgia, Georgia . . ."

I gazed at my former student, who looked like a sleeping angel with his fair skin and feathery eyelashes. *The whole night through . . .*

As he continued to sing along, his fingers lightly tapped the steering wheel, and a ray of light from the streetlamp shone down on his wedding band.

As Charlie crooned his last, I thanked Ádám for the ride and gifts, adding, "It's been a long day and—"

"Well, what do you think of him?" Ádám said, ejecting the CD.

"He's got a distinct style, a kind of edgy Ray Charles."

Ádám went on to say that he and his friend Dénes were going to hear Charlie the next week at Old Man's Music

Pub and invited me to join them. I must have visibly jolted because he quickly added that Dénes was a divorced college friend who had recently returned from traveling three months in New Zealand. If Ádám was setting the scene for a romantic encounter between Dénes and me, he didn't have to go to so much trouble. "What about next Tuesday night?" he said. "Maybe you have a girlfriend, and we can make it a foursome."

I'd gotten in the habit of spending that night with Gretchen. Perhaps she'd agree to a change of venues, I explained.

"What's she like, this Gretchen?" I described a lively, smart, thirtyish American of part-Hungarian descent with exotic dark looks. "Perfect. Talk it over with her, and we'll take it from there."

Ádám got out of the car and swung over to the passenger side. After asking for my phone number and a quick exchange of chaste kisses, he promised to call on Monday.

"Whatever!" I waved from the gate. As soon as he pulled out of the parking spot, I immediately dialed Heléna.

∞

"He's choosing you, the Ádám," she said the next day over lunch at my favorite pancake place, Nagyi Palacsintázója, which overlooked the Danube from the Buda side.

I scoffed at the suggestion. "That sounds pretty sexist, as if I have no say in the matter."

"My dear, here in Hungary, the man always choose the woman." Heléna dug into her *sós rakott*, or "salty stack," with much enthusiasm. I opted to satisfy my sweet tooth.

"But he's married, Heléna. He wears a wedding band. If there were any indication that Ádám was having marital problems or even separated, it would be different. But there's no way to know because he never mentions his wife. Maybe I should ask."

"*Whoa!*" Heléna dropped her eating utensils and wagged a middle finger at me. "Don't *ever* do, Linduska! In Hungary, you don't ask married man about wife. It's forbidden."

"But it's okay to sleep with him?"

Heléna rolled her eyes. "What is big deal Ádám is married? My best lovers, like the István, had wife."

And look what happened, I almost blurted out. Instead, I lathered Nutella on my pancakes. "This isn't really about Ádám, but his way of tricking me into meeting his friend."

"My dear, Ádám using Dénes as bait."

"What do you mean?"

"Ádám wants you but is afraid to ask directly, so he confuses you about his true feelings."

"That's not very nice."

"No, but I'm familiar this type." She waved her fork at me. "You shall see."

After Heléna left for work, I gravitated toward St. Anne's Church across nearby Batthyány Square. Flocks of pigeons darted atop the twin spires that rose from the Baroque façade, a shiny Eye of God symbol appearing to burst between them. I opened the massive door in search of a quiet place for reflection, but the sanctuary was closed. Before leaving, I dipped a finger into the scalloped dish of holy water and crossed myself. Turning toward the exit, I was surprised by a statue behind the door. *Mother Mary!*

I reached up and touched her feet, which were surrounded by lilacs and roses on the wooden pedestal. Aside from the wreath of gold stars hovering above her head, she looked much like she had that night in Somerville, clad in a blue mantle over white undergarments, which tied at the waist. *How I long to run into your comforting open arms!* I hung my head and thought of the impending date with Ádám. *Please, Mary, watch over me and stop me from doing something I'll truly regret. I feel weak around Ádám and don't know if I can resist temptation.*

After praying in silence, I grabbed my workout bag and headed to Dagály, where I hoped the endorphin rush I got from swimming would cool my misguided desires.

∽

Gretchen was dressed as a '40s pinup in a ruby-red dress with matching open-toed pumps. Her glossy black hair was tied back with glittery bows. "You look ravishing," I remarked as we waited for Ádám and Dénes outside Old Man's Music Pub.

"And you're looking more like a native," she said, noting my ultra-tight black pants and maroon Lycra shirt. I glanced at the local females packing Akácfa Street and agreed.

Suddenly, we heard someone singing a few bars of "Georgia" and turned to find Ádám sauntering toward us in a brown leather jacket and matching cowboy boots. "American style," he said, looking down at his footgear. My mouth dropped open, which he took as an opportunity to draw closer and kiss me, Hungarian style. He was more restrained when introduced to Gretchen.

"Where is Dénes?" she said.

Ádám glanced at his watch. "Don't worry, he's coming." He looked over his shoulder. "Before you meet him, there's something you should know."

"You mean, the divorce?" I said.

"No, not that." Ádám's voice trailed off as he saw his friend approaching. When he waved to Dénes, Gretchen and I turned around. Hovering over us was the tallest, lankiest creature I'd ever seen. I noted, with relief, the absence of eyeglasses.

"Hi Dénes, I'm Linda." I extended a hand, wondering if I'd need to climb a ladder for him to hear me.

"Nice to meet you," he replied.

"And this is my friend Gretchen."

"A pleasure," she said, squinting upward, as if she needed binoculars.

"*Én is,*" Dénes concurred.

The bouncer pointed to the bar's subterranean entrance, which was decoupaged with old Beatles and Rolling Stones album covers. We sat at our reserved table, an old converted stove near the stage. A rusted trumpet and a stringless mandolin hovered above; large display windows full of rock 'n' roll memorabilia from the '70s and '80s lined the walls.

Ádám rushed to find the waitress, who returned with four generous Mojitos. Then he raised his glass and proposed a toast: "To better Hungarian-American relationships."

"I think you mean relations," I corrected my former student.

"No, I meant what I said." *Maybe I'm a better English teacher than I thought.*

Gretchen tapped her glass with a spoon. "And Happy Birthday, Linda!" I flashed her a shush-up look, but it was too late.

"I didn't know it was your birthday," Ádám said, putting down his menu. "Why didn't you tell me?"

"It's not until next week."

"Aha." Ádám tilted his head, as if calculating my years in bodily measurements.

Sensing my unease, Gretchen quickly opened her menu. "Goulash for me!"

Ádám ordered the same for everyone, including another round of the rum, lemon, and mint concoctions. As he caressed the neck of the glass with his fingers, I noticed he wasn't wearing his wedding band. *Has my wish come true?*

While Charlie's ensemble warmed up, Gretchen and Dénes huddled into what looked like a lively discussion. Ádám downed his drink and took my hand, leading me through a haze of smoke toward the matchbox-sized dance floor. "I asked Charlie to play our song," he said, wrapping his arms around my torso from behind in a spooning position. I glanced over at the table; fortunately, our friends were facing the other direction.

As "Georgia" filled the room, my former pupil held me tightly in his arms, moving a warm hand up and down the back of my slinky top. His other played with a few strands of my chestnut hair. As Charlie cooed about Georgia on his mind, it was clear that Ádám had something else on his. His sensuous lips nibbled their way across my face, and he massaged the back of my neck in the gentle manner I'd often fantasized about, lingering on each vertebra.

"You feel tense," he said as the pianist modulated into his solo. "What's the matter, Linduska?" he cooed into my ear.

I glanced at a photo of James Brown, who conjured up all sorts of naughty thoughts. "It's just that . . ."

Ádám pulled away slightly, his breath smelling sweetly of mint. "Am I bothering you?"

"No, on the contrary, I'm enjoying your touch way too much." I fell into his arms with a sigh.

"Then what is it?" He caressed my cheek.

"It's . . ." *Oh, help me, Mary!*

"Do you find me attractive?"

"Yes, very."

"Then I don't understand."

When the music stopped, I pulled him into a side room. "I can't do this, Ádám. It's not right."

"Do what?"

"This!" I raised our two clasped hands and pointed to our image in the faded wall mirror. "Unless I'm mistaken, you're still married." I paused, waiting for him to refute that truth or explain what was going on with his wife.

His eyes lingered on a young couple kissing at a nearby table made from a former Singer sewing machine. "Is that what's bothering you?"

"Yes. If you're married, that's a pretty big obstacle for me to overcome."

"Hmm." He wiped his dark brow and stared vacantly at the dance floor.

"Ádám." I turned his head toward mine. "You *are* married, aren't you?"

"*Igen.*" He looked at me with sad eyes but offered no further explanation. Then he pulled me toward him and drew circles on my cheek. "Is it that you have a boyfriend?"

"No. That's not the point anyway."

"Then what is?"

Be strong, Linda! You need to settle down, not settle for! I pushed his hand away from my face and held it firmly. "I like you a lot, Ádám. If you were available, I would easily fall for you. But I'm looking for a permanent relationship with a free man."

"And until that happens?" He flashed that provocative smile that had sent shivers up my spine during many a class.

"I'm not interested in having a casual affair."

"I take you seriously, though. You're the only other woman I'm interested in."

"That's still one too many."

In the distance, Gretchen was doodling on her placemat and craning her head in all directions. Eager to drop the dead-end discussion, I suggested we get back to our friends and call it a night.

Ádám insisted on paying the tab as a birthday treat and drove us home, stopping first at Dénes's posh Gellérthegy address, and then dropping off Gretchen. At two in the morning, he and I once again found ourselves parked outside my building. He turned off the ignition and lights.

"Does this mean I won't see you again?" he said, pushing back into his seat.

"You have to understand that it's frustrating for me to be around you, wanting to be close but not being able to."

"That's your decision." He raised my hand to his lips, kissed it tenderly, and then helped me out of the car. As we approached the gate holding hands, I wondered what kind of woman he was married to and why he had left her that evening to be with me. Against Heléna's advice, I decided to satisfy my curiosity. I glanced at my Swatch, then at Ádám.

"If you don't mind my asking, what does your wife think about your being out so late?"

"She doesn't know."

I twitched. "How's that possible?"

He considered his answer before speaking. "Because she's been in the hospital for the last month."

My mouth dropped open, and I fumbled for my keys. "Is she okay?"

"Hopefully. She's having complications with her first pregnancy."

My heart grew cold; my hands froze. "When is she due?"

"In three months."

Ugh! I felt disgusted for being part of Ádám's charade; although nothing sexual had happened, it very easily could have. "I hope everything works out . . . for *her*." I fidgeted with the gate keyhole and turned to face him. "If she asks about tonight's social plans, what will you tell her?"

"That I was out with Dénes." Good ole Dénes. Ádám's bait and alibi.

I looked away from him, quickly unlocked the gate, and rushed to slip through. Ádám reached out his arm to stop me. "Just one little kiss?" he said, searching my eyes for an ember of interest.

"No way!" I pushed his hand away and entered the front yard, slamming the gate door behind. Lester saw me and scooted under the fence, escaping from the huge black dog suddenly growling on the other side. Thwarted, the canine turned his attention to Ádám and began gnawing at his jeans.

"Can I call you?" he eked out, trying to shake off the dog. I bent down and scooped Lester up into the safety of my arms; he tucked his head into my left shoulder. As I turned from the driveway, I made the "Whatever" sign that I'd taught Ádám and his colleagues.

"Oh, not that dreaded American word!" he begged, rattling the gate door. "Anything but that!"

As I crossed the backyard to my apartment, I smiled brightly and waved goodbye, relieved to have one less complication to consider during my upcoming solo trip to Amsterdam.

Part Five

The Brit Who Liked Me

Truth is a great flirt.

Franz Liszt

Dear Diary, Part One

Amsterdam
October 17th

Dear Diary,

Anne Frank once wrote: "Paper has more patience than people." I'm now going to put that adage to the test by not writing or calling anyone while I'm here in Amsterdam (at least for as long as possible). Let's see how I manage with only you to confide in.

Today, my first day in Holland, I visited Anne's former hideaway, now a museum on Prinsengracht. She would have been touched by the very long queue of tourists (half a million a year!) waiting to see the place where she had penned her diaries, as she thought "no one would be interested in the musings of a thirteen-year-old girl." She also would have been overjoyed to see her beloved chestnut tree still gracing the street, where people now indulge at outdoor cafés on surrounding bridges, boats glide along the canal, and bicyclists zip by in the shadow of the Westerkerk.

Inside the Annex, or Achterhuis, I slipped through the secret bookcase and imagined the Frank family's arrival in July of 1942. It's unbelievable that they were able to survive for over two years in such cramped quarters, even inviting four others to join them. Because they were forbidden from leaving the Annex, let alone peering out the curtains, Anne had created her own way of staying connected with the outside world by clipping photos of Shirley Temple, Greta Garbo, and other movie stars from smuggled magazines, and pasting them on her bedroom walls. Viewing the still-visible pictures so many decades later tugged on my heartstrings.

The kitchen looked as if Anne were about to show up at any moment and make a batch of her "notable biscuits." Very little had changed since August 4, 1944, the day she and the others were arrested there and dispersed to different concentration camps. I tried hard not to think of the fatal outcome for all but Anne's father, Otto, and focused on the countless pages of paper that comprised Anne's diaries. Not only had she filled the original "Kitty," but had continued sharing her innermost thoughts in exercise books and on tracing paper.

After this pilgrimage to the Annex, I returned to my B&B located in a residential part of the city. Nothing fancy, but easy on the pocketbook. At the top of the very steep staircase is a shared kitchen with a computer terminal. Although it was fairly dark, a strong light emanated from the monitor. Sitting at the keyboard was a man I mistook for the manager. I asked him if it was possible to make a cup of tea.

When he turned to face me, his eyes sparkled, and the top of his head lit up like a halo from the electric light. "I'm not sure. I'm only a guest here," he said, rising from his chair to rummage through the cabinets. He must be the tallest person I've ever seen at close range, about the same height as Dénes, but more comfortable with his stature. My cheeks crimsoned when his legs brushed past my waist. He plugged in the hot water heater, and in a distinct British accent, introduced himself as "David." "From the sound of it, I'd say you're from America," he said. "Let me guess—East Coast?"

"You're pretty perceptive." I extended a hand. "I'm Linda, most recently from Boston."

He told me that he had grown up in Oxford, lived in the States for four years while attending graduate school at Georgetown University, and then moved back to a London suburb. After a while, he sat back down at the computer, his long, shaggy black hair constantly falling in front of his horn-rimmed glasses. "What brings you to Holland?" he asked.

I explained that I'd come from Budapest to sightsee for a long weekend while waiting for a teaching job at IH to be confirmed. He, on the other hand, is in serious negotiations for a management consulting job with a local company and hopes to relocate here. In the past week, he's had three interviews and is now waiting for his prospective employer to check his references before making him a firm offer.

"I guess you could say I'm a tourist here, too," he said, "biding my time until the job comes together." He seemed confident, but not cocky, about his chances, and from the thrashing he was giving that poor keyboard, I'd say he's one helluva computer wiz.

During our conversation, David's sirloin-sized hands were constantly busy typing. He apologized for his rudeness, saying that he and a faraway friend were "instant-messaging." (A girlfriend, perhaps?) Then he abruptly logged off, cut the power, and turned toward me. "Budapest . . . hmm," he said. "Never been. What's it like?"

This launched a three-hour conversation in which we talked about our recent travels and family backgrounds.

He was most attentive and at the end of the night asked, "*How* long did you say you're staying here?" Maybe it was the way he gently rubbed his chin when I reminded him of my three-night reservation that led me to believe he was a little disappointed that only two nights remained.

Whether or not I see David again, it was the most stimulating talk I've had with an available man in ages. At least I think he's single—he doesn't wear a wedding ring, although I know some husbands play hide-and-seek with theirs, like the naughty Ádám.

Around midnight, we walked to our respective rooms (his down the hall). He wished me "Cheerio" and said we'd meet again, as he's staying a few more days at the hotel. *Swoon.* I'd already decided to cancel my plans to attend the Beethoven recital at the Concertgebouw tomorrow night. Instead, I'll loiter in the kitchen to increase my chances of that happening.

I sank into my bed and after daydreaming for a time, picked up these blank pages. A very good "Cheerio" night indeed!

Yours,

Linda

∞

October 18th

Dear Diary,

Well, my loitering paid off in a big way! After a long day exploring this beautiful city (despite the incessant rain), I returned to the B&B around seven in the hope of seeing David. When there was no sign of him, I hung around the kitchen and wrote emails for the next few hours.

Shortly after eleven, a distinct shuffle echoed

through the staircase. "I'm glad you're still up," David said, struggling to catch his breath. He went to unload his umbrella and briefcase, promising to return for "a wee chat."

I logged out of my account and went to steep yet another cup of tea. When he came back, he inquired about my day and in the middle of my response, chimed in, "You still haven't seen the Van Gogh Museum, and you're leaving for Budapest on Sunday? That only gives you tomorrow to discover more of Amsterdam."

I scrunched up my face. "Yes, three days aren't enough to squeeze in everything."

He walked over to the ever-ready coffee pot and helped himself. "Since I'm free tomorrow," he said, "why not go sightseeing together?"

Ja! After discussing the many possible tourist destinations, David promised to put together an itinerary, which we'll review tomorrow after breakfast. I'm so full of anticipation—I just got here and already have a date! (At least, I think it's a date. Then again, I could be chaperoned by his whole family à la Gabi.)

Yours,

Linda

∞

October 20th

Dear Diary,

Yesterday was a banner day! You'll notice I'm writing this on Sunday, when I was originally supposed to fly back to Budapest, but I'm staying on another week. *Yippee!*

Early yesterday morning, David knocked on my door. Fortunately, I was freshly showered and ready for action in my "uniform" (olive pants and black wool sweater). He unfolded a city map and suggested a walking route that took in most of the cultural sites I was eager to see.

Soon we were standing beneath *Blossoming Almond Tree* at the Van Gogh Museum. Ever since Mom and Dad took me to the Museum of Modern Art in New York as a child, Vincent has been my favorite painter. David is also "keen on" Van Gogh. (He uses that expression a lot. I could listen to his accent for days, months, years. I could drown in it . . .)

After two hours gazing at three floors of sunflowers, self-portraits, and wheat fields, David suggested we start our tour in the medieval section of Oude Zijde. The area was quite boisterous with a mix of policemen, Rastafarians smoking dope, and young Russian men hurling empty beer cans, which seemed odd given our proximity to the sacred fourteenth-century Oude Kerk. Curious, we followed them down a street lined with red neon lights.

"Oops, must have made a wrong turn," David said, burying his face in the map to hide his apple red cheeks. My eyes were peeled to the spectacle of mostly middle-aged female foreigners poured into skimpy leather dominatrix outfits. One stood in a doorway punching messages into a Big Mac mobile phone as she fondled her breast. Another was grinding into a cushy sofa while wetting her lipstick-stained mouth with an elongated tongue in suggestive, circular motions.

David tried hard not to stare and took my arm, but it wasn't so easy to maneuver out of the Red-Light labyrinth. When he asked directions from a young Asian transvestite wearing a "Pizza Slut" T-shirt, I tried to suppress a giggle but couldn't hold back at the windows full of penis-shaped beer openers and silver dildos poking out of bongs.

"Let's get out of this dodgy place," David said,

whisking me inside an antique bookstore near the Royal Palace, where I naturally gravitated to the comprehensive Dickens collection. Seeing me flip through a few chapters of *Great Expectations*, David's thin eyebrows jerked upward. "Oh no, not Pip!" he exclaimed, as if he'd caught me shoplifting.

"Why yes, I've been a big Dickens fan since reading *A Christmas Carol* in sixth grade. I'm always on the lookout for an affordable first edition."

"You might want to save your money," he said, patting my hand.

"But he's one of England's greatest treasures," I insisted.

David feigned a gasp. "In my humble opinion, too many of my fellow Brits think so." He made a beeline for the sci-fi shelves and began singing the praises of Ray Bradbury, his favorite writer. "There's something to be said about being too British." Well, couples can't always agree on everything. (Did I say *couples*?)

After we'd both bought a few paperbacks and returned to the cobblestones, David began sniffing in various directions. I thought he had a runny nose, but soon the unmistakable bittersweet smell of reefer was also tickling my nostrils, an unpleasant sensation I recalled from dorm life in college. However, David was "keen on" experiencing a coffee shop offering various kinds of marijuana, so he picked Extase on Oude Hoogstraat and inside we went.

The menu was quite extensive ("space cakes," "white widow," "lemon haze"), but after a short discussion, we opted for a different sort of pot (tea, of course!). We sat at the metal tables in the low green light, big grins on our faces, inhaling as much as our lungs would allow. I'm sure the twentysomethings in their purplish dreadlocks, skeleton tattoos, and nose piercings got a kick out of the two fuddy-duddies sitting among them. Eventually,

I started coughing from all the secondhand smoke, and David suggested we leave. Well, at least I can say I "inhaled" in Amsterdam!

All that smoke must have roused David's lung passages, because as soon as we got outside, he lit up yet another Marlboro. (He apologized for this nicotine habit of twenty years, which probably explains the yellow-stained teeth that mar his otherwise fetching face.) At the end of the Leidseplein, I recognized the stylish Art Deco Café Americain from its orange and white striped canopies. David saw the gaga expression on my face and at once extinguished his cigarette, took my arm, and swept me up the red-carpeted steps into the swanky, cavernous dining room.

We sank into our green leather chairs under stunning brass lamp fixtures, which looked like inverted Japanese parasols and hung from teal-colored archways. Near the front window, artsy-looking guests sat at a long wooden table and perused stacks of international newspapers and magazines. David glanced at the menu, then slapped it down. "Fancy a pea soup?" he said with much enthusiasm. I bit my tongue to keep from sticking it out. Yes, it's a Dutch specialty, but after all that walking, I was craving a decadent, multiplex club sandwich. (Not to mention my concern about the flatulence factor.)

During lunch, an older gent in a black silk smoking jacket strode to the ebony grand and began serenading us with a medley from *Porgy and Bess*. I remembered how Dad used to croon "Bess, You is My Woman Now" to Mom and twirl her around the room during their Expat New Yorker meetings. As I imagined him and I swaying to Gershwin during our father-daughter dance at my wedding celebration one day, David burst out, "Pea soup, what bliss!" Although I didn't share his sentiments, I must admit that the *erwtensoep* was the best I've ever tasted.

In between hearty spoonfuls, David studied the map,

wondering aloud how many more tourist sites we could cram in. "You've been to the Rijksmuseum, haven't you?" he asked. I shook my head side to side while swallowing a platoon of peas. He looked at his wristwatch, but alas, the museum was closed. "You absolutely must see *The Night Watch* by Rembrandt."

David's comment, dear Diary, afforded me the perfect opportunity to get to the bottom of his intentions. I took a long sip of wine for fortification and said, "Looks like I'm running out of time this weekend and will have to come back to Amsterdam."

He immediately took the bait. "Then why not extend your stay now? While you're waiting for the teaching job at IH to be confirmed, you can stay in Amsterdam, like I'm doing."

I hadn't been thinking along those lines, but the idea appealed to me, despite the cost of changing the return flight and missing more BACS rehearsals. (There's a full lineup of upcoming concerts, including Bach's *Magnificat*, and I won't be able to participate if I don't attend. Gábor is a stickler about that.) After weighing the pros and cons, I told David I'd consider remaining in town if our B&B had available rooms.

"If you're concerned about finances, you can stay with me later in the week." He avoided the expression of surprise on my face and motioned to our waitress for the check. "I've had my eye on a place but can't sign the lease until my work situation is finalized, hopefully by the middle of this week."

My head started spinning while calculating the extra expense of staying, my jobless status, the commitment to the chorus, and David's implying we'd be sleeping in close proximity. I'm *very* attracted to him, but we haven't even kissed yet. It's a lot for my rusty brain to go from knowing him only a few days to thinking about living with him in a couple more. Nor have we discussed our romantic expectations, although my sense is that he's unattached and looking for a life partner.

David put my reservations to rest by reassuring me it was a two-bedroom flat. He invited me to check out the layout, as the realtor had given him a key. Out of curiosity, I accepted. Soon he led me there via Vondelpark, where amorous young couples sprawled out on spacious lawns lined with towering willows and oaks, kids kicked soccer balls, and young mothers pushed baby strollers. We exited at the northwest corner of the park and turned into a cozy neighborhood with predominantly low-level brick homes and heaps of bicycles chained to lampposts. I made a note of the nursery school tucked away near a secondhand shop and the charming Madelief Restaurant. All the while, my heart and head were battling over what was best to do—the former wants to stay and get to know David better, but then the latter chimes in like the Westerkerk Bell Tower striking twelve.

I was delighted when David announced that he lived on Frederiksstraat (another omen to this Chopin fan). When we got inside his flat, I immediately understood the whole roommate scenario and relaxed, as there were neighbors all around, windows galore, and a garden. David was quite eager to show me the guest room and said he'd already picked out an IKEA bed. He's been a real gentleman, opening doors, paying the tabs, telling me to "mind the puddles."

"Yes, I'd like to stay on," I said as he showcased the sparkly kitchen appliances, "depending on how soon the job at IH starts."

David slammed the refrigerator door shut. "Oh, joy!" he burst out, seeming a little taken aback by the sudden meltdown of his English reserve. (Despite his claim to the contrary, his Union Jack stripes do show now and then.) We smiled at each other in the low light for what seemed an eternity. If ever there were a moment for two destined lovers to fall into each other's arms, this was it! Instead, he fumbled for the keys, saying he still had a few hours of "number crunching" to do.

When we returned to the B&B, I checked with the manager, and fortunately, there's a room vacancy this week. I also phoned KLM and learned that my ticket is open-ended, so I canceled my original flight today and am staying one more week, maybe longer. *Exciting!*

I'm glad I have you to confide in, as this has all happened so quickly, and I've not had time (nor interest, I might add) to tell my friends. For now, let this be our secret.

Yours,

Linda

∾

October 23rd

Dear Diary,

Unlike Monday and Tuesday's city excursions and forays into secondhand shops (I'm out of clean clothing), I spent most of the day on a guided bicycle tour that wound through miles of windmills to a typical Dutch dairy farm north of Amsterdam. When I returned to the B&B in the early evening, I heard David's keyboard strokes from the staircase.

"Great news!" he said, jumping up when I entered the kitchen. "The job is mine." Before I had a chance to rush over and plant a big, wet congratulatory kiss on his lips (maybe a rain check this weekend?), he added, "I've arranged for us to move into the new flat on Saturday."

I put down the bag of Edam cheese samplers and

loosened my neck scarf. "This calls for a celebration. How about my treat this evening?"

"Great." David reached down to turn off the computer, turned his head sideways, and raised an eyebrow. "Fancy a pizza?"

We wound up at a cozy neighborhood place with candlelit tables covered with red and white checkered cloths that reminded me of Boston's North End. David escorted me to a cozy corner table, where we ordered a bottle of Chianti and two goat cheese-pesto pizzas. As usual, he asked all about my day, but tonight I wanted to hear how his new job offer came together. He wasn't too specific but seemed relieved about the prospect of receiving a regular paycheck. (He's been out of work for three months.)

He soon changed the subject to his creative ideas for updating and redesigning the interior of his new flat. Tomorrow the furniture is being delivered; boxes from the UK arrive on Friday, a workstation on Saturday. "That leaves only linens, towels, and dishware." He jotted down a list on a paper napkin and asked if I'd join him for a "big shop" at IKEA. I told him I'd be delighted, as he seems eager to have my input on color schemes and other domestic issues. The kitchen's not exactly my forte, but if I'm going to be spending a lot of time on Frederiksstraat, it makes sense to be involved in the initial decision-making process. As we were speaking, my mind drifted over to David's new home, where I imagined playing hostess at all the festive dinner parties and patio barbecues we'd organize. I'd invite Heléna and Gretchen for long weekends; maybe even Jenni would fly over, since she had been so taken with Amsterdam a few years earlier.

We called it an early night, as David said he had to stay up a bit to "catch up on paperwork," while I'm pooped from the twenty-mile bike ride today. I still haven't confided in anyone, only you, dear Diary. My Hungarian friends are probably wondering where Linduska is, but as long as there's no start date at IH (I phoned them today and everything's status quo), and I have a free place to stay, why rush back? I'd rather stay here and see where this is all leading. My sense is to the altar :-)

Yours,

Linda

∞

October 24th

Dear Diary,

What a difference a day makes! My head's whirling like a windmill. I have a big decision to make.

This morning I was checking my emails when I received a lengthy one from Adél. She's wondering where I am, why I missed both BACS rehearsals this week, and when I plan to show up. *Uh-oh.* I don't want to burn my bridges with her, as she had to pull some strings (and I don't mean violins) to get me into the chorus without an audition.

Truthfully, I've been so smitten with David that I've neglected what's going on back in Budapest. My musical immersion there is very important to me, but on the other hand, it's not every day I meet a suitable, attractive man who's not hiding a pregnant wife or living with his Papa. Adél's message forces me to put my priorities into perspective.

The most startling news was the bit about the chorus traveling to Israel in December. There had been rumors about BACS participating in the Liturgical Festival there, but I had tuned them out because of all the recent

235

violence in the Middle East. Adél told me that if I'm interested (all expenses paid for three weeks by the Israeli government), auditions are being held on Tuesday, only five days away. *Help!*

I have to confess that it's been my lifelong hope to visit the Holy Land. When I was living in America, that prospect seemed unrealistic because of the long distance and expense involved. But to sing Rossini, Mozart, and Fauré amid the backdrop of such ancient history is a dream come true. How can I let this opportunity pass me by?

The other side of the shekel is that I keep hearing Angelica's words echoing in my ears: "Tall man with glasses." David is the tallest, most visually challenged man I've ever met. I don't want to disregard Angelica's insights and leave Amsterdam prematurely, especially when so much of what she predicted has already come true.

Anne Frank often wrote of the "eternal struggle" between the heart and mind. Yes, there is a time and place for both, but how to know when that is? I'm tempted to ask my friends for their advice, but the conservative New Englanders would advise me to return to Hungary at once, whereas the lusty Magyars would command me to stay. Then I'm back to square one. I'm so torn right now that all I can do is to pray for guidance.

It's getting late, so I'll sign off. David is at his flat, organizing the furniture, my bed included. I'll broach the subject of Israel with him tomorrow and try to catch him after breakfast when my head's clearer. Wish me luck!

Yours,

Linda

∞

October 25th

Dear Diary,

A few hours after my last entry, I awoke to muffled noises down the hall. I threw on my robe and quietly opened the door to see a sliver of light coming from David's room. It sounded as if he was on the phone, whispering. I wondered with whom he would be conversing at four in the morning, but then quickly returned to peaceful slumbers. This disturbance caused me to oversleep, and I missed him at breakfast. I left a note on his door, asking him to find me as soon as he returned from work (he didn't give me his number there) and spent most of the day emailing Adél back and forth, googling information on Jerusalem, and listening for David's inimitable gait.

That evening, he breezed into the kitchen, looking so happy to see me that I wasn't quite sure how to bring up the subject. The way he was perfectly poured into his charcoal gray suit made me feel like backpedaling. *Almost.* But I had already decided that I'd never forgive myself if I didn't at least try out for the Israeli tour.

Before he could speak, I said, "David, I received some interesting news yesterday and was hoping to share it with you last night, but you were at Frederiksstraat."

He glanced down at my note, then swiftly at me. "Everything all right?"

"Yes, although I have to return to Hungary sooner than expected."

"The job came through?"

"Not exactly." I explained about the missed rehearsals and the opportunity to sing in Tel Aviv and Jerusalem. "If I want to be part of the tour—and I do—the auditions are early next week."

David's face twitched in a way I'd not witnessed before; he pulled out a chair. "This *is* a surprise," he said, sinking down. "But, of course, I understand your passion for music and travel." He didn't mention one thing about Israel or question why it was important for me to go there. We've never openly discussed our religious leanings, although he has shared that he was raised Anglican but only attends church services on major holidays. Some of his other comments lead me to believe he's a Doubting Thomas.

I reassured David that my decision was nothing personal; on the contrary, I was looking forward to staying with him on Frederiksstraat.

"I hope you'll at least spend inaugural night there," he said. "The furniture from IKEA has been delivered and needs to be assembled. I could use your help."

"Count me in," I said, winking. "I'll stay one night but need to fly back on Sunday."

After chitchatting a bit, he left to unpack more boxes. We agreed to meet tomorrow after breakfast and go to his place via taxi. I can hardly wait!

Shalom,

Linda

∾

October 27th

Dear Diary,

I'm writing this from the airport. The taxi just dropped me off, and now I have two hours before boarding my KLM flight back to Budapest.

What a memorable night David and I had! When we got to his flat yesterday morning, he began by giving me the grand tour. It's amazing how much he's been able to accomplish while starting a new full-time job. The living room is comprised mostly of bookshelves ("With not a

Dickens among them!" he joked) and a large mahogany table where we ate our meals. The guest room, with its matching teak dressers and nightstand, looks out at the back patio surrounded by elm trees. *Lovely!*

David didn't show me his room; in fact, the door was shut most of the time. I don't know if it was too messy and didn't feel like prying. However, he explained that he's storing his computer system in there for the time being and will move it elsewhere after the workstation is delivered.

After reminding me of my promise to help build the bed, he guided me into "my" room, full of all sorts of carpentry tools he'd borrowed from the realtor. We tried to make sense of the instructions, which were in Swedish, but it wasn't easy, and for a while the project seemed pretty hopeless. I wondered if I would be camping out on the floor or if perhaps this would afford me a good excuse to sleep with David. However, I think we both realized *it* wasn't going to happen—I was leaving the next morning, and we're both looking for more than a one-night stand. Nonetheless, my hormones were raging, especially when he was flat on his back, pounding nails into the oak frames. As I held up the diagram of screws and bolts, it was all I could do to keep from pouncing. I wondered if he was thinking along the same lines, but he continued to focus on building the bed. At one point, he said, "This gives new meaning to the expression, 'You made your bed, now lie in it.'" *And how!*

Finally, after three hours, David declared it was tea-coffee time and proceeded to make me a cup of Earl Grey, exactly how I like it. I have to say, I'm impressed that he's been paying attention. After a while, he took my hand and pulled me out onto the patio. It's small with barely enough room for a grill. We continued holding hands until he felt the urge to light up. (This nasty habit is really the only strike against him, but unlike my Hungarian friends, he never smokes indoors.) It was a bit cold, and David fetched me one of his wool pullovers. A bottle of Merlot, too.

After the vino took effect, I became more relaxed and flirtier. As he pointed up to Orion's Belt, I visualized what a kiss from him would entail. Could he bend down without getting a major crick in his neck? Would I need a stepladder? After David opened a second bottle, I stopped thinking of smooching logistics and started wondering when he was going to sink his lips into mine. But he kept going on about parallel universes and distant galaxies, two subjects he's very passionate about, but which do absolutely nothing for my libido.

Then I remembered how Anne had described her close nights with Peter in the Annex, watching the stars and moon together, her head leaning against his shoulder, their fingertips caressing one another's faces. This went on for quite a while before they finally kissed. I also want to build a strong emotional connection before adding the physical one, which more often than not complicates matters. I knew I was leaving the next morning, and if David and I had made love, it would have been impossible for me to get out of bed and fly back to Budapest. I sensed he didn't want to rush either, so other than long, desirous stares, we didn't gravitate to one another's bedrooms.

I know this story of yet another close call will sound crazy to my Hungarian friends. I can already hear Heléna chiding me for not handing David a package of rubbers and imagine Béla racking up yet more evidence in support of his lesbian theory. But I must stay faithful to my mantra to "settle *down*, not settle *for*." If David is indeed the "tall man with glasses" (and my hunch is that he is), there will be countless opportunities for intimacy.

Nonetheless, it was with a heavy heart that we parted ways at three o'clock. I lay on the brand-new, not-so-comfortable bed, too distracted to sleep. Later when I got up to use the WC, or water closet, I noticed that David's bedroom door was ajar. An invitation, perhaps? He was snoring so loudly I knew I wouldn't get any sleep if I joined him, even if we only cuddled.

After we rushed through breakfast the next morning, David waited with me at the taxi stand. We didn't make any definitive plans to get together, although he expressed an interest in attending the chorus's Bach *Magnificat* concert next month at the Liszt Academy. He gave me a big bear hug, and off I went to Schiphol Airport.

As I wait for my flight, I want to thank you, dear Diary, for being such a trustworthy confidante. Sharing this budding romance with you has given me a chance to know myself better and learn to trust my instincts. I'll write again during my next trip to Amsterdam, which will hopefully be very soon. David says I'm welcome at his place any time, so stay tuned for the next installment, whenever that is.

Your grateful friend,

Linda

Magnificat

Gábor leapt onto the stage of the Liszt Academy's Great Hall to enthusiastic cheers and applause. Adorned in a black tux and white bow tie, his right hand clutched a baton; his left blew kisses to a pretty young blonde in the front row. From behind the Dohnányi Orchestra, I looked up to see if he had charmed the gold-plated leaves off the ceiling and if they'd begun to rustle and float down upon the rapt audience.

"Does he ever stop?" I whispered to Adél, who shimmered in a black sheath with the trademark BACS maroon scarf draped over a bare shoulder.

"I hope not," she said with glazed-over eyes. "What I wouldn't give for some of that attention." I scrunched up my face. "Believe me, there's a queue—a long one." *Now I know I'm back in Budapest.*

As Gábor approached the podium with the four sumptuously attired soloists, Adél discreetly applied more lipstick behind the Bach score. "I'm glad you're here with us, Linda," she continued. "I know it wasn't an easy decision to leave David in Amsterdam."

No, it hadn't been, but there I was, about to sing at the musical institution bearing the Master's name. David had understood that this was one of the biggest pinch-me moments of my life and promised to pull strings at work in order to attend. Although the odds were stacked against his making a last-minute appearance, I still held out hope that he'd somehow finagled the time off and was among the attendees.

My eyes peered out from under the majestic German pipe organ and combed through the rows of concertgoers immediately in front of the Orchestra, but the only familiar faces were Heléna and Gretchen. Above the SRO crowd in back, two pairs of topless Egyptian statues performed Herculean feats by holding up balconies that ran along both sides of the Hall. In the top tier, I watched Gabi and Júlia, on break from a night of home decorating, settle into their seats.

"And to think you'll soon be singing the *Magnificat* in Israel," I heard Adél say.

I turned toward her and crossed my fingers. Even though I hadn't amply prepared for the tour audition, Gábor had seemed sufficiently impressed with my rendition of "Chestnuts Roasting on an Open Fire" to forgo the usual sight-reading test. I'd taken that as a good sign.

"We'll know the results tonight," she continued, fanning herself with a program. "Gábor promised to post them in the dressing room after the performance." I tried not to think about the tour and turned my attention to our Maestro.

Gábor tapped his baton against the music stand and pulled on his cuff links—our cue to open the scores. After nodding to the soloists, he turned toward the chorus with an encouraging smile. As we waited for him to raise his wrists, the entire room inhaled in unison.

The forcefulness of the trumpet entrance had an immediate effect on the six enormous crystal chandeliers, which appeared to sway, illuminating the skylights inscribed with the Hungarian words for Beauty, Rhythm, and Poetry. I reveled in the captivating aura of the Hall and every note that Johann Sebastian had composed. After the last "*In saecula saeculorum*" echoed up to Gabi and Júlia, I turned to the friend who had made this experience possible. "And to think Gábor got through the whole piece without throwing his baton or screaming '*Gyerekek!*' at us, Adél."

"Isn't he something?" she said dreamily.

The audience thought so, "iron clapping" in sync, slowly at first, then with a marked *accelerando*. Our conductor wiped the sweat from his face, loosened his bow tie, and then disappeared from the stage with the soloists. They returned to a standing ovation and a barrage of colorful bouquets. When the applause died down, we filed through the exit, where he congratulated the tenors and basses with slaps on the back; each female received kisses, except for me, who got a limp handshake.

"What was that about?" I asked Adél, a bit concerned that Gábor's reserve might mean I didn't make the tour.

"Don't take it personally, Linduska. You're still a new chorus member."

After briefly chatting with Heléna and Gretchen, who congratulated us backstage, I followed the other singers to the rehearsal room, where an assortment of black stockings, padded bras, and skimpy lace panties flew through the air on one side, white-collared shirts and silver cummerbunds on the other.

Adél was conditioned to such a display, but William rolled his eyes and reached for his sports bag. "A warm-up scene from *Caligula*, perhaps?" he whispered. "I don't feel the need to show everybody my boxers. Let's get out of here."

I glanced around the room. "Agreed. We expat prudes need to stick together."

After changing into casual clothes in private WCs, we returned to the dressing room. The air was thick with anticipation as Gábor hung up the list of those members who'd made the cut for the Israeli tour.

"Good luck, William," I said, knowing how much he had practiced for the audition, even hiring a private music tutor.

"God willing."

From across the room, Adél scoured the roster of names. She abruptly stopped and shook her head sideways; William and I rushed over. "You aren't on the list," she said, shrugging.

"There must be a mistake," I insisted. "Please check again." The three of us pored over it, certain that William's and my foreign surnames had been listed differently. But after a few moments, the reality sank in: he and I weren't going to Israel.

"I'm shocked," Adél said, wrapping her arms around us. "And sorry, too, if I was leading you on. I was so sure you would make the cut." She threw her hands up toward the full-length mirrors. "I don't understand what happened."

"It's okay," I said, fighting the welling up of tears as the other choristers celebrated their good news with group hugs and cheers. I could only imagine how William felt, as he never had any spare money for travel abroad. I patted him on the back while Adél searched for Flóra amid the mob of scantily clad torsos.

Minutes later, she explained that we hadn't been accepted due to "seniority;" like me, William was also one of BACS's newest members. "But let's see what I can do," she promised.

"Linda and I aren't looking for special favors," he told her, nodding toward me.

"No, definitely not," I agreed.

She leaned over my shoulder and whispered, "But maybe I am." With a wink, she disappeared into the throng surrounding Gábor.

"Looks like I'll be going back to England for Christmas after all," William said, without trying to mask his disappointment.

"Oh, Christmas . . ." I'd been so sure of joining the tour that I hadn't allowed myself to think of other holiday options. I dabbed the concert scarf to my mouth and stifled a sob. "Let's get some fresh air, William."

We walked outside to Frank Liszt Square, where the neon lights of KFC beckoned nearby. "Shall we gorge away our sorrows with a big basket of fried chicken parts?" he said.

"No thanks," I said. "I'm in a funk and need to be alone for a while."

"Yeah, that's probably best." William wiped the mist from his glasses and kissed my hand. "Well then, catch you at rehearsal next week."

Against a crush of concertgoers, I made my way back to Tulip Street and despite the late autumn chill, sat on the patio steps and gazed up at Orion's Belt. No matter where I was and what was pulling on my heartstrings, the constancy of that constellation always soothed my anxieties. Weeks earlier, when David and I had stood outside Frederiksstraat entranced by a similar view, I'd imagined the stars showering down and wrapping us in a lover's embrace.

As disappointed as I was that I hadn't been selected to sing in Israel, I was haunted by the way I'd abruptly left Amsterdam for the audition. David had been so eager for me to stay longer, even buying an extra bed that he didn't need. I felt like a fool for leaving the only guy in the whole universe I was interested in. "I hope I haven't blown it," I said aloud, lowering my head toward my bent knees.

The cold breeze eventually swept me inside, where I undressed while watching BBC News. An item about the Middle East caught my attention, and another pang of regret surfaced. I removed the concert scarf and draped it over the armoire door; as I patted out the wrinkles, a ladybug crawled up and down its muslin fabric. Years earlier, I'd read about a lottery winner who had woken up on the morning of an enormous jackpot to find hundreds of ladybugs climbing her bedroom walls. Even though only one was in my room, I considered it an omen—it was November, yet somehow the creature had found its way into my home.

I put a finger under its minuscule legs, and as it tickled me, watched the ladybug flare its wings. Then I understood: *Without a doubt, I am going to Israel.*

Chapter 29

A Kiss From Mary

A few blocks from Kikar Zion Hotel, William pointed to the marketplace and darted far ahead of Zoltán and Zsuzsa—our respective roommates—and me. Since arriving in Jerusalem two weeks earlier, Gábor had strictly forbidden chorus members from using public transport, noting the recent increase in suicide bombs detonated on local buses. Fortunately, he had leased a large van for shuffling singers to and from concerts and rehearsals. During the days, however, my friends and I explored the Mount of Olives, Kidron Valley, and the Arab Quarter by foot.

"William, wait for us!" I shouted, rushing after him on Jaffa Street. A woman with dark exotic features gracefully wove her way through the noisy traffic while balancing piles of pita bread on her covered head. Young *Hasidim* with twisted hair curls, or *payot*, ran in front of their fathers, men in black wearing wide fur-brimmed hats who appeared to have no peripheral vision. As my words faded into the bustle of hundreds of footsteps pounding against the honey-colored stone pavement, I caught up to William and pulled on his raincoat belt. "Hey, stop jerking your head from side to side and drawing attention to yourself. You're putting us all at risk." I motioned to Zoltán and Zsuzsa behind us.

"Apparently, you've not been reading the headlines." *No, intentionally not.* He stopped for a moment and threw his faux Burberry scarf over a shoulder. "And what about you, screaming in that God-awful American accent: "Weelliuum! I mean—*Hellooo!*""

Although he had been getting on my heightened-alert nerves with his nonstop paranoia, I was grateful for William's company these past two weeks. Several chorus members had backed out of the tour at the last moment, allowing us both to participate. His comforting British accent was also a constant reminder to keep the faith regarding David, whom I'd not heard from in over a month.

"Okay, you two," Zoltán said, his timid voice straining above the *muezzin's* call to prayer wafting over the minarets and palm trees. "I thought we agreed not to speak English in crowded places."

"I like," said Zsuzsa, who spoke passable English, but preferred conversing in French. She swung her long auburn braid in coquettish fashion over her delicate frame in Zoltán's direction.

I led my friends across the street to Jaffa Gate, one of eight carved out of two and a half miles of fortress-like granite walls enclosing the Old City. "Listen up," I said, requesting a breather. "We're all on edge from the constant fear of terrorists lurking about, the long rehearsals, and lack of sleep after last night's performance at the Opera House."

"Don't forget the hotel food," William added.

We all stuck our tongues out. Realizing I couldn't stomach another meal featuring canned peas, I turned to a map of the Armenian Quarter. "I say let's go out for some real food today. My treat."

"*Merci,* Linduska," Zsuzsa said, pecking my cheek. The guys stuck their thumbs up.

We passed the Tower of David, which had actually been built by King Herod to fortify his royal palace, and walked briskly toward our destination, where the smell of grilled kebab and garlic mingled with sweet hibiscus in the blustery air. "Here's that tavern we were eyeing yesterday," I said. Its windows were darkened, but the manager came out to reassure us they were open. We descended into the snug subterranean space, which looked much like an Orthodox chapel with ornate hanging lamps and displays of religious icons, paintings, and crucifixes on the stucco walls.

After we ordered four teas and luncheon platters of lamb and hummus, Zsuzsa pushed back into the wooden seat, slipped out of her sandals, and put her feet up. Zoltán, who harbored a not-so-secret crush on her, jumped at the chance to massage them. William turned toward me with a raised brow. "Any emails from Amsterdam today?"

"*Nem,*" my roommate answered for me. From our nightly pillow talk, patched together from Hungarian, English, and French words and phrases, Zsuzsa knew all the David updates, or lack thereof.

"Have you tried getting in touch with him?" Zoltán asked in his high, youthful voice.

"I wrote David immediately after my job came through at IH and again before leaving for Israel." I glanced over at the artificial Christmas tree flashing its silver lights by the cash register. "I can't believe it's the day before Christmas Eve and still no word."

"Oh." Zoltán saw my eyes well up; his did, too. "I'm sure he's so busy with his new job and flat that he's not even thinking about the holidays."

"Or even better—he's sent you a care package full of your favorite British teas, a few Dickens novels, and Marmite, of course," William added, smiling.

"No lose hope, Linduska." Zsuzsa reached over to stroke my shoulder. "I'm sure a good reason."

The waiter arrived with our sizzling plates, which we dug into with rapture. "At least being in Israel with the nonstop singing and touring helps take my mind off him." *Not so easy in this City of David.*

"Maybe you can impress him by writing about our great performance last night at Tel Aviv's Opera House," Zoltán said.

"Wasn't that splendid?" William added, squirting ketchup on his fries, as well as my napkin. "Other than a few bloopers, mostly coming from me, I'd say we were in top form."

I put down the massive kebab skewer. "Yes, once I got over my fears of perishing in a terrorist attack, it was pure magic."

After we debriefed about our performance of Rossini's *Stabat Mater*, William steered the subject back to David. "In defense of my fellow Brit, I say give him the benefit of the doubt." The others nodded. I appreciated their efforts to cheer me up but was relieved when the waiter approached with the bill, which I settled.

"*Köszönöm*," Zsuzsa and Zoltán said in unison.

"Let's hope and pray this wasn't our Last Supper," William added.

"Speaking of which, let's head to the Coenaculum, site of the real thing." I referred to the map and pointed out the route down the Armenian Quarter's Patriarchate Road toward Zion Gate.

Back on the cobblestones, the soft breeze intensified the musty aroma floating in gentle puffs, which we followed to St. James Cathedral. Inside the mysterious, cross-shaped twelfth-century church, priests wearing pointed black caps dispensed incense under a dome emblazoned with the Star of David. Oil lamps with decorated ostrich eggs dangled from the ceiling; colorful tiles lined the walls. Tourists congregated near the chapel where the head of James, Armenia's holiest Saint, was buried. Another chapel contained the body of Jesus's brother, also named James.

Leaving the Old City, we headed toward Mt. Zion, arriving at the dining hall thought to be the place where Jesus and his Disciples had gathered for their last Passover feast together. We vanished through the stone arches, each seeking our own private niche for prayer and reflection. A short distance away, we paid our respects to Oskar Schindler in the Catholic cemetery, and in keeping with Jewish tradition, placed rocks atop his tombstone. Etched on his grave were the words: *The Unforgettable Lifesaver of 1200 Persecuted Jews.* The tranquility was disrupted by the blaring of ambulance sirens, a never-ending, nerve-racking part of Jerusalem's soundtrack. "Shouldn't we be getting back?" William said with fear creeping back into his voice.

"We've still got time," I said, checking my watch. "Rehearsal isn't until six."

"Look!" Zsuzsa pointed to a flock of sparrows hovering over an enormous bell tower. "What church that is?"

"The Dormition Abbey," Zoltán said, squinting his dark brown eyes at the fortress-like structure with four corner towers. "It was called the 'Mother of all Churches' during Emperor Constantine's day. The Virgin Mary is believed to have died on that spot."

"I thought Mary died in Ephesus," I told my friends. "I went to her home near there about a year and a half ago." I remembered having felt her serene presence all around me and couldn't imagine that she'd died anywhere other than Nightingale Hill.

"There's some debate about the actual place," William said.

"Let's go in," Zsuzsa said, not caring if the real thing was there or in Ephesus.

William opened the massive wooden door, and we entered the exquisite neo-Romanesque church. I emptied my pockets of shekel coins, exchanging them for four white candles, which I shared with my friends. The candlelight infused the interior with an unearthly glow. The only tourists, we each walked in a different direction around the nave, pausing at various Stations of the Cross.

I closed my eyes outside St. Joseph's Chapel and found myself mouthing the refrain from Bach's *Magnificat*. William, who stood outside the chapel in honor of John the Baptist, joined in with a soft tenor whisper. Zsuzsa, holding a candle up against the Zodiac symbols etched on the multicolored marble floor, added her lovely soprano voice when we sang "*Anima mea Dominum.*" From the brilliant mosaic of Mary holding Baby Jesus, Zoltán conducted us with his candlestick. At the end of the movement, he cued our finish, pretending to play the final solo measures on an imaginary trumpet. As the brass section "roared" to its climax, the rest of us clapped.

"A good warm-up for next week's performance," I said.

Moments later, Zsuzsa noted a side door, and we descended the spiral staircase into the damp, chilly crypt. My companions quickly walked around the statues of Jesus and the Saints before heading back upstairs. I was drawn to the commemorative wreaths swathed in red, white, and green on the altar of the Hungarian Chapel. As I struggled to make out the Magyar text, I felt a tap on my shoulder and jumped. An older man in a dark blue uniform apologized for startling me and informed me that the church would soon be closing.

"I'm sorry, I didn't realize. I'll join my friends upstairs." As I walked through the claustrophobic room toward the exit, he followed close behind and again touched my shoulder. This time my heart leapt into double time.

"Sorry to bother madam," he said, tipping his head forward. "I am only wondering if madam is a Christian."

I stopped, wary as how best to respond, given the religious tensions in the area. "Why do you ask?"

He moved away and motioned toward a fenced area in the middle of the room. "If madam is a Christian, she can receive a kiss from Mary." He clasped his hands together and raised them toward the heavens. "Wouldn't madam like a kiss from Mary?"

I looked around, unsure of what he meant. "Why yes, I guess so."

"Then come this way." He opened the black gate surrounding the ivory and cherrywood image of Jesus's mother, who was reclining atop her multicolored mosaic deathbed, which in my fascination with the side chapels, I hadn't noticed. "Quickly!" With clammy palms and jittery legs, I followed him inside. Interlocking his fingers into a steeple, he pointed toward Mary's empty, life-size sarcophagus. "Now madam can kiss her."

Under a magnificent golden mosaic of Jesus surrounded by six women from the Old Testament, I bent over and pressed my lips against Mary's. An electrical spark shot down my throat, pulsating its way toward my fingertips and toes. Dizzy, I stood up slowly, one hand around my neck, the other clasping a fence railing.

"Is madam okay?"

The intensity gave way to a flood of warmth that gushed toward my pores, infusing me with a deep sense of calm. I remembered having felt the same way only once before: that night in my bedroom in Somerville, during the breakup with Hank.

"Yes, more than okay," I said, bowing my head with appreciation. As he continued sweeping up, I drifted toward the door and turned for one last glimpse of the Sleeping Virgin. Then it dawned on me—I'd been so focused on finding the "tall man with glasses" that I had neglected the second part of Angelica's prediction: the Russian icon.

From now on, I promise to pay more attention, Mary.

Chapter 30

Dear Diary, Part Two

Amsterdam
March 22nd

Dear Diary,

I never would have guessed it would take five months to return to Amsterdam! But I'm back on Frederiksstraat, sneaking a few moments to write while David is napping.

About two weeks ago, he finally emailed to say that as much as he wanted to visit me in Budapest, he couldn't bear the thought of getting on another plane. Instead, he suggested I visit him and promised to "roll out the red carpet." I jumped at the opportunity.

When I got to David's flat from Schiphol Airport in the early morning, he greeted me at the door in his bathrobe. At first, I thought it suggestive, but after our conversations, now realize that the poor guy's utterly exhausted. His employer is sending him to two or three countries per week. Although he's been to some beautiful cities like Paris and Rome, he rarely gets to enjoy them because he's holed up in an office night and day. He's very disappointed that he has to travel again on Monday, as we'd hoped to spend more time together (I'd taken a few extra days off from IH). He blamed it on "seniority," which I know something about.

Even though it was a glorious, sunny Saturday, we spent most of it inside, talking about his work stress and how he's (not) coping with it. He's not too specific about his job or work destinations. When I inquired about his colleagues, he gave me an odd look. I thought he'd already be making friends.

The place looked not much different than when I'd left in October—boxes galore, empty fridge, still no shower curtain. When I asked David for a towel, he flinched and apologized that they were all in the laundry bin. Then he fetched an old terry cloth robe and asked if I minded using that. *Bachelors!*

We did get out for a scrumptious Italian dinner in the New Market, where he opened up a bit more after a few gin and tonics and shared that he'd been "in a deep funk" over the holidays (a combination of work pressures and loneliness) and hadn't felt like celebrating. This was the closest he came to explaining his lack of communication during that time. If only he'd reached out to me! He did acknowledge my Christmas card, though, which was taped to his fridge.

I wish I had something juicier to share, but again, not even a kiss. Last night we chatted until two, when he suddenly stood up and declared that he needed to "plop into bed." I still feel a strong attraction but definitely sense he's holding back. Why, I don't know. In any event, I have one more day to try to figure this out. For now, I'll sign off and go buy pastries from the corner bakery, as there's nothing here for breakfast.

More soon.

Linda

March 24th

Dear Diary,

Sorry I'm writing this last entry from Tulip Street, having arrived here a few hours ago, but I wanted to spend as much time with David as possible before leaving Amsterdam.

He wound up sleeping until noon yesterday, when I finally knocked on his bedroom door and announced that breakfast was ready. From inside I heard a big thud, followed by, "Oh, shit!" David jumped out in his briefs, dragged a comb through his unkempt hair, and picked at something stranded between his two front teeth. While I set the table with an assortment of strudel, he apologized for not having stocked the fridge or cupboards.

Over breakfast, he asked how I had slept. "Like a log," I lied, as it had been difficult knowing he was in close proximity.

"Not me."

"Why not?"

"Oh, no particular reason," he said with a suggestive wink. The body heat generating from his massive, hairless chest was so electrifying, I wanted to crawl into bed with him and melt into a puddle. The timing, however, wasn't very conducive to a first romantic interlude. He reached for his robe and while pouring himself a mug of coffee, asked if I was interested in a day trip to Utrecht. After a leisurely meal, we went downtown and caught a southbound train to that charming city, a mosaic of canals and bridges with shops and cafés that wound along the Oudegracht, or "Old Canal." We choose an eatery with a perfect view of the Gothic Domkerk and its three-tiered bell tower, which was closed by the time we arrived. I was disappointed, as I am convinced that the Russian icon Angelica had foreseen is here in Holland. After all, I found the "tall man with glasses" :-)

Everything was going well until our lunch was disrupted by David's mobile phone blaring out the *Star Wars* theme. He told me the call was urgent and walked away, engaging in a heated discussion. "Sorry about that," was all he said twenty minutes later, when he returned to our canal-side table.

I didn't dare pry, but after a few minutes, it rang again; David rolled his eyes, grabbed the phone, and disappeared. This time he explained that it was his ex, which was confusing, as he'd reassured me last fall that they had broken up the year before. "It's her birthday, and she's upset I'm not celebrating with her in Devon."

I wondered why she'd assume David was available, but I smiled and said, "Oh, sorry if I'm taking you away from—"

"That's not at all what I meant," David said, patting my hand. He silenced his phone and put it down. "I wouldn't be visiting her anyway. She keeps forgetting she's not my girlfriend."

"Obviously, she still has feelings for you," I said, topping off our Pinot Grigios.

"I don't know." He tapped his fingers against the white linen cloth. "I hadn't been getting that impression. I think she's just lonely."

After clearing the air, he once again told me he "longs for the day" when he can settle down and start a family. He even mentioned Utrecht as a possible place to put down roots and asked if I could envision living there. *Yes!* I hope to be first in the queue when he gets freed up. I asked what was preventing him from fulfilling his dream, but he fumbled and steered the discussion back to how his job made it difficult to seriously pursue personal goals.

"It sounds like you're leading a double life," I remarked in an off-handed manner.

"How do you mean?" He lit up another Marlboro (he's smoking more than ever) and looked at me with curiosity.

"Well, you say you want a family life, but from what

you're telling me, the one you're living prevents you from attaining it."

"Hmm . . . a double life," he said. "Never thought of it in those terms." He changed the subject, and after trying to make sense of the train schedule, we headed to the station.

It was almost eight when we arrived at his flat, where we sat, shocked and awed by the news images coming out of Iraq. "At least you and I are on the same side," David said, taking my hand. We watched TV a little while longer until he excused himself to pack and rest up for his business trip to Italy the next day. We headed to our respective bedrooms, and I set my alarm to see him off at six.

He was in such a rush this morning, we barely had time for words, although he promised to visit Budapest ASAP. "I'd like to see this Gábor in action," he said before collapsing his long legs into the taxi.

So, another chaste visit and sleepless night. Despite our not "closing the deal" (as the eloquent Béla is so fond of saying), I'm very glad I returned to Amsterdam. While it would have been wonderful to consummate our mutual attraction, I'm following David's lead because he's clearly not ready for a commitment. His opening up to me about his depression at Christmastime shows he trusts me and that our relationship is deepening. Yes, it's frustrating, but I believe that staying the course is the best route. Patience, Linduska, patience.

"*Tot ziens*" for now. Let's hope it's not too long before I write again, either here during David's visit, or when I'm next in our beloved Amsterdam.

Yours,

Linda

János Keresztelö (John The Baptist)

"I think I'm gonna cave and call Angelica," I told Gretchen in between bites of a tasty chicken kebab sandwich at Szeráj, one of the few affordable eateries on the Boulevard open during the long Easter weekend. She and I were both teaching full-time at IH, and I had hoped to fly to Amsterdam to visit David during spring break. "I can't stand all this waiting. Yes, David's a workaholic, but this lack of communication is ridiculous."

"How long did it take him to write this time?" Gretchen asked, leaning over the table and dissecting his latest email.

"Three weeks. By the time he wrote, it was too late to request time off from IH. My patience is wearing thin."

"Oh, dear." She read aloud about his *"frenetic work situation and fond memories of our trip to Utrecht,"* and his closing words: *"Once again, it was wonderful to see you. I'll visit you in Budapest as soon as I get some free time and my personal orientation straight. With love, David xxx."*

Gretchen threw down the paper next to her meze plate and dug into the yogurt-doused eggplant dish. "Hmm . . .

interesting choice of words," she said, pointing to the last sentence.

"Yes, 'straight' jumped out at me, too."

"Are you thinking what I'm thinking?"

I told Gretchen that the idea of David being gay had only crossed my mind after reading this email, never while I was in Holland. He had been way too attentive and flirty. *Could I have been so blindsided?* I had known many gay men while working for an HIV/AIDS organization in the '90s and was sure I would have sensed if David were also.

"Maybe he chose Amsterdam as a place to come out," she said. "You know the Dutch are more open about their sexuality than the Brits."

I looked up at the photo of Turkey's beautiful Bodrum Beach on the bright green walls and was reminded of Fokas Beach in Tinos and the revealing conversations Eve and I had enjoyed with Sven and Marten about life in Amsterdam. "True."

"That doesn't explain the ex-girlfriend, though," Gretchen said, "and David's comments about wanting a home and family." She cradled her fair chin with her palm. "If he's leading you on but engaging in a different lifestyle, he must be living a double life."

"A double life," I murmured, remembering David's rapt line of questioning after I'd uttered those same words weeks earlier in Utrecht. "That's it, Gretchen," I said, snapping my fingers. "He's leading a double life. Only how and why, I have no clue."

"Well, Sherlock, you could call and ask him." Her voice strained against "*Şımarık*," the Turkish Pop hit by Tarkan blaring from the loudspeakers.

"And blurt out, 'Are you gay?' I would never do that. I'd want to see his reaction." I took a sip of tea from the hourglass-shaped cup. "His reticence and reserve are driving me nuts."

Gretchen pointed to *xxx* at the bottom of David's email. "On the bright side, he added another *x* and is now signing 'With love.'" I appreciated her efforts to cheer me up.

After downing a plate of baklava, we headed out to the deserted boulevard and eyed the windows of the Európa. My mouth watered at the sight of so many chocolate Easter bunnies and chicks, but my favorite café was closed. As we were about to cross St. Stephen's to check out the Vígszínház's theater schedule, a familiar buzz drowned out our footsteps. Gretchen's head spun around. "Watch out!" she said, pushing me back with an extended arm. "That wheelchair is heading straight toward you."

"No worries, Gretchen. That's my friend." I rushed over to the man who had brought me such unexpected joy on Women's Day. Before I could greet him, János reached for a paper bag under his seat. "Everything okay?" I asked.

Ignoring my inquiry, he whipped out a bottle of perfume, took aim at my white silk blouse, and started spraying. "*Kellemes húsvétot!*" he said, wishing me a "Happy Easter." Overcome by the aroma of roses, I pulled at my soaked shirt but was no match for Avon.

My startled eyes searched Gretchen's for a glimmer of understanding. She laughed from a safe distance. "It's a time-honored Hungarian tradition," she explained as she approached with care. "On Easter Monday, males spray females with perfume to bring them luck and enhance their chances of fertility."

"Then I'm the luckiest, most fertile woman in all of Europe." I beamed a grateful smile at János. He tipped his Yankees baseball cap and started wheeling away.

"You're supposed to return the favor with some chocolate," Gretchen said.

"Let me take a look." I fumbled through my bag for some stray Milka pieces as I followed János down the street to a flower stall, where he stopped to speak with the owner.

She waved as I approached, and then turned away to give us a moment of privacy.

"Pick one," I told János, holding out my fists. He nodded to the right one, which I opened, and reached for the chocolate. I took his hand and rubbed it against my cheek. "*Kedves* János," I told the dear man. "You've given me so much hope." *You've blessed me.*

He flashed an uncertain look and crossed his hands over his heart. I watched as he slowly turned around and accelerated toward the Metró station. When he disappeared, I meandered back toward Gretchen.

"Oh, Gretchen," I said, choking back tears. "János is much more than he appears to be, too."

His Double Life

After peeling off my perfume-soaked clothes and showering, I searched my address book for Angelica's phone number. Noting the six-hour time difference in Massachusetts, I dialed, hoping not to disturb one of her psychic sessions; she answered on the second ring.

"Hi, Linda, you've been on my mind. Thanks for your postcard. How was Israel?"

I filled her in on the highlights of the chorus's three-week tour, from candlelight vigils at the Church of the Holy Sepulchre and slipping messages into the Western Wall, to singing Mozart and Fauré at Henry Crown Symphony Hall.

"Splendid! Now aren't you glad you went? You were so worried about terrorism."

"Luckily there was no incident during our stay. However, shortly after we left, there was a double suicide bombing in a commercial part of Tel Aviv."

"Yes, I saw that on the news." I heard Luna meowing in the background; Angelica purred a few words of reassurance to her pet, and then said, "What can I do for you, Linda?"

Without going into much detail, I explained about meeting David, my recent trip to Amsterdam, and the long communication gaps. She asked me to call back thirty minutes later, after she'd had a chance to "tune in."

Our chat reminded me that it was Whiskas time for Lester. After dishing out a few heaps of lamb into his bowl, I fell back into the armchair and deeply inhaled the intoxicating scent of lilacs. When the clock ticked five, I reached for the landline.

Again, Angelica asked me to sit up straight, without crossing my arms or legs, and to imagine us enveloped in a warm glow of white light. After a few minutes, she broke the silence with a hearty giggle. "Oh, he likes you, Linda. David really likes you."

"Then he's not gay?" I blurted out.

"Definitely not."

"Whew!"

"Wow, he's super tall, isn't he?"

"Yes."

"Nice-looking fellow."

"No argument there."

Silence. "I see him surrounded by computers. His eyes are very tired. Actually, his whole energy is tired." I bit my tongue. "He's weighed down, like he's not able to be free. Does that make sense?"

I hesitated in revealing too much. "I've gotten the impression that he would like to settle down, but that something—or someone—is preventing him."

"Let me take a closer look." I imagined Angelica's feathery eyelashes batting against her fair skin. She remained quiet for a good minute.

"You still there?" I finally asked.

Her voice faltered. "Linda, it's clear now. There *is* something you don't know about David." I pushed back into the chair and grabbed the armrests. "He's not who he says he is."

My heart began pounding out staccato rhythms; the receiver shook in my hands. "You mean, he's leading a double life?"

"So to speak . . ."

"Oh my God! He's married and has a family somewhere."

"No, nothing like that."

I pulled at the phone cord, twirling it in my sweaty hands. "I don't understand. If he's not gay and there's no third person involved, what's the matter?"

"I can't tell you."

"You can't or you won't?"

"Both."

I scooped up Lester and settled him on my lap. "Is he ill?"

"No, just exhausted."

I was desperate to keep Angelica on the line, hoping she'd clarify, but she insisted on ending the call. "I need to get off," she said, curtly. "I'll write soon and explain. Goodbye!"

To the sound of the busy signal, I stared out at the birch trees, utterly confused and dumbfounded. I couldn't fathom her strange, cagey behavior. "What's so terrible about David that Angelica is afraid to tell me?" I addressed Lester, patting his nose.

A feeling of impending doom enveloped me for the next two weeks, until the much-anticipated envelope arrived one afternoon on my doorstep. Although there was no return address, it was postmarked "Cambridgeport." At once, I knew it was from Angelica and tore it open. She had wrapped a few blank sheets of paper around an index card. As I unfolded it, my eyes were drawn to the single word centered in block letters: INTERPOL.

Sisu (Chutzpah)

One month later, Heléna greeted me at her door with the expensive bottle of Tokaji she had been saving in the cellar since Róbert's birth for his rite of passage into manhood. "It finally happened," my friend informed me, grinning from ear to ear. "The Emma promised to have sex with Róbert on night of senior party. He's no longer virgin." She poured out some of the good stuff they had savored earlier that morning after his return home.

Holding up the same crystal flutes she had used the first night we met, we toasted in English and Hungarian, Heléna congratulating me on my near-perfect *"Egészségedre"* pronunciation. "I learned from the best," I said, winking.

"Oh, Linduska," she sighed. "I'm so glad you stay a little longer in Europe."

"Me, too." I reached for a cocktail napkin. "Not only do I get to spend more time with you, but I have the trip to the Baltics to look forward to."

On my birthday, Dad had agreed to extend my stay so I could sing Beethoven's "Ode to Joy" with BACS and a chorus of two thousand in Heroes' Square in mid-August.

The composer's choral finale from his Ninth Symphony was one of my favorite pieces and seemed the perfect send-off. In return, I'd promised Dad I would move back to America immediately after. He had also asked me to make a special trip to Vilnius, birthplace of his father Vincent, to learn what I could about his family history from the local archives. I agreed to go in early August before the concert.

Heléna leaned forward on the sofa and patted my knee. "It's such a pity David never got in touch. Wasn't he going to visit you in July during his holiday?"

"Yes, he promised," I said, "but he totally blew me off and never responded to my messages about his travel plans."

"But if he really is spy, like the Angelica say, then you have explanation."

I shook my head. "You know, I'm not sure if any of what Angelica said about him is true. The idea of David being something other than how he presented himself is creepy."

"That's because he's good spy."

"*If* he is." I jiggled my glass, dislodging the last droplets of champagne. "In which case, I'm not interested."

Heléna walked toward the kitchen area and returned with a tray of Pick sausage and cheese sandwiches. "How exciting, to be wife of spy," she said.

"Only in the movies, Meryl." In addition to David's broken promises to visit, I thought of his inability to settle down, his pounding on the computer in a late-night flurry of emails as I'd tried to sleep on Frederiksstraat. Even if his odd behavior made sense in some mysterious way he couldn't share with me, my heart still ached from the way he had seemingly cut me out of his life.

Seeing me tear up, Heléna raised an arm toward the floral curtains rustling in the warm breeze. "Don't be sad,

Linduska. You're going to Finland!" I winced. "Lucky you. It's always been my dream to go Nordic countries."

"Really?" It sure wasn't mine. When I'd booked my trip to Vilnius, the travel agent had encouraged me to fly into Helsinki, the "city on sale" that week, instead of Warsaw. At first, I'd hesitated. *Why would I want to visit some ice floe adrift in the Arctic?* However, when she told me I would save one hundred dollars, I caved.

"Just imagine, the people there so civilized, so sophisticate, so tall." *Tall?* "So clean country, not like here." She motioned to the graffiti-ridden concrete parking dividers outside.

"I'll drink to that." I emptied my glass; Heléna rushed to replenish it.

"I hear Finland famous for *sisu*," she said, draping a few slices of Swiss cheese over a sesame bun. I leaned over and did the same.

"What's *sisu*?" I imagined a salmon salad or herring casserole from the Baltic's ice-cold waters.

"I don't know exact word in English, but it's like when you Americans say someone has balls."

"I think you mean 'guts' or 'chutzpah.'"

"Maybe. Whatever it is, you need man with *sisu*." Heléna pushed out her chest and beat it à la Tarzan. "Clock ticking, soon you return to States. No time for reserved man now."

Suddenly, the bedroom door opened, and Róbert entered, a big smirk on his slightly stubbled face. I stood up to greet him and raised my glass to the ceiling. "How about a toast to the new man of the house?"

Heléna poured her son the remainder of Tokaji, and the three of us huddled into a small circle, clinking our glasses together. After hearing general details about Róbert's "first time," we reminisced about our early days as neighbors, my foray onto the ice-skating rink with Róbert, and the *American Pie* fiasco.

"I still can't believe you played the uncut version," Róbert said, rolling his eyes and suddenly fancying himself mature.

"What will we do without our Miss American Pie?" Heléna asked her son, blotting away an imaginary tear.

As their voices receded, I wistfully recalled my first time making love with the young man I thought I might marry. And here I was, decades later, a celibate "virgin" of three years, wondering when my dry spell would end.

Part Six

The Finnish Line

*For where your treasure is,
there your heart will be also.*

Gospel of Luke 12:34

Chapter 34

Catch of the Day

Enshrined on its own hillside in Helsinki Harbor, the Uspenski Cathedral towered over the nearby Art Deco university buildings and docked cruise boats, its magnificent golden cupolas glistening in the Northern sun. After buying a ticket for the noon ferry to Tallinn, Estonia on Linda Lines Express, I wove my way through the maze of orange vendor tents at the Fish Market and headed up the steep cobblestone steps to the nineteenth-century religious landmark, the largest Orthodox Church in Western Europe.

The absence of ordered pews gave the space a cavernous feel. Royal red carpeting cut a path to the altar as Archangel Michael and Angel Gabriel watched from the colorful iconostasis. An enormous, gilded chandelier hung from the sky-blue dome, from which an array of golden stars appeared to burst. The aroma of musk lingered from dangling incense holders.

A handful of visitors lit long brown candles in front of icons of Russian saints and paintings depicting various Bible scenes. I bought a honey wax taper from the cashier and looked around for an inspirational spot to reflect and pray. A petite *babushka* wearing a colorful headscarf directed me to a shimmery icon on the north side of the church. "It work miracle," she promised.

The serene faces of the Madonna and Baby Jesus peeked out through a delicate mesh of tiny pearls and gold and silver sequins. Countless crosses, rings, bracelets, and tie clips hung from the images, offset by a soft blue velvet frame. A small label identified the treasure as *Theotokos of Kozeltshan,* honoring the Mother of God. For what I presumed was the last time, I thought about Angelica's prediction that a Russian icon would lead me to the "tall man with glasses." During the last two and a half years, I'd visited many Protestant and Catholic churches, but very few Orthodox ones.

Staring now at the loving face of Jesus's mother, I felt reassured that my journey had come full circle. I lit a candle and bowed my head in gratitude for the amazing adventure that had allowed me to live in Liszt's homeland and volunteer for the institution bearing his name, pay tribute to Anne Frank at the Annex, and sing many of my favorite pieces in Israel. I also gave thanks for the friendships forged with Heléna, Gabi, Adél, and Gretchen that I hoped would last a lifetime. The compassion of Bea, Gyöngyi, and János would forever be an inspiration. I'd even return to the States with some teaching experience under my belt.

Although part of me was disappointed that I hadn't met the man Angelica had envisioned, I would never forget the Dutch Treats, cavorting with My Spy in Amsterdam, Ádám's fib, and other Magyar close calls. Sure, I would be going back to the States without a ring on my finger, but with a smile forever etched on my heart. *I'm ready to return home now, Mary.*

In sharp contrast to the cathedral's dimly lit interior, the outside terrace was awash in sunlight, affording a bird's-eye view of the Helsinki Cathedral's expansive dome in Senate

Square. I reached for my Pentax and added a new roll of film, but the camera suddenly stopped functioning. At the nearby Tourist Information Office, a clerk suggested I buy a new battery from Stockmann's Department store at the other end of the street.

The windows along the stylish Esplanade were teeming with bold-patterned Marimekko skirts and jackets, reindeer skins from Lapland, Sibelius CDs, and Iittala ceramics with a fanciful owl theme. Wholesome-looking couples sipped wine and flirted in brimming outdoor cafés. Colorful floral patches carpeted the grounds beneath statues of Finland's most revered poets and war heroes, with not a squirt of graffiti or dog poop on them. For what many described as a sleepy town with extreme weather, Helsinki looked to be a thriving and bustling cosmopolitan city; I regretted not having allowed myself more time to explore. As I changed my camera battery, Heléna's words came back to haunt me: "If you don't take photographs, it means you're going back." *Yes, I'd like that.*

With forty-five minutes to spare before my boat left for Tallinn, little time remained for picture taking. However, the famously seductive Havis Amanda beckoned, her coquettish come-hither look having lured sailors into port for over a century. Considered a symbol of Helsinki by the locals, the bronze statue of a naked mermaid was surrounded by a sea of squealing seals and open-mouthed fish spouting water into the fountain below her feet.

As I steadied my camera to capture the alluring arc of Amanda's voluptuous bottom, a bright red flash filled the viewfinder. When it wouldn't go away, I looked up to find an attractive man wearing a windbreaker of that same color walking toward the Fish Market. Suddenly, everything and everyone—the shops and park around us, the children throwing coins into the fountain, the approaching tram—froze in time and space. All I noticed was the tall man in red; everything else receded from sight. Intrigued, I shoved the Pentax into my bag and felt compelled to follow him.

On the street corner, I patiently waited for the light to change, as I had read that Scandinavians were averse to jaywalking. This gave me extra time to check out the forty-something guy who flaunted a marathon runner's physique under his beige athletic shorts. He probably sensed my eyes checking out his sculpted calves and boring into his backside, because he turned to look at me. I quickly glanced down at his left hand; the absence of a gold band buoyed my hopes. When the light flashed green, we walked in sync across the street toward the market.

After leaving the intersection, we parted ways—or I thought we had—until I caught him peeking at me from the reindeer skins vendor across the path. I spun around and walked in the opposite direction toward a pile of *Suomi* T-shirts, curious to see if he'd follow; he didn't. Instead, he came toward me from the opposite direction, smiling shyly as his shoulder lightly touched mine as he passed by.

A glance at Helsinki Cathedral's clock starkly reminded me that less than thirty minutes remained until boat launch. Despite the time crunch, I was determined to see if the good-looking stranger would approach. Spotting a fresh-squeezed orange juice stand, I purchased a large cup and stopped in my tracks, giving him the opportunity to take the bait. Seconds later, he was at my side.

"*Hei,*" the Finn greeted me, bending his tall, lean frame down to meet me at eye level.

"Hey," I said, using a word sounding exactly like the one he had uttered.

"Do you speak English?" he asked in a shaky voice.

"I certainly hope so. I'm American." I extended a hand. "My name is Linda. And you?

"Otto."

"Otto," I repeated, remembering Anne Frank's beloved

father. "You sure are a popular guy, Otto. Your name is everywhere." I pointed to the OTTO machine across the street and told him that earlier in the day I'd withdrawn some cash from one of his ATMs.

A flicker of a smile graced his serene, suntanned face. "Sorry, no relation. My name means 'to take' in Finnish." My mind raced through all the places Otto could take me, starting with his bedroom.

"What brings you to Finland?" he asked as we strolled past the crêpe eatery with its quaint blue and white checkered tablecloths.

"I flew in last night and am on my way to Tallinn, and from there, Vilnius." I pointed to the Linda Lines fleet beyond the brick Vanha Kauppahalli, or "Old Market." "My boat leaves in about twenty minutes." *Oh, how I wish it didn't!*

"Hmm." Otto pushed his wire-rimmed glasses against a perfectly symmetrical nose. "Vilnius is an unusual destination. Most tourists head to Stockholm or St. Petersburg."

As I started to explain the family research project I'd be pursuing in Lithuania, my entranced mind noted that the bespectacled Otto was also a good six inches taller than me. In the middle of recounting my grandfather's saga, I switched gears, and suddenly found myself emphasizing my return to Helsinki five days later. "Do you live nearby, Otto?" I asked, hoping he would offer to show me around the city the following week.

Otto explained that he lived in the Töölö part of town but had grown up in Pihtipudas, a small village in Middle Finland, whose name he uttered with pride. "I moved here one year ago because of my prosticutor job," he said, nonchalantly.

I cocked an eye. "Come again?"

"I'm a prosticutor."

He must have noticed the cloud of bewilderment overshadow my face because he quickly whipped out his business card. The scales of Justice reassured me that Otto worked in the courtrooms, not the city sidewalks.

"Oh, you mean *prosecutor,*" I restated, hoping he'd catch the difference.

"Yes, that's it." He turned over the card and with a jittery hand, scribbled his home address on the back. As he gave it to me, he asked about my background and job situation. When I told him I was an English teacher in Budapest, he fidgeted with his windbreaker zipper. "Please excuse my English—it's my fourth language," he confessed.

"It's okay," I said. *You'll have years to improve if I have anything to do with it.*

Otto stopped at one of the seafood tents and insisted on buying me a salmon sandwich for my journey. Unsure of the lunch menu on the boat, I accepted the *graavilohi sämpylä* made with lightly smoked salmon on rye bread sprinkled with salt and dill. "My weekly ration," he explained. "I walk here every Saturday to treat myself." *TGIS!* I thanked him and put the food in my bag. When we turned around, the Makasiini Terminal loomed in front of us. I reminded Otto of the few minutes remaining, and he offered to escort me there.

"Will you be going back to your teaching job in Budapest this fall?" he asked in a voice straining against the squawking seagulls circling above us.

"No. I'm moving back to America at the end of this month." As soon as I uttered these words, I immediately regretted sharing information that could easily deter him from seeing me again. Fortunately, he persevered.

"Is there a job waiting for you back home?"

"No. I'm actually a bit nervous about reentering the workforce." I explained the type of work I'd done at The Guidance Center and other nonprofit groups. "My parents are eagerly awaiting my return," I added, remembering the promise I'd made to my father and how he had already extended my stay abroad so I could sing in the Beethoven concert.

Otto suddenly stopped, lightly rubbed the salt-and-pepper stubble on his chin, and then blurted out: "I live alone and have no family."

Relieved that he most likely was not hiding a pregnant wife in the hospital or living with his Papa, I said, "I'm in the same boat."

He craned his long neck and examined the fleet of hydrofoils. "Which is your boat?"

I laughed and touched his sleeve. "It's an American expression that means I'm in the same situation."

Otto's body language eased up as he opened the door to the terminal, which was teeming with Asian tourists and tipsy Finns returning from Estonia with boxes of tax-free booze and cigarettes piled high on wheel-away carts. I walked to the locker where I had stowed my suitcase earlier that morning; Otto reached in to retrieve the bag.

"*Kiitos,*" I thanked him, proud of another Finnish word I'd acquired since my arrival.

"*Hyvä,*" Otto replied in surprise. "Good that you already know some Finnish."

As we approached passport control, Otto and I stopped in our tracks. His pale blue eyes smiled, but were tinged with disappointment. *Should I cancel this ferry trip and go tomorrow instead?* It was tempting, but the ten-hour bus journey from Tallinn to Vilnius didn't leave much wiggle room. Plus, I had already prepaid my hotel rooms.

As the loudspeakers blared final boarding call, my mouth became parched, and I pulled at the collar of my beige swing coat. *Say something, Linda! Show some* sisu! Hordes of tourists rushed by with their suitcases; I reached down for mine. "Well, Otto . . ." I cleared my throat several times. "It was nice . . ."

Otto moved in closer, his kind, intelligent eyes narrowing into a serious expression. "Will you be spending time in Helsinki before flying back to Hungary?"

Bingo! I'd already booked a hotel room in Tallinn for the last night of the trip, as accommodations were significantly cheaper there, but would gladly cancel it and find one in Helsinki. After all, I'd saved one hundred dollars by flying there instead of Warsaw. "Yes, I'm coming back on Thursday."

"Can I see you that night?"

"I'd really like that." As I jotted down my email address, Otto reminded me that his was on the business card and asked me to write once I got settled in Vilnius. "Definitely," I said, my pulse returning to normal.

He pulled me close and kissed me Finnish style, once on each cheek. "I'm waiting your email," he whispered as I stepped toward the customs booth.

With a Cheshire-like grin, I spun on my heels and waved back at Otto, shouting, "See you soon!" before making it onto the boat with a few minutes to spare.

As I sank into my economy seat and reviewed the events of the last thirty minutes, my whole being buzzed in sync with the vibrations coming from beneath the ferry. *Did it all really happen, or am I dreaming?* I consulted Otto's business card for proof that he did, in fact, exist. Eyeing the Scales of Justice logo, I realized that most likely nothing would come of our meeting the following week. Otto's roots were firmly in Finland, and I was moving back to America. After having my expectations so thoroughly dashed by David, it was probably best not to pin any hopes on this date.

Soon the ferry picked up speed, and the bright orange tents of the Fish Market faded into specks on the horizon. To the east, Suomenlinna fortress sprawled out over small stone islands across the velvety surf as ships cruised in and out of Helsinki Harbor. I craned my neck for one last view of the brick façade and twinkling gold cupolas of the majestic Uspenski. As I remembered my prayer at the miraculous icon earlier that morning, a warm gust of wind swept through my being; I closed my eyes and visualized Otto's kind face and sweet smile. Liszt's *Liebestraum* filled the air, but as I listened more closely, it was Angelica's prophetic words tapping on my eardrums: "Tall man with glasses."

"Ode to Joy"

"**G**ood luck!" the taxi driver shouted as the door slammed behind me. I struggled toward the dock, my arms bulging with *käsitöö* from Tallinn's Old Town markets. It had been difficult to pry myself away from all the handcrafted bargains—embroidered holiday linens, brightly colored dish towels, wool mittens—and the charm of Estonia's medieval capital city.

The entrance to the Helsinki-bound ferry was roped off, no one on duty. Finally, an older man in a neatly pressed white shirt, dark blue uniform, and sailor's cap began removing the boarding signs. "You're late," he said, moving an index finger sideways at me. "Passport control is closed."

I looked at my watch. "But the boat doesn't leave for fifteen more minutes!"

"Sorry. Foreigners are supposed to be here thirty minutes prior to departure to clear customs." He encouraged me to wait for the next boat, which left four hours later. In my email to Otto, I'd promised to phone early in the afternoon upon my arrival in Finland. From there, we'd make plans to get together that evening.

"Please, sir, I really need to get on that boat. Someone's waiting for me in Helsinki."

The man, who clearly was the boat's captain, stopped thumbing through a stack of tourist brochures and cocked an interested eye. "Where are you from, miss?"

"The United States."

"What are you doing in Estonia? Not many Americans pass through here."

I explained the purpose of my visit to Vilnius, adding that he and I were "practically cousins" on account of our Eastern European backgrounds. "Oh, *please, please, please* let me on this boat, sir." I sent out a silent prayer to St. Olav's Church in the distance, its four-hundred-foot black steeple rising out of a blur of bloodred tiled roofs.

He smacked his lips and stared blankly into my pleading eyes before sticking out his hand. "Passport please!"

After thanking him profusely, I boarded Linda Lines, which glided into Helsinki Harbor less than two hours later. As soon as I passed through customs at the Makasiini Terminal, I tried to find a pay phone—not an easy task in the land of Nokia. The receptionist in Otto's office answered on the first ring.

"*Terve, Helsingin Kihlakunnan Syyttäjänvirasto,*" she said. I tried to follow along with the wording on Otto's business card, but Finnish appeared as difficult as Hungarian.

"Hello, I'd like to speak to Otto—" I struggled to pronounce his family name.

"Yes. One moment, please," she answered in perfect English.

I inhaled deep breaths while the call was being transferred. After a short delay, Otto whispered, "Linda?"

"*Hei!* I just arrived in Helsinki and am calling about tonight."

"Okay."

"Do you still want to get together?"

"Yes." I waited for a suggestion of a possible venue, but none was offered.

"What time is good for you?"

"Six."

"Where shall we meet?"

"I come to your hotel. Where you are staying?"

"At the Helka." I had picked that accommodation after noting its close proximity to Otto's address on Google. "Do you know it?"

"Yes." Pause.

"Well, see you at six then."

"Goodbye."

Before I was able to ask further details, Otto had hung up. *Odd.* I slumped over to gather my bag, headed outside into the sunshine, and hailed a cab to my hotel. Our brief conversation—if one could call it that—left me feeling uneasy about our date. Otto had sounded as enthusiastic as someone scheduling a colonoscopy. *Don't stress out, Linda, it's only one night. Tomorrow you'll be back in Budapest, and then on your way home to America.*

After checking into my room, I laid out a long black skirt and a soft purple Lycra top with matching knit jacket on the bed. Then I showered and sat down by the phone in my robe. Today was my parents' wedding anniversary, and I wanted to congratulate them first thing East Coast time.

Mom picked up after many rings. "Hi, dear. Are you still in Vilnius?"

"No, I'm back in Helsinki, but only for one night."

"Helsinki? What are you doing in Finland?"

There was no reason to tell Mom about the date with

Otto, especially in light of his curtness. "I'm cramming in some sightseeing before flying back to Hungary tomorrow."

I heard her fidgeting with the phone while sharing asides with Dad. Their voices sounded animated; perhaps I'd interrupted a reenactment from their wedding night. "How was your trip to Lithuania?" Mom continued. "Did you learn anything about your grandfather?"

I was loath to disappoint, but the clerk at the Vilnius Archives had looked at my documentation and instructed me to go to Nana's birthplace in Russia. "Sorry, Mom, but I didn't have enough time to apply for a tourist visa and arrange another side trip."

"No worries, dear." She handed the phone to Dad, who barely referred to my trip, but instead told me of a surprise visit from Hank, who had popped in to see them a few days earlier.

"Your mother and I were both on the porch when your old Geo Prizm pulled into the driveway."

"What did *he* want?" I moved the skirt aside and sprawled out on the bed.

"He told us that your old Somerville building is going condo, and since he can't afford to buy in, he's moving out. While he was packing, he came across some of your belongings. Nothing important." I wondered if Hank had an ulterior motive; apparently Dad did, too. "He seemed eager to know when you're returning."

"You didn't divulge any details, did you?" I sat up, noting that Otto was meeting me in twenty minutes, which probably meant he was already downstairs, as Finns were known to be fashionably early.

"No, I was vague."

Whew. As much as I would always care about Hank, I hadn't left him and moved overseas only to return to America and revisit the past. I couldn't imagine any scenario in which I'd want to be with him again, even if he suddenly proposed marriage and children. "No worries, Dad. You and Mom enjoy your special day, and don't give Hank another thought."

After hanging up, I slipped into my outfit, jacked up the blow dryer with one hand, and applied mauve lipstick with the other. *Presentable enough.* Then I rode the elevator down five flights to the lobby.

Otto was sitting in a cream-colored leather chair, flipping through the *Ilta Sanomat*. When our eyes met, he dropped the tabloid and walked over.

"*Hei*, Otto. How are you?" Like me, he was freshly showered and casually dressed.

A faint smile flitted across his face, and he reached for my hand. "Much better now that you're here." He opened the glass door and led me onto the busy sidewalk. Before I knew what was happening, Otto pulled me close, tilted my head back, and started kissing me. *Passionately.* I pushed into the balls of my feet, reached up, and wound my arms around his neck. Our hip bones pressed together; I curled into his sturdy shoulder as he tenderly caressed my cheek and moved a hand through my windswept hair. The roar of rush hour traffic whizzed through my ear canals, or maybe it was the blood rushing to my head. The love carousel I'd been on these last few years jolted to a full stop. I tried grasping details of my Odyssey: the lilacs draping over my balcony on Tulip Street; the lingering hazelnut taste of Eszterházy torta; the sound of János's wheelchair approaching on the Boulevard. But like my body, my mind went numb.

Eventually, Otto's faint voice surfaced. When I looked up, he turned toward the Finn Kino Cineplex across the street. "Do you want to see a movie?" he seemed to be asking. Dizzy from our lip-lock, I grabbed a window grating on the façade of the Helka. I knew that a foray into the darkness of the cinema would shortly translate into a roll in the *hei* either in my hotel room or Otto's place. Although my body was screaming to give in to the moment after three long years of celibacy, my head warned me to slow down and get to know more about this man, who seemed full of surprises.

"If you don't mind, I'm quite hungry and would prefer getting a bite to eat," I said.

"Okay, I know the perfect place." Otto led me by the hand through the Töölö area of the city. Stopping at the bottom of a small hill, he pointed to a peach-colored Art Deco building he identified as his home. I thought he might invite me in, which would have been tempting, but instead, he turned onto another street, where dozens of young boys were playing soccer in the schoolyard. My date stopped and pushed his soft lips against mine. I felt a bit self-conscious; public displays of affection appeared rare in the more reserved North.

"Don't you feel a little shy in front of these kids?" I asked Otto.

"No. I think it's good they see love, don't you?"

Love? I was curious to know Otto's true motives—one minute he wanted to sit mutely in the theater, the next he was taking me on a grand smooching tour of his city. He was definitely an enigma and one I was determined to solve before flying back to Budapest.

After walking down the main coastal road, we turned into Sibelius Park, where an abstract monument comprised of hundreds of steel tubes had been erected in memory of the country's most famous composer. Swarms of tourists, mostly Asians, snapped photos of one another standing underneath the twenty-five-foot-high structure in the shape of a willow tree. Others pressed their mouths against the pipes and shouted upwards to the cloudless sky.

"Do you like Sibelius?" Otto asked.

"Yes, *Finlandia* in particular. But I'm more of a Chopin-Liszt fan."

Otto inquired about my musical background and seemed especially interested in the chorus's participation in the Liturgical Festival in Israel. "Oh, so you've been to Jerusalem," he said, raising his wispy eyebrows upward. "I've been two or three times."

I told him how my initial excitement at being accepted on the tour had given way to intense jitters, both onstage and off. "The possibility of a terrorist lurking in our midst was always on our minds."

Otto stopped and took my hands in his. "But aren't you glad you went?"

"Yes. It was, without a doubt, the highlight of my musical life." We shared similar stories about visiting the Stations of the Cross on the Via Dolorosa and gathering fallen olive branches at the Garden of Gethsemane. "Now my chorus is getting ready to perform 'Ode to Joy' as part of the St. Stephen's celebrations in Hungary. The goal is two thousand singers in Heroes' Square."

"When's the concert?" Otto asked, a look of concern sweeping across his face.

"On the twentieth." *Less than one week away!* Even though I had missed several rehearsals while on my trip, Gábor had promised that I could participate.

Otto grew quiet and pensive as we descended back toward the sea, the silence only broken by a handful of geese honking from the expanse of grass along the rugged coast-line. When we arrived at a sauna bathhouse, he explained Finland's long-standing tradition of heating one's body in a small wooden room, and then plunging into the sea or lake, even in wintertime.

"Brrr!" I said, pretending to shiver. Otto leaned against a birch tree, pulled me into his chest, and wrapped his long arms around me. Through the soft cotton of his red, white, and blue striped shirt, I heard his pulse quicken. After a few moments, he gently pushed some windswept chestnut strands from my face and moved my chin upward.

"Will you go with me to Pihtipudas this weekend to meet my mother?" he asked, his pale blue eyes fixed on mine.

At first, I had trouble deciphering what Otto had said and asked him to repeat it. Even after a second time, I was stunned. I didn't know what I thought I'd heard, but an invitation to meet his mother hadn't been a remote possibility. In our short time together, he'd not once mentioned her, nor did I have any idea where exactly Pihtipudas was and how we'd get there. My top priority was getting back to Budapest; I reminded Otto of my flight the next day.

"I'm aware of that," he said, "but I'm hoping you'll want to stay and see more of Finland."

Remaining in Helsinki meant rebooking my flight; I scrambled to calculate the cost. I still had money left in my savings account, so finances weren't the pressing concern. The safety issue crossed my mind, and I imagined Eve warning me: "Run for your life! He could be an ax murderer!" Having called Otto's office earlier that day, I was convinced he was a prosecutor of criminals, not a perpetrator of crimes. "Let me think for a moment," I whispered, embracing Otto, whose heart now leapt into double-time.

"The Finnish countryside is very beautiful," he continued, "especially in summer. You can try our lakeside wood sauna. We can also go canoeing, pick berries, swim." While I was flattered by Otto's efforts to entice me, I also felt he was rushing. Hank hadn't introduced me to his mother until we'd been together three years. Perhaps this was the way relationships operated in the land of *sisu*; I remembered Heléna's insistence that I needed a man with this national character trait. Otto knew I was scheduled to leave the next day and probably opted to go full throttle. I understood, and sensed he did too, that my flying back to Budapest and then moving to the States would preclude us from pursuing a romance. If I didn't accept Otto's invitation now, there would unlikely be future ones. *Why am I hesitating?* Mom hadn't been deterred when she met Dad, even though he was from the other side of the tracks. Nor had Liszt when he met Princess Carolyne and gave up the concert stage for her.

Beethoven's Ninth flitted into my head. Yes, I'd be disappointed if I couldn't participate in the performance. Torn by my desire to sing with the masses or act out more earthly ones with Otto, I closed my eyes and considered how I'd feel if I never saw him again. With some regret, I remembered how my decision to rush back to Budapest after meeting David had negatively impacted our relationship. Mixed with the smoke emanating from the sauna arose the strong inner voice: *"Don't leave Otto for a concert! Seize this opportunity—it's your last before you go home."* Yes, it was time to forget Ludwig and pen my own "Ode to Joy."

I looked up into Otto's expectant eyes. "Yes, I'd love to go."

He seemed as surprised as I was by my reply, and a smile as bright as the midnight sun lit up his relieved face.

Leaving details for later, we continued our kiss-stained stroll along the coast until we reached a wedding cake-styled Victorian café with picturesque views of Töölö Bay. Vases of fresh and dried roses lined the well-worn wooden porch steps. The aroma of freshly baked quiche and apple pie beckoned us inside. An elegant antique table stood in command at the center of the room, where guests sliced and served up huge silver platters bursting with sweet and savory treats. The need for sustenance won out over our sugar cravings, and we cut two pieces of spinach and feta quiche.

An oak hutch displayed floral-patterned teapots and a variety of teacups, from delicate white and blue porcelain china to glass ones with bronze Russian holders. Empty vodka bottles labeled "Chopin" with the composer's likeness lined the top of an upright piano.

"This looks like your kind of place," Otto said, winking. He staked out a spot on the sun-drenched porch and pushed our white wicker chairs together to maximize rays. We huddled and kissed in between bites and sips while feeding crumbs to the baby birds bouncing from table to table. "So, you've told me a bit about your grandfather from Vilnius," he continued, "but where was your grandmother from?"

"Russia."

Otto put down his fork and dabbed his thin lips with a linen napkin. "Have you been to the Uspenski Cathedral?"

"Yes, I visited there just before meeting you." *And lit a candle at the miraculous icon.*

Otto leaned over and kissed my forehead. "On the way back to your hotel, we can stop at my place, and I'll show you my Russian treasure, if you'd like."

Uh-oh. I wondered if "treasure" was a Finnish code word for "etchings" and visualized Mom wagging a finger at me. Were Otto's intentions, like the impending visit to his mother's—honorable—or was this soft-spoken, polite Finn really a smooth international operator? I had prepaid for my room at the Helka and had every intention of sleeping there.

"Okay," I finally said, rounding up the last bit of pie crumbs. "We can stop briefly at your place en route to the Helka."

The sun was still high in the sky by the time we left the

café. We retraced our steps and continued our smoochfest, arriving at Otto's building on Vänrikki Stoolin Street.

"I'm warning you, I live in a bachelor flat," he said, opening the front door. As we climbed four flights of stairs, I braced myself for a pile of dirty dishes lining the kitchen sink or a mirrored disco ball hanging above the bed, but immediately upon entering the studio apartment, I understood that "bachelor" meant "small." Otto gave me a quick tour of the tiny space, which was furnished with a lone blue love seat, a wooden desk, and a table with two chairs pushed under the sleeping loft. The kitchenette consisted of a mini refrigerator and a two-burner stove. Had it not been for the fifteen-foot ceiling, the space would have felt claustrophobic.

Otto rummaged in a drawer and directed my attention to the two narrow windows that looked out over the neighbor's rooftop.

"Nice view," I said, watching the seagulls circle against the finally setting sun.

"That's not what I want you to see." He approached the wall and held a lit candle to the picture hanging between the windows. "Look," he said, touching its simple wood frame.

Ave Maria! The icon of Mother Mary holding Baby Jesus wasn't at all like the glistening one I'd prayed to at the Uspenski, but a Byzantine rendition in earthy tones, also radiating love and serenity. "Where did you get this?" I asked, my eyes drawn to the delicate star-shaped beads sparkling on Mary's caramel-colored mantle.

"At a church in Zelenogorsk, Russia." *Russian icon.* Otto adjusted his wire-rimmed glasses, which twinkled in the reflection of the lit icon. *Glasses.* I moved my eyes slowly up and down his lean, long torso. *Tall . . .*

Tall man with glasses . . .

Tall man with glasses . . . and Russian icon!

I walked closer to the icon and gazed into Mary's watchful eyes. Her Son's arms reached up and wrapped around her neck. His cheek brushed against hers.

Otto tenderly touched Mary's hand and smiled. *Here's a man who also reveres Mary.* A sensation of warmth pulsated up and down my body as it had in Somerville years before, and again in the crypt at the Dormition Abbey in Jerusalem. *Otto is my kindred spirit!* I put my hand to my mouth and gasped. "She's so beautiful," I murmured, understanding that my Odyssey had reached its final destination.

With a newfound calm, I cozied up to Otto, and after kissing him for a few minutes, pointed to the sleeping alcove above. "Isn't it time we go up there?" I suggested.

We embraced knowingly, and then slowly climbed up the sturdy ladder to the loft, outfitted with piles of foam pads that together posed as a makeshift mattress. Three months later, it would be here—after meeting Otto's mother in Pihtipudas, celebrating his birthday in Russia, and finally moving my belongings from Budapest and squeezing them into my new Helsinki home—where Otto would whisper the words I'd so longed to hear: "I think we should be going married."

A Promise Kept

Three years later ...

Otto extracted himself from the minibus, his long legs a bit wobbly as he struggled to regain his balance in the parking lot. Despite having spent the last few days sunbathing in Marmaris, Turkey, the vertiginous four-hour journey had sapped the suntan off his now-ashen face. I rushed over and kissed his cheek.

"It's easier going downhill," I said, pointing to countless red poppies blanketing the hills and fields. "I promise it's worth all the trouble to get here." I took my husband's clammy hand and led him to the statue that had welcomed me to Nightingale Hill five years earlier.

Otto gazed at the bronze image of Mary, whose open arms warmly welcomed us; a gently sculpted mantle draped around her flowing garments. "I'm feeling better already," he said.

As we walked into the stone chapel, I noted with relief the dramatic drop in temperature compared to my previous visit with Eve. The scarcity of tourists in early spring allowed us to linger by the altar and sit quietly without being disturbed by overly zealous pilgrims.

"Is this chapel what you wanted to show me?" Otto asked after we had lit candles and prayed.

"No, that's further down the way." I motioned to a more populated area where a dozen people were filling plastic bottles with water and filling the crevices of the stone wall with small pieces of paper. "Soon we'll join them," I continued, "but first I'd like to sit a while."

I dropped beneath the same fig tree where I'd become so mesmerized years earlier and drew Otto close to me. It didn't take long for us to tap into the divine reverie. We inhaled the sweet fragrance and felt the soft breeze caress us. Now was the perfect moment to divulge the reason for this return pilgrimage to Mother Mary's house.

"When I came here as part of the Turkish tour with Eve, I was looking for the 'tall man with glasses,' as you know," I began. He squeezed my hand. I pointed to a group of Asian tourists in the distance and explained what they were doing. "You see, people from around the world travel to this sacred spot and leave messages for Mary at the Wishing Wall in the hope that she will fulfill them."

Otto fumbled in his shirt pocket for a pen. "You want to leave a wish today?"

"Oh no, dear. My wish already came true." I pointed to the simple gold band on my ring finger, then to his.

Otto's eyes brimmed with tears. He withdrew his sunglasses for a quick cleaning, and then repositioned them over his nose.

"When I was here last time, I wrote Mary a note asking for a loving husband—a kindred spirit." Otto knew all about Angelica's prediction that a Russian icon would lead to my future husband. "Naturally, when I saw the image of Mary and Baby Jesus hanging in your living room, I thought, 'Here he is! The man who will understand. My intended.'" My voice started to crack. "What I haven't told you is that I promised Mary that if my wish were granted, I'd return with this kindred spirit to give thanks."

Otto was silent a long time and finally whispered, "That's beautiful, Linduska." He brushed a stand of hair away from my misty face. "Now that we're sharing, there's something you should know."

"Oh?" My eyes widened as I considered what Otto's confession might be.

"Remember when you first saw the icon in my flat, and I told you it was from Zelenogorsk?" I nodded. "If you recall, I was traveling with my work group, and we stopped at the Church of Our Lady of Kazan on our way back from St. Petersburg." He patted his forehead with a handkerchief and inhaled a deep breath. "What I didn't tell you was what had happened moments before I bought the icon."

My heart skipped a beat, and I motioned for Otto to continue.

"As a shy Finnish man, this is a little difficult for me to express, but here goes." Otto looked around, as if someone he knew might be lurking in the bushes, and then lowered his voice. "After exploring that Orthodox church, my colleagues returned to the bus, leaving me alone for a while. I sat on one of the few available seats, surrounded by icons of Mother Mary, and felt inspired. Like you, I was in my forties and was losing hope of finding a life partner to share these experiences with." He motioned to the statue of Mother Mary by the entrance. "So, I prayed to her for a wife because I felt that as a woman, she would understand and help me. Moments later, as I was leaving the Cathedral, I was drawn to an icon by the cashier and felt compelled to take it home with me."

"Amazing." I caressed Otto's rosy cheek. "Our prayers were not only answered, but in the most extraordinary way." I smiled at the image of Mary on my ring and gave it a twirl. *Blessed.*

We sat for a long time, gazing at one another, the serene environs, the birds darting over the ravines, the other pilgrims. Finally, the minibus driver waved from the parking lot and pointed to his wristwatch; the bus back to Marmaris was leaving in fifteen minutes. I stood up, straightened my black pants, and aired out my blue silk shirt. Otto kicked some sand from his sandals.

"Now let's go and fulfill my promise to Mother Mary."

Otto and I walked to the water taps and splashed our exuberant faces with the holy spring water. Then I looked around for the area where I'd placed my original wish—during my Odyssey, before I'd found the "tall man with glasses," before seeing his Russian icon. Before we'd gotten married a few months later, and I had officially moved to Helsinki.

My husband watched me with intent as I unfolded a piece of hotel note paper from my bag. Before leaving it—and Ephesus—behind, I shared my poem with him:

ODE TO JOY—to *Mary*

I felt the sway of distant lands,
That I've since kissed away.
Another beckoned farther still,
My destiny to stay.
Amidst the loaves and fishes,
My heart leapt in my chest.
Her serene image reassured,
The union would be blessed.
Thank you, Mother Mary,
For keeping me on track.
And granting me my dearest wish,
As I was turning back.

With love and forever gratitude,

Linda / Linduška

Acknowledgments

So many dear ones showered me with love and kindness to ensure that my Odyssey was fun, meaningful, and unforgettable. Thank you from the bottom of my heart.

There are not enough pages in this book to express my gratitude to my dear parents, Gloria and Joseph Tyrol, without whose generosity and encouragement there would not have been an Odyssey to write about. Thank you, Mom, for the gift of music and filling our home with beautiful songs—from Liszt to Gershwin—and your patience and dedication in teaching me piano. Dad, you were the best jazz whistler ever! I love and miss you colorful characters and carry you in my heart always.

Jenni Caldwell, you were the best friend a gal could ever have. Thank you for all the teatime tête-à-têtes and the miracle at Mount Auburn. I'd give all the tea in China for one more hug.

Angelica, your vision of true love in the tea leaves and others that followed changed my life forever. Thank you for inspiring me to leap forward and not turn back. Also, for the gorgeous red hat.

In loving memory of Josie Kurkinen, who spent countless hours reading and discussing these pages with me while completing her psychology doctorate. How I wish you were here to celebrate *Odyssey's* launch into the world, my lovely friend.

To everyone who accompanied me on my Odyssey (whether or not mentioned in these chapters), my deepest appreciation for your friendship and hospitality: Mariann Sziklay, Ágnes Draskóczi, Zsuzsa Hardy-Orosz, John Williams, János Hős, Gretchen Meddaugh, Maria Petz-Stifler, the Bohács family, the Döbrőssys, Judit and David Sutherland, Uli Nater, Devon Krohn, the late Martin Hodge, Vali Sarus, Nathan Resika, Bence Sziklay, Jane Thomson, and Lia Genovese.

János (the Baptist), Bea, Gyöngyi, and Anett, you touched my life in a special way. Thank you to Judit Kovacsics for Slovenia and the spirited soirées with the late Viktor Bohács. *Vielen Dank* János Strohmayer and Sophia Verykios, the host/ess with the most/ess. Many hugs to Claire Preisser, my partner in pastries—from Prague to Vienna. A shout-out to Cousin Renate Eppich and the Antoniou clan for my goddaughter's memorable (and loud!) baptism in Athens. Sigrid Shone, you owe me a soak in Széchenyi, no excuses! Paula Ziehr, thanks for the memorable night with "Nimrod" in Berlin. *Danke* Anja and Markus Contius for sharing your favorite Hamburg haunts.

Hats off to Maestro Gábor Hollerung and my Budapest Academic Choral Society mates for the singular experience of making glorious music together. Thank you to my students and fellow teachers at The Bell School and International House in Budapest.

I am forever indebted to Deborah Grose and Elizabeth Titus, my touchstones in Boston, for listening to and comforting me during many stressful visits back home. I'm dreaming about a Jaffrey reunion and logging some serious sun, swim, and sightreading time together.

My sincerest thanks to the following who cheered me

on during the creative process, including the beta readers who offered invaluable feedback: Cynde Sadler, Tina Tabler, Sirkka Numminen, Mary Woolley, Lisa Newton, Russell Shane and Delaine Winkler Shane, Ilena Patti, Pimma and Peter Knight, Bard bestie Cathy Stork Waters, Bard bros John Leaman and Lance Tait, Barbara Hirschmann and David Elinson, April Eberhardt, Paula Vincent-Cowan, Riita Tammisto, Suzanne Fluhr, Moran Winsteen Albin, Bernadette Jokinen, Lisa Muszynski, Chisato Kondo, Paula Saukkonen, Wendy and Val, Diane Englert, Patty Tyrol, Kelly Mosher, Jeanmaire Hryshko, Siru and Tapani Erling, Mariann Lindroos, and Esko Kurkinen.

Tuija Jämsén and Kaisa de Paez Jämsén, I really lucked out in the sister-in-law lottery. *Gracias* Tuula Jakowleff and all the lovely Agora gals. A warm thanks to the American Women's Club in Finland for being a home away from home for many of us expats. Blessings Reverend Deena Galantowicz for listening and offering clarity and courage at a critical time. It took ten years, but I finally hit the "Send" button! Helinä Wacklin, *kullan murunen*, I miss our musical Mary moments. Milka Alanen, what a serendipitous meeting in Tinos! Thanks for the travel tips and photos.

Tack Kammarkören Idun and *kiitos* Viva Vox and Lauttasaaren Laulajat choristers for all the beautiful music (with apologies for my odd pronunciation). To my cherished St. Nicholas Church family, you continue to grace my life with comfort and joy. Agnes Goerke, you light up my Christmas every year.

Many thanks to Katherine Don, "The Book Don," and Dr. Marlene Broemer for their editor's expertise in polishing these pages. Also to Alexa Bigwarfe and her creative team at Write|Publish|Sell for their guidance in helping me publish my first book and waving their magic marketing wands. Cheers to my launch team for their support and the musicians who livened up our launch day celebration. Catherine Pettersson, you deserve a round of applause for making the Stockholm Writers Festival a welcoming place where writers feel supported and appreciated. Anthony Marini, thanks for coming out of IT "retirement" to set up my website. Markus Paez, thanks for all those late-night runs to Verkkokauppa.

The spirit of Franz Liszt hovered over my fingers at both keyboards—computer and piano—while I was writing *Odyssey*. Since my youth, I have been listening to and playing the Master's music. I hope these pages do justice to his enormous genius and talent. Please visit the Music Academy in his name if you are in Budapest, or virtually: https://zeneakademia.hu/en.

Otto, my beloved husband—*rakkaani, kaikkeni, aarteeni*—from that first auspicious meeting, you have been the biggest blessing in my life. So many thanks for your sweetness and sensitivity, and for insisting that I write this hopeful love story and share it with the world. *Rakastan sinua aina, immer, ja ikuisesti.*

And to Mary, my other mother in Heaven, all honor and glory be yours *in saecula saeculorum.*

Lastly, thank you, readers, for going on this journey of words with me, when so many other books beckon.

Book Discussion Questions

(Spoiler alert!)

1. Have you ever visited a fortune-teller? If so, did their predictions come true? If you have not, would you consider a psychic reading?

2. Have you ever lived overseas? If you are currently an expat living abroad, what motivated you to leave your homeland?

3. Jenni warns Linda, "If Hank can't commit after seven years, ten or fifteen might not be enough either." Do you agree with Jenni's assessment of his and Linda's future as a couple?

4. After close encounters with Attila and Marek, Linda suspects that American women are stereotyped as sexually "easy." Have you come across this attitude in your travels?

5. Twice Linda finds herself in precarious situations with men: first, with the stalker in her neighborhood, and then with Attila at the spa. Would you have handled these interactions differently?

6. Why do you think Gabi's family chaperones him and Linda on their Opera date? Do you think this is a cultural issue?

7. Linda engages in heated discussions with students about their derogatory comments and views toward certain ethnic groups. Have you come across these issues in your workplace?

8. Of all the book's locations (Amsterdam, Budapest, Jerusalem, Helsinki, etc.), which do you find most alluring? When it is safe to travel internationally again, where will you go first?

9. When Linda realizes that Sven has stood her up, she decides to confront him. Have you ever faced up to a man who treated you that way, and if so, what was the outcome?

10. Are you familiar with the life and music of Hungarian pianist-composer Franz Liszt? Did reading about him inspire you to listen to his works?

11. Linda accepts Ádám's invitation for a double date because she believes he is trying to match her up with his friend Dénes. Heléna thinks otherwise. Do you think Linda was naïve in accepting Ádám's invitation?

12. Have you ever lusted after a married man? If the attraction was mutual, how did you both handle your feelings?

13. After getting to know David in Amsterdam, Linda becomes increasingly frustrated by his lack of communication and senses he is holding back. Do you think Angelica's perception of his "double life" is correct, or do you suspect some other reason?

14. Who is your favorite/least favorite supporting character in the book, and why?

15. Linda travels with the chorus to Israel during a time of heightened turmoil and violence. Would you have stayed home?

16. Do you believe in love at first sight or destined love?

17. After seeing a vision of Mother Mary early in the story, Linda becomes drawn to all images of her. Do you think this experience helped her recognize the Russian icon at the end?

Visit https://lindajamsen.com/bonus
for a special peek at Linda and Otto's wedding
photos, just for *Odyssey of Love* readers!

Triptych

Healing Pilgrimages of Hope, Faith, and Love

Now seven years married, Linda confronts several health challenges and family crises at once. Haunted by the sudden deaths of her beloved father and best friend Jenni, and fearing more devastating loss, Linda turns to her faith for hope and healing. Listen as she beseeches the Black Madonna of Częstochowa, Poland for a medical miracle. Follow her to the mystical mountains of Medjugorje, where she seeks spiritual guidance and makes her first confession. Accompany her back to Boston, where her heavy heart finds solace in an unexpected blessing—one that will sustain her for years to come.

To receive updates about *Triptych*, sign up here:
www.lindajamsen.com

LINDA JÄMSÉN is an American expat writer and classically trained pianist. Growing up in New York, she was inspired by the beautiful playing of her mother, who became her first piano teacher. Years later, she studied with German Diez and Luis Garcia-Renart at Bard College, where she received a B.A. in Music. Her most memorable "gigs" include playing in Istanbul's Crimea Memorial Church, at Vantaa Prison in Finland, and atop the staircase of the Massachusetts State House.

Linda is also an avid choral singer. She has performed with the Budapest Academic Choral Society, as well as Finnish Chamber Choirs Viva Vox and Idun, and participated in musical tours in Israel and the UK. She looks forward to returning to the stage with her singing mates when it's safe and hopes for an opportunity to perform in Beethoven's "Ode to Joy," which continues to elude her.

She lives on an island in Helsinki with her husband, the "tall man with glasses," and their treasured Russian icon. *Odyssey of Love* is her literary debut.

Learn more about Linda at:
www.lindajamsen.com
@lindajamsenauthor
www.facebook.com/OdysseyOfLoveBook

Made in the USA
Middletown, DE
29 December 2021

57022915R00191